Schumpeterian Analysis of Economic Catch-up

One of the puzzles about why some countries have stronger economic growth than others revolves around the so-called "middle-income trap," the situation in which a country that has grown strongly gets stuck at a certain level. In this book, Keun Lee explores the reasons why examples of successful catching-up are limited and in particular, why the Asian economies, including China, have managed to move, or are moving, beyond middle-income status but economic growth has stalled in some Latin American countries. This is one of the first studies to demonstrate using patent analysis that the secret lies in innovative systems at the firm, sector, and country levels which promote investment in what the author calls "short-cycle" technologies and thereby create a new path different from that of forerunning countries. With its comprehensive policy framework for development as well as useful quantitative methods, this is essential reading for academic researchers and practitioners.

KEUN LEE is a Professor of Economics at the Seoul National University and Director of the Center for Economic Catch-up. He is a globally recognized expert on the economics of catch-up and Asian economies. Professor Lee is also a member of the UN's Committee for Development Policy, a co-editor of the journal *Research Policy*, and a member of the governing board of Globelics, as well as the Asia-Pacific Innovation Network.

"This book lays out a convincing new perspective on the conditions behind the remarkable development of manufacturing in South Korea and Taiwan. The well documented argument is that in several of the industries where firms in these countries were very successful, technology at the frontier was going through a transition, with the technology coming in requiring a different set of skills and capabilities than the technology becoming obsolete. This diminished the advantage of the old industrial leaders and provided a window of opportunity for effective entry in these two economies. The story Keun Lee tells is fascinating and thought provoking."

Richard Nelson, Professor, Columbia University

"Based on convincing theoretical and empirical analyses, Professor Lee argues that Korea and Taiwan's success hinges on their shift, after reaching middle-income status in the 1980s, to specialize on shorter cycle technology-based sectors, which rely less on existing technologies, allow their economies to leverage the greater opportunities that arise from the emergence of new technologies, and enable them to continue the catching up process. This book is original, makes important contributions to the development literature, and should be read by anyone concerned about how to help a country overcome the middle-income trap."

Justin Yifu Lin, Peking University and
Former Chief Economist, the World Bank

"The manuscript is original, relevant and impressive because Keun Lee consistently proves his argument with analyses conducted at three connected levels: countries, sectors and firm. Keun Lee inserts findings into a broader discussion of economic catch up, and on the role of public policy. The book encompasses other large emerging countries that were not (yet) as successful as Korea and Taiwan, such as India and Brazil, or that are on the road of sustained catch-up such as China."

Franco Malerba, Editor, *Industrial & Corporate Change*

"This book is essential reading for any scholar interested in the economics of technological catch-up. While the core argument interestingly emphasizes the length of technological life cycles, Keun Lee here provides a fascinating treatment of the role of different types of firms and countries in the capacity for catch-up."

John Cantwell, Editor-in-Chief, *Journal of*
International Business Studies

"Based on a profound theoretical understanding of the process of technological change and using careful and innovative empirical methodologies, the book provides a very sophisticated framework to understand the process of technological innovation and learning at the firm, sectoral, and national levels. It is a path-breaking work that should be read by everyone who is interested in understanding the process of economic development."

Ha-Joon Chang, University of Cambridge
and author of *Kicking Away the Ladder*

"The book presents an original analysis of the catch-up processes pursued by Korea and Taiwan (with a discussion extended to China and India) demonstrating (using patent data analysis) that successful catch-up involves strong attention to targeted knowledge capture and build-up of capabilities. The argument is that catch-up is always strategic, in that there must be smart choices made over which technologies to target, and the role of what are called high, middle and low roads. It is sure to become a classic in the field."

John Mathews, author of *Tiger Technology*
and Professor at Macquarie University

Schumpeterian Analysis of Economic Catch-up

Knowledge, Path-Creation, and the
Middle-Income Trap

KEUN LEE

CAMBRIDGE
UNIVERSITY PRESS

CAMBRIDGE
UNIVERSITY PRESS

University Printing House, Cambridge CB2 8BS, United Kingdom

Cambridge University Press is part of the University of Cambridge.

It furthers the University's mission by disseminating knowledge in the pursuit of education, learning and research at the highest international levels of excellence.

www.cambridge.org
Information on this title: www.cambridge.org/9781107042681

First published 2013

A catalogue record for this publication is available from the British Library

Library of Congress Cataloguing in Publication data
Lee, Keun, 1960–
Schumpeterian analysis of economic catch-up: knowledge, path-creation, and the middle-income trap / Keun Lee.
    page cm
Includes index.
ISBN 978-1-107-04268-1 (Hardback)
1. Technological innovations–Developing countries. 2. Economic development–Developing countries. 3. Schumpeter, Joseph A., 1883-1950. I. Title.
HC59.72.T4L37 2013
338'.064091724–dc23   2013015851

ISBN 978-1-107-04268-1 Hardback

Contents

Figures

Tables

Foreword

JOHN A. MATHEWS
Macquarie University

One hundred years ago in 1912 a very young Joseph Schumpeter published an epochal book, *The Theory of Economic Development*, in which he laid bare the mechanisms through which capitalism expands and renews itself. In the intervening century, the system he described so well has expanded worldwide, and is now drawing in China, India et al. Yet while Schumpeter's emphasis on innovation and creative destruction was entirely correct, his dismissal of follow-up strategies as "mere imitation" has not stood the test of time. First Japan, then Korea and Taiwan, and now China are all pursuing highly sophisticated strategies of resource leverage and knowledge appropriation that have enabled them to catch up with the industrial leaders (in the cases of Korea and Taiwan) or to be well embarked on the process, in China's case.

One hundred years later, Keun Lee finally provides a clear account of just how they are doing it. His book draws from his own and colleagues' empirical investigations of Korea's catch-up strategies, and engages with the wider literature on industrial and competitive dynamics. The book presents a sustained and original analysis of the catch-up processes pursued by Korea and Taiwan (with a discussion extended to China) demonstrating – using patent data and analysis – that successful catch-up involves strong attention to targeted knowledge capture and build-up of broad capabilities. Keun Lee demonstrates that countries that catch up do so by targeting specific technologies that are characterized by what he calls short cycle times – meaning that they have a high rate of product and process turnover (as measured in terms of patenting rates). Using the examples of Korea and Taiwan, Keun Lee shows how the two countries acquired their initial technological capabilities for the decade 1975 to 1985 in technologies such as automotives, steel, and chemicals (of lengthening cycle times) but passed their first transition, or turning point, in the mid 1980s when they started systematically targeting technologies with shorter cycle times (electronics, semiconductors, flat panel displays, IT) which required them to build broad capabilities in these fast-moving technologies. They then passed a second transition, or turning point, at around the year 2000 when they started concentrating on the most advanced technologies with longer cycle times, thereby approaching the technological frontier (as now achieved by companies such as Samsung, Hyundai and LG in Korea, and Acer, or AU Optronics in Taiwan). This is an instructive and very significant and original contribution (see Figure 6.1).

Keun Lee's contribution goes beyond arguments that emphasized how latecomers should target technologies that were standardized ("dominant technologies") – developed by scholars such as Alice Amsden, Sanjaya Lall, Linsu Kim, Richard Nelson, and myself. Keun Lee's new emphasis on technology cycle time clarifies why some technologies work better than others as vehicles for catch-up. He argues that countries like Korea and Taiwan go through a kind of "technological detour," pursuing the highest levels of technological capability only after mastering the medium levels associated with short-cycle technologies. By contrast, countries that go straight for the highest levels (as revealed in their patenting records) tend to burn out and fall behind (as he argues has been the case for some Latin American countries). By the same token, countries that go for only the lowest-level long-cycle technologies (like basic steel-making or automotive assembly) then get stuck at this technological level. In this sense his argument is the very opposite of the celebrated "product life cycle" approach associated with Ray Vernon of Harvard, where it is argued that countries emerge from poverty by focussing on the most mature parts of the product life cycle. Lee's argument is that this constrains countries' further development, and they end up caught in the "middle-income country trap."

Lee's argument also has something to say about countries that are at the earliest stage of development, where they need to focus on what he (and Justin Yifu Lin of the World Bank) call trade-based strategies, or what used to be called simply the pursuit of comparative advantage. These strategies can lift incomes in countries as they build industries in the simplest kinds of activities, exploiting their low labor costs – but need to be complemented, according to Lee, by promoting new industrial shoots where the focus is on successively shorter-cycle-time technologies. Otherwise countries again run the real risk of being stuck at a certain level of development and lacking the technological base for moving forward.

There are three points to make about this fresh argument from Keun Lee. The first is that it is firmly technology based – and thus leaves behind many of the less than helpful ideas associated with the Washington consensus, where the focus was exclusively on macro-economic variables at the expense of concern for development of technological capabilities. This makes it profoundly Schumpeterian in spirit. The second is that it is concerned with industrial development as a process of changing industry structure through targeted initiatives. In this sense it is profoundly Gerschenkronian, always being focussed on the latest technologies that offer opportunities for leapfrogging. Thus it places industrial policy firmly back on the development agenda. The third is that it views the role of the state in economic catch-up as essential, where strategies are driven by collective entrepreneurship exercised through ministries, state-funded R&D centres, and universities, all pursuing various levels of technological catch-up. Strategies that leave out this essential role for the state in catch-up are doomed to fail, according to Keun Lee – and he is right.

This book is well argued. The data are presented using country-level, sector-level, and firm-level analysis (e.g. Samsung and its knowledge trajectory tracked by patenting). The argument is that catch-up is always strategic, in that smart choices must be made about which technologies to target based on their characteristics (e.g. long-cycle technology vs. short-cycle technology), and the role of what are called the high, middle, and low roads in accomplishing the catch-up. It is sure to become a classic in the field.

Preface

This book originated with a research grant I received from the National Research Foundation of Korea (No. B00007). Given only to a selected number of "star" scholars, this Ministry of Education funded grant requires scholars to write a single-authored monograph over a five-year period. Before I received it, I had, like most economists, focussed my energies mainly on writing journal articles. Although I had published my doctoral thesis as a book some time ago, I felt that writing an article for a journal was a far more valuable contribution than writing a book. Needless to say, I did not like the idea of writing one, and without the grant, this book would not have existed.

I have since realized my folly. Writing a monograph became an opportunity to synthesize my work and to compile the ideas I have scattered across journals. In one sense, this book is an outcome of the Korean government's "industrial policy" in the area of education. While the focus of Korean industrial policy during the catch-up period was to promote specific industries, the current priority of the Korean government is to boost the level of academic scholarship.

Given the background of the book, and its focus on economic catch-up, it is somewhat ironic that it devotes so little space to industrial policy itself. The reason for this is that several important works have already been written on industrial policy in East Asia, such as those by Ha-Joon Chang (1994) and Alice Amsden (1989). Adopting a Schumpeterian approach to innovation systems, this book provides a more theoretical and generalizable account of the divergent process of catch-up as it occurs in different countries or parts of the world. In addressing the important question of why some countries have been more successful than others, the book identifies several key innovation systems. The cycle time of technologies is one such variable. This refers to the speed with which technologies change or become obsolete over time, and the speed and frequency at which new technologies emerge.

This book demonstrates that successful economies and firms have tended to specialize in, or gradually move into, sectors based on short-cycle technologies.

The argument that qualified latecomers can advantageously target such sectors and specialize in them is based on the fact that the dominance of the incumbent can be disrupted by the opportunities presented by ever-emerging new technologies. Latecomers do not have to rely too greatly on the existing technologies whose use is dominated by the incumbents. The new opportunities present new growth prospects, and a lower reliance on existing technologies may lead to the faster localization of a knowledge-creation mechanism. This property could also mean lower entry barriers and the possibility of greater profitability since there is less conflict with the technologies of advanced countries, fewer required royalty payments, and even a first-/fast-mover advantage or product differentiation. As an analogy, research by Jones and Weinberg (2001) on the age–achievement relationship in the natural sciences demonstrates that young scientists (who can be seen as being similar to late entrants attempting to play catch-up) tend to make more contributions at a younger age when they practice in the fields of abstract /deductive knowledge than when they attempt to make a mark in the more inductive fields that draw on accumulated knowledge, and in which existing knowledge is slow to reach obsolescence.

This book often uses Korean and Taiwanese firms and industries as examples of successful catch-up, leaving us with an intriguing question: did the policy makers in these countries have the criterion of short cycle time firmly in mind as they planned and conducted industrial policy? While the answer to this question is no, they were in fact always asking themselves, "what's next?" They looked keenly at which industries and businesses were likely to emerge in the immediate future and thought carefully about how to enter the emerging ones. Without specifically planning to do so, in effect the policy makers were always pursuing the short-cycle industries as these were often the ones that relied the least on existing technologies.

The key strategies for economic development identified in the current study differ from those traditionally recommended. We maintain that trade-based specialization is more suitable for low-income countries than middle-income countries. This study then makes its biggest contribution to the literature by taking the first step to explicitly and theoretically addressing the specialization conditions for middle-income countries. We recommend that they specialize in technological sectors that rely the least on existing technologies, and that afford the greatest opportunities associated with new technologies. In this way, our findings complement the growth identification and facilitation framework of Justin Lin, in which policy makers are advised to target an industry that is new to a latecomer country but mature in a forerunning country. This allows the latecomer country to begin the process of moving into shorter-cycle sectors. This book argues that after a certain amount of technological capability has been built up in the latecomer economy, it can then target another industry that is new to both the latecomer and forerunning economies. This is an effort at leapfrogging, and China is already doing this in various industries. Thus the distinctive policy argument of this book is that sustained industrial catch-up requires not only an entrance into mature industries, but also an effort to leapfrog into emerging industries that are new to both advanced and developing countries.

I would also like to contrast this book's emphasis on innovative systems with that on inclusive systems in the book *Why Nations Fail* by Acemoglu and Robinson (2012). First of all, their book does not explain how a country can move toward more inclusive institutions, which is also pointed out in a book review by Bill Gates. Furthermore, I observe that the inclusive or extractive dimension may be relevant more for low-income countries or pre-modern economies existing before the world became interdependent and globalized, and that contemporary middle-income nations fail not so much because of extractive institutions but more because of weak innovation systems, since these also affect their international competitiveness. This contrasts with differences in the degree of inclusiveness among them, which are not that substantial.

This study also provides a yardstick with which one can assess whether a middle-income country is stuck in the middle-income trap, or whether it is in fact moving beyond the middle-income stage to achieve high-income status. We label this phenomenon the technological turning point, or the point at which cycle time, as measured by the patent portfolio of a country, reaches a peak and turns to technologies with shorter cycle times. Korea and Taiwan passed this turning point in the mid 1980s, and China seems to have reached this point in the mid 1990s. The Indian graph also shows a peak in its cycle time in the late 1990s, but a downward trend is not yet clear enough for us to declare that India has passed its technological turning point.

While this book defines economic catch-up as a narrowing of a firm or country's gap *vis-à-vis* a leading country or firm, the concept has a long history, going back to the famous work of Gerschenkron (1962) and, Abramowitz's (1986) influential article ("Catching up, Forging ahead, and Falling behind"), which popularized the concept of catch-up and made it part of the standard vocabulary of development economists. While the article examines the relative performance of European economies after World War II, this book is about non-Western latecomer countries. It conducts a multinational, quantitative analysis of economic catch-up across three dimensions (i.e. firms, sectors, and countries) based on a single consistent framework focussed on the innovation system. This multi-level analysis identifies a consistent set of catch-up determinants and operationalizes them using patent data, with technological cycle time (short cycles) serving as the transition variable, and the localization of knowledge creation and technological diversification serving as end-point variables.

This book offers both new and refined methodologies for quantifying the conceptual elements of innovation systems and Schumpeterian economics, which can be used to conduct econometric analyses across country, sector, and firm levels. While these methods are useful for researchers, the book also contains important insights for practitioners and policy makers. In particular, Chapter 7 offers suggestions on building up the technological capability required for the journey toward economic catch-up. It focusses on the role of the government, of public research institutes, and of public–private partnerships. We consider capability building to be one of the most binding elements in catching up growth.

This book owes a lot to an intellectual tradition that may be called neo-Schumpeterian or evolutionary economics, and in particular to the works of Richard Nelson, beginning with the book he co-authored with Sidney Winter (1982) called *An Evolutionary Theory of Economic Change*. I am a latecomer in this school and I came to study the book only in the early 1990s – a full decade after it was first published. My intellectual journey started in that period, and I evolved from being a student of the economics of transitioning former socialist economies, to being a student of the economics of innovation in latecomer economies. Interestingly, both areas can be subsumed under the heading "economics of catch-up". While the former is about the catch-up of economic systems, both focus on reducing the performance gap between latecomers and the forerunning economies. This book argues that you cannot catch up by trying to directly emulate or replicate the economic practices of the forerunning economies. Catch-up comes only if you take a different path.

My personal encounter with Nelson came another ten years after my encounter with his book, at the 2004 Globelics Conference held in Beijing. After the conference, I became a key participant of the research group on catch-up that he initiated, as well as of the Globelics conferences led by another mentor of mine, Bengt-Ake Lundvall. The catch-up group held its first meeting at the campus of the Columbia University in May 2005. The meeting resulted in several books on multiple subjects, specifically sectoral innovation systems and catch-up (Malerba and Nelson 2012), intellectual property rights (IPR) and catch-up (Odagiri et al. 2010), and innovative firms and catch-up (Amann and Cantwell 2012). It also spawned another forthcoming book on university–industry linkages and catch-up. I have contributed a chapter to each of the four books and have learnt tremendously from the community which meets annually at the Globelics meeting. Earlier sections of the book have been presented at these meetings, and they have provided me with a great opportunity to pursue my own intellectual catch-up through exposure to the leading ideas of eminent scholars in the field, such as John Cantwell, Giovanni Dosi, and Franco Malerba. It has been my good fortune to receive both direct and indirect feedback on my research from these scholars.

A number of other scholars have kindly provided me with comments on the manuscript version of this book. Specifically, Nelson led me to explore more literature on the Schumpeterian theory of the firm, and to further revise a chapter on firm-level analysis. He introduced me also to Tushman's works, which offered the insight that competence-destroying discontinuity may lead to the rise of new entrants. As one of the pioneers in the subject of technological catch-up, John Mathews read several versions of the manuscript and suggested a number of important changes to the overall structure of the book. He led me to reevaluate the priority given to key concepts of the book, and I benefitted from his encouragement and feedback at various stages of writing this manuscript.

Among his feedback, Adam Szirmai's remarks on the generalizability of the technological turning points led me to think more deeply about this issue and I added a separate chapter on the subject (Chapter 9). I recently found out that postwar Japan also specialized in much shorter-cycle technologies than European countries, although by then it was too late to add this. Kangkook Lee and Kyooho Park have also commented on early versions of this book. I have to thank Park in particular because we first identified the importance of technology cycle time during our collaboration.

The econometric analysis conducted in this book would not have been possible without a data set of US patents. This was compiled by the NBER research group, in particular Bronwyn Hall, who also provided comments on Chapter 4 after I presented my findings at a conference in Hitotsubashi University. Some variables used in the book were directly retrieved from the data set, with my research team reclassifying them at the firm, sector, and country level. I would like thank my students for managing the data set and conducting the statistical analysis, particularly Junki Park, Buru Im, Raeyoon Kang, and Hochul Shin.

Earlier versions of sections of this book have been presented at various academic meetings and the final versions have benefitted greatly from participant feedback. I would like to thank Eduardo Albuquerque, Hyunbai Chun, Susan Cozzens, John Foster, Xudong Gao, Shulin Gu, Mei-Chih Hu, K. J. Joseph, Taehyun Jung, Byung-Yeon Kim, Chulhee Lee, Xibao Li, Maureen McKelvey, Justin Lin, Xielin Liu, Mehdi Majidpour, Mammo Muchi, Rajeshwari S. Raina, Sadao Nagaoka, Barry Naughton, Hiro Odagiri, Walter Park, Rajah Rasiah, Bhaven Samphat, Elias Sanidas, Daniel Schiller, Jung C. Shin, Lakhwinder Singh, Joseph Stiglitz, Bart Verspagen, Yi Wang, Brian Wright, Guisheng Wu, Xiaobo Wu, Yao Yang, Gabriel Yoguel, and Jiang Yu. Notable occasions on which feedback was received include the 2012 International Schumpeter Society held in Brisbane, several Globelics conferences (Beijing, Kuala Lumpur, Mexico City, Buenos Aires, Dakar), the IEA–World Bank Conference on New Thinking in Industrial Policy, the EPIP conference in Tokyo, the Atlanta Conference on Science, Technology, and Innovation Policy, the Cicalics Workshops (Hangzhou and Beijing), the Africalics Academy (Nairobi, Kenya), the Asia-Pacific Innovation Conferences (Singapore and Seoul), the Gordon Research Conference (New Hampshire), and the

EBES Conference (Istanbul). The book benefitted also from presentation at many seminars held at Tsinghua University, the China Academy of Sciences, the University of Gothenburg, UNU-MERIT, the American University, the Amirkabir University of Technology (Teheran), Punjabi University, Kyoto University, CCER and the School of Economics of Peking University, UFMG (Belo Horizonte), Korea University, Lund University, Hanover University, Seoul National University, and NIS-TADS (New Delhi).

I would also like to thank the staff at Cambridge University Press, whose valuable work has made this book available to the world, including Chris Harrison, Claire Poole, and Tom O'Reilly. A couple of editors have helped me by lending professional English-editing services to this work. In particular, I thank Amrit Kaur for this service. The last acknowledgement (but certainly not the least) goes to my lovely wife, So-yeon, who always stands by me with her prayers.

Keun Lee,
On the hills of Gwan-ak Mountain, Seoul, Spring 2013

PART I

Introduction and perspectives

1 | Introduction

1.1 The motivating question: sustaining the catch-up

While the rapid economic growth achieved by the newly industrialized economies in East Asia is widely appreciated, there has been concern recently about why such a "catch-up" is not happening elsewhere.[1] Despite high levels of development aid, policy changes, and reforms along the lines suggested by the "Washington Consensus," poverty prevails in many countries, the gap between rich and poor countries is widening, and many middle-income countries are not living up to expectations.[2] One reason why good policy prescriptions, such as opening up of the economy for international integration, may fail is argued to be poor institutional conditions, including insecure property rights, and an absence of the rule of law.[3] Thus, the recent literature on economic development has debated the relative importance of institutions, policy, and geography as competing determinants of economic growth, or as factors that contribute to a possible reversal of the fortunes of former colonies and other Third World countries. A stream of research has emerged that verifies the importance of institutions, and has become influential to a certain degree.[4] This "institutional supremacy" view has provided a theoretical justification for "second-generation" reforms and led to the so-called augmented Washington Consensus, which replaced the original Washington Consensus that had lost credibility.

The augmented Washington Consensus includes additional elements such as corporate governance, anti-corruption measures, flexible labor markets, compliance with World Trade Organization agreements, financial codes and standards, the prudent opening of capital accounts, non-intermediate exchange-rate regimes, independent central banks, inflation targeting, and social safety nets. These elements remain a part of a "shopping list," rather than a "recipe," for successful development. Rodrik (2006) contends that the augmented Washington

3

Consensus emphasis on institutions is its fundamental weakness, because even the most ambitious efforts at institutional reform can be faulted *ex post* for leaving something out. He also observes that the cross-national empirical literature has failed to establish a strong causal link between the implementation of any particular feature in an institution and sustained economic growth. Criticism of the relevance of institutions has also emerged in view of the questionable robustness of the proxy variables used to measure the degree of institutional development. Furthermore, Glaeser et al. (2004) propose that human capital is a more robust variable for long-term economic growth. The Commission on Growth and Development, established under the auspices of the World Bank, acknowledges the importance of government activism and industrial policy, while expressing caution over hasty liberalization and privatization.[5]

Two similarly important arguments have arisen from this body of literature. One is by Rodrik (2006), who claims that the Washington Consensus is dead and that we should identify "binding constraints" for growth in each country. The other argument is by Lee and Kim (2009) and Lin (2012a; 2012c), who state that the attempt to determine universal growth factors is absurd, and that development policies should consider the structural differences between developed and developing countries. Lee and Kim (2009) used country-panel analysis to prove that these different factors are important or binding, depending on the stage of development. They found that, although secondary education and political institutions seem important for lower-income countries, technological development and higher education are more effective in generating growth for upper-middle-income and high-income countries. In a sense, Lee and Kim (2009) suggest technological capability as the binding constraint on growth for middle-income countries. We build on these findings in our own study as it contributes fundamentally to the question of how to sustain economic growth in developing countries and avoids the more traditional focus on the state–market dichotomy.

Both the augmented list of the Washington Consensus and the 2008 Growth Commission report by the World Bank view the learning and promotion of technological capabilities by private firms as a matter of some, but not pre-eminent, concern. However, evidence from East Asia (as a success and in contrast to Latin America) indicates that this issue is the real binding constraint on sustained growth. Although

Hausmann, Rodrik, and Velasco (2008: 324) used growth diagnostics to identify specific binding constraints for each country, different bottlenecks or binding constraints can be identified for groups of countries, not just for specific countries. The idea of identifying bottlenecks or binding constraints makes sense because many developing countries are able to show growth spurts over a limited period (usually less than a decade), but are then unable to sustain this growth over a longer period.[6] Rodrik (2008) also cites the greater importance of sustaining rather than initiating growth.

We discuss this question of sustaining growth because many countries are able to grow and attain middle-income status, but subsequently fail to achieve high-income status. Examples from Latin America include Brazil and Argentina, where growth more or less stalled during the 1980s and the 1990s.[7] These countries are caught in the so-called middle-income country trap, a situation in which middle-income countries face a slowdown of growth as they get caught between low-wage manufacturers and high-wage innovators because their wage rates are too high to compete with low-wage exporters and their level of technological capability is too low to allow them to compete with the advanced countries.[8] However, this has not been the case for all developing countries. Several have successfully escaped this trap and moved beyond middle-income status to join the rich-country club. These include Korea and Taiwan, where per capita income trebled in the 1980s and 1990s after they started the decade on par with a number of Latin American countries.

Following this, the first question we ask in the present study is: what sustains such "catch-up" performance. Although the poverty trap and its relevance to low-income countries have been well-studied, few empirical studies have focussed on sustaining economic growth beyond the middle-income level. Neither the World Bank-sponsored Growth Commission report, nor a book by the leader of the commission (Spence 2011), discusses how developing countries can sustain growth beyond the middle-income levels. Nevertheless, the issue of the middle-income trap has attracted increasing attention and fueled a number of recent studies, including one by the World Bank (2010; 2012).[9]

One may question why growth beyond the middle-income status is important, or more important than spurring growth in low-income countries. A simple answer is that without clear prospects for middle-income countries of reaching higher levels of income, the promotion of growth may make less sense or present limited benefits for low-income countries. A more specific answer, however, is that the growth of low-income countries can be facilitated and sustained only when some middle-income countries can progress beyond producing and exporting low-cost, labor-intensive goods and services. The progress of the middle-income countries attenuates the "adding-up problem" that occurs when all developing countries flood the market with similar goods that they are comparably good at producing, thus reducing the relative price of these goods and making the sector less profitable (Spence 2011: 122–5). Only when middle-income countries become more successful and move away from the sale of these low-end goods to the next stage of making and selling higher-value-added or high-end goods can lower-income countries continue to grow from the sale of low-end goods.

From this viewpoint, China needs to move quickly beyond its specialization in low-cost, labor-intensive goods toward the development of higher-end goods so that latecomer countries can avoid competition with Chinese goods. Such a succession has happened in Asia, with the Koreans and Taiwanese taking over from the Japanese who came before, and the next-tier countries filling the vacuum left by South Korea (hereafter Korea) and Taiwan.

1.2 The middle-income country trap and sustaining the catch-up

Record of catching-up and the existence of the trap

The word "catch-up" has a long history, going back to the famous work of Gerschenkron (1962). In *Economic Backwardness in Historical Perspective*, Gerschenkron describes the economic growth of continental Europe in the late nineteenth century as it caught up with the UK. Following this work, the influential article by Abramowitz (1986), "Catching up, Forging ahead, and Falling behind", popularized the concept of catching up and made it part of the standard vocabulary of development economists.[10] Fagerberg and Godinho (2005: 514) define catch-up as a narrowing of a country's gap in productivity and income *vis-à-vis* a leading country, and convergence as a trend toward a reduction in differences in productivity and income in the world as a whole. This definition is consistent with that presented by Odagiri et al.

(2010: 2), who describe catch-up as the process by which a late-developing country narrows its gap in income ("economic catch-up") and technological capability ("technological catch-up") *vis-à-vis* a leading country. These studies suggest that catch-up can be measured by several indicators such as income, productivity, and technological capability. The measurement method selected should depend on the purpose of the research, and whether a nation, sector, or firm is involved.

Table 1.1 compares the gross domestic product (GDP) per capita of Korea and Taiwan with that of other countries between 1960 and 2010. In 1960, the per capita income in both Korea and Taiwan was about $150, which was substantially lower than that of most other comparable countries such as the Philippines ($257), Malaysia ($299), Chile ($550), Brazil ($208), and South Africa ($422), and closer to the level of Ghana ($180). However, by the early 1980s, Korea and Taiwan had reached the level of middle-income countries such as Brazil and Chile, and had even surpassed other previously richer countries in Asia, such as the Philippines and Malaysia. Regardless of whether the measure used is GDP per capita as measured in constant dollars or the more internationally comparable purchasing power parity (PPP), the fact remains that Korea and Taiwan were able to make the jump in two short decades, achieving per capita incomes upward of $10,000.

By the year 2000, the per capita incomes in PPP terms of comparable countries, such as Brazil, Argentina, Malaysia, and South Africa, was only one-half or one-third that of Korea or Taiwan. As shown in Table 1.1, between 1980 and 2000, most Latin American middle-income countries increased their GDP per capita only in nominal terms. In constant dollar terms (either PPP or ordinary constant dollars), the income levels of several Latin American economies, except Chile, made very little progress. For instance, Brazil's GDP per capita in constant dollars according to 2000 prices was $3,536 in 1980, and only $3,696 in 2000. Brazil, like many Latin American countries, had been caught in the middle-income trap.

The more recent decade of the 2000s seems to have been better for most Latin American economies (Table 1.1). In terms of per capita GDP (based on PPP), the increases in this decade tended to be larger than those of the 1980s and 1990s. Figure 1.1 displays per capita income trends for various middle-income countries. Brazil, Argentina,

Table 1.1 *Growth indicators in selected countries: GDP per capita*

	GDP per capita (current US$)				GDP per capita (2000 US$)				GDP per capita (2005 international PPP$)		
	1960	1980	2000	2010	1960	1980	2000	2010	1980	2000	2010
Korea	155.2	1,674.4	11,346.7	20,540.2	1,153.7	3,358.2	11,346.7	16,219.4	5,543.6	18,730.4	26,774.0
Taiwan	164.0	2,385.0	14,704.0	18,588.0	1,107.0	4,188.7	14,704.0	20,294.1	7,426.5	23,022.8	32,117.7
Asia											
Philippines	257.0	689.5	1,048.1	2,140.1	691.7	1,098.4	1,048.1	1,383.4	2,827.0	2,697.4	3,560.5
Thailand	101.1	681.4	1,943.2	4,613.7	320.9	785.0	1,943.2	2,712.5	2,220.6	5,496.8	7,672.9
Malaysia	299.1	1,802.8	4,005.6	8,372.8	812.6	1,909.6	4,005.6	5,184.7	4,866.9	10,208.7	13,213.9
China	92.0	193.0	949.2	4,433.0	105.5	186.4	949.2	2,426.3	524.0	2,667.5	6,818.7
India	83.1	270.8	450.4	1,375.4	181.0	230.0	450.4	794.8	879.4	1,722.1	3,038.8
Latin America											
Brazil	208.4	1,931.0	3,696.1	10,992.9	1,447.8	3,536.0	3,696.1	4,716.6	7,566.5	7,909.1	10,092.7
Argentina		2,735.8	7,695.6	9,123.7	5,251.9	7,540.7	7,695.6	10,749.3	10,075.4	10,282.4	14,362.6
Chile	550.4	2,466.5	4,877.5	12,639.5	1,841.1	2,500.3	4,877.5	6,430.1	5,653.8	11,029.4	14,540.2
Mexico	339.8	2,825.9	5,816.6	9,132.8	2,456.0	5,024.4	5,816.6	6,105.3	10,238.5	11,852.7	12,440.9
Africa											
Ghana	180.5	407.0	259.7	1,319.1	281.8	241.7	259.7	359.9	992.8	1,066.8	1,478.5
Nigeria	91.4	849.9	371.8	1,242.5	279.5	416.3	371.8	540.2	1,645.4	1,469.3	2,134.9
South Africa	422.1	2,926.8	3,019.9	7,271.7	2,203.7	3,463.2	3,019.9	3,753.4	8,762.6	7,641.0	9,496.9

Source: National Statistics of Republic of China (http://eng.stat.gov.tw) for Taiwanese data. All other data are from the world development indicators (WDI) compiled by the World Bank.

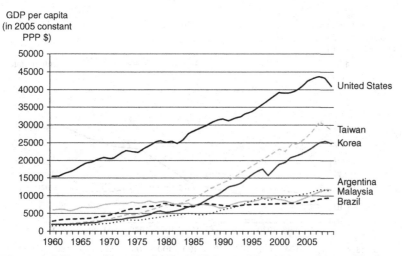

GDP per capita
(in 2005 constant
    PPP $)

Figure 1.1 Trend of income levels in Taiwan, Korea, Argentina, Malaysia, Brazil, and the USA.
Source: Prepared by the author using data from Penn World Table 7.0.

and Malaysia recorded positive growth, albeit slower than Korea or Taiwan. However, even this decade cannot be considered one of significant catch-up if we compare the per capita income of the two middle-income countries in Figure 1.2 (Malaysia and Brazil) to that of the USA. For instance, the income level of Brazil in 2009 relative to the USA was 22.7 percent, and the figure had remained almost unchanged in the twenty years since 1990. In fact, its relative income had gone down slightly in 2000 when it reached 19.9 percent. The best year for Brazil was 1980, when its income level relative to the USA was 32 percent, a level to which Brazil has never recovered since.

Turning next to Malaysia, we see that although the country grew very fast in the 1980s and 1990s, income levels stalled more or less in the mid-1990s. In 1980, its income level relative to the USA was 17 percent (Figure 1.2). This figure reached a peak of 25.7 percent in 1995 before declining to 24.8 percent in 2000 and recovering to 25.2 percent in 2005. Malaysia per capita income has made minimal progress from 1995 levels and reached only 27.5 percent in 2009, leading the World Bank to place Malaysia firmly among the countries which had fallen into the middle-income trap (Yusuf and Nabeshima 2009).

These cases imply that positive growth does not guarantee catch-up, and that faster growth is necessary if a developing economy is to catch

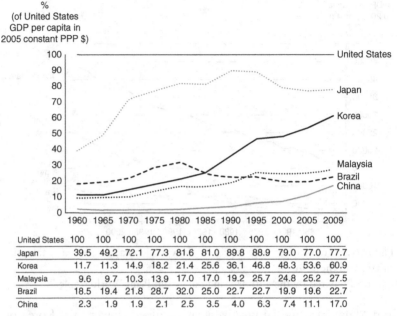

%
(of United States
GDP per capita in
2005 constant PPP $)

	1960	1965	1970	1975	1980	1985	1990	1995	2000	2005	2009
United States	100	100	100	100	100	100	100	100	100	100	100
Japan	39.5	49.2	72.1	77.3	81.6	81.0	89.8	88.9	79.0	77.0	77.7
Korea	11.7	11.3	14.9	18.2	21.4	25.6	36.1	46.8	48.3	53.6	60.9
Malaysia	9.6	9.7	10.3	13.9	17.0	17.0	19.2	25.7	24.8	25.2	27.5
Brazil	18.5	19.4	21.8	28.7	32.0	25.0	22.7	22.7	19.9	19.6	22.7
China	2.3	1.9	1.9	2.1	2.5	3.5	4.0	6.3	7.4	11.1	17.0

Figure 1.2 Trend of income levels in Japan, Korea, Malaysia, Brazil, and China as percentages of US income levels.
Source: Penn World Table 7.0.

up with its forerunners. Based on these cases, we infer that countries are most likely to fall into the middle-income trap when their income levels rise to about 20–30 percent of the US level. Only a few countries, including Korea and Taiwan, have served as notable exceptions to that rule by continuing to catch up beyond that range. Although the per capita income of Korea was only 21 percent of the US level in 1980, it tripled to 61 percent in the subsequent thirty years (Figure 1.2). When we draw a similar graph with Japan as the benchmark, we find the income levels of Korea and Taiwan 30 percent that of Japan in 1960, over 60 percent in 2000, and approaching 80 percent in 2009.

The risk of the middle-income trap is not limited to only a small number of countries, but is also relevant to many countries in the world. The recent report on China by the World Bank (2012:12) compares the relative income levels of a number of countries (compared with the USA) in 1960 to the levels in 2008. According to this analysis, as many as thirty countries fell into the trap. Specifically and more interestingly, the table indicates that the phenomenon of

Table 1.2 *Growth rates by income group*

	GDP per capita		Annual growth rate
	1980	1995	(1980–1995, %)
High-income countries	14,985	20,593	2.14
Lower-middle-income countries	958	1,280	1.95
Upper-middle-income countries	5,001	4,616	−0.53

Note: GDP per capita in constant 2000 US$. For details on each country and data sources, see Appendix Table A1.1.

Table 1.3 *Comparison of average growth of the three groups*

	High-income countries		Middle-income countries		Korea, Taiwan, Hong Kong, and Singapore	
	1980	1995	1980	1995	1980	1995
Real GDP per capita (in constant 2000 US$, average)	16,308.6	21,432.0	3,075.6	2,980.4	7,041.5	15,560.0

Note: GDP per capita in constant 2000 US$. For details on each country and data sources see Appendix Table A1.1. Data of the four Asian Tigers are excluded from the high-income group.

income-growth stagnation is more apparent in the group of upper-middle-income countries, or those with an income level of 20–30 percent of that of the USA. From 1980 to 1995 the average growth rate of the per capita incomes of upper-middle-income countries was negative, with the average income level decreasing to $5,001 in 1980 and $4,616 in 1995, both in year 2000 constant dollar terms (Table 1.2). In contrast, lower-middle-income countries with per capita incomes of between $1,000 and $3,000 in 2000 exhibited positive growth in this period, although their per capita income growth (1.95 percent) was lower than that of high-income countries (2.14 percent). In the same period, the income levels of the four Asian Tigers more than doubled (Table 1.3).

This trend of growth rates declining as a country moves from lower-middle to upper-middle income levels suggests also that it becomes more difficult to sustain catch-up when a country is getting close to the frontier level of income. How can we explain the difficulties faced by middle-income countries, and how can such countries make a break-through in this dismal situation? This book attempts to answer this question, in part by asking also how a few countries, such as Korea and Taiwan, have managed to escape the trap, and how they continued to catch up despite the odds.

Korea: taking a new path since the mid 1980s

In the debate on the determinants of long-term economic growth, Acemoglu, Johnson, and Robinson (2001) use the contrast between North and South Korean institutions to argue for the importance of institutions for long-term economic growth. In contrast, Glaeser et al. (2004) used North and South Korea as the basis for the converse argument that institutions are not in themselves a key cause of growth. Instead, economic growth itself facilitates the establishment of institutions or democracy in formerly authoritarian states such as South Korea. Glaeser et al. use the case of South Korea to criticize the view that institutions are of primary importance for economic growth. They argue instead that human capital is a more robust factor. While North and South Korea have pursued different growth strategies, the impact of policies alone in each of these states is not easy to understand because institutions also differ markedly across them in matters such as the protection of private property rights.

Looking at South Korea (hereafter referred to as Korea), we see that it is similar to other developing countries in that it specializes in manufacturing labor-intensive goods for export, and in that it har-nesses the advantage of low wages to this end. However, Korea faced external imbalances in that it had a persistent trade deficit throughout the first two decades of its industrialization in the 1960s and 1970s. These two decades not only were periods of rapid growth but also of slow catch-up in income levels compared to Japan, which was also growing fast during this period.[11] Faster catch-up occurred only after the 1980s when Korea shifted to higher-end goods backed by the in-house research and development (R&D) of its private firms. Prepar-ation for catch-up started in the mid 1970s as the government emphasized technological development by conducting publicly funded R&D in government research institutes and transferring the results to private firms. In the 1980s, the government switched from conducting public R&D to promoting private R&D by enabling tax incentives. Since then, it has even initiated joint R&D activities involving private firms and government research institutes for larger, riskier projects. In the mid 1980s, the R&D–GDP ratio of Korea surpassed 1 percent, and the private sector share of total R&D expenditure surpassed 50 percent. Most Latin American countries did not increase their R&D expenditure by as much, and as of 2000, none of them had an R&D–GDP ratio higher than 1 percent.[12]

If we use the development of IPR as an indicator, the catch-up experience of Korea can be described as having four distinct stages.[13] The first stage occurred from the 1960s to the mid 1970s, when Korea's rapid economic growth started. This period was characterized by the very poor technological capability of its domestic inventors. The inflow of foreign technology was low, and foreign inventors had no interest in applying for IPR in Korea. There were few regular patents and more petit patents or utility models being filed, with a large share of these patents being attributed to Korean inventors. Although the number of utility models created each year was as large as 4,000 on average, the number of regular invention patents was only one-third of that figure.

The second stage occurred from the mid 1970s to the mid 1980s when foreign inventors dominated patent application and registration in Korea. Korean firms started at this time to actively seek the importation and transfer of foreign technologies in order to achieve imitative innovation. With the growth of the technology market, the inflow of foreign technology increased, and foreign inventors became increasingly interested in applying for IPR in Korea, so that the foreign share of patents registered in Korea reached an average of 70 percent each year. The remaining patents were registered by Korean inventors, most of whom were individuals acting on their own accord, as corporations were not yet running in-house R&D centers and were rather primitive in their technological capabilities.

The third period, from the mid 1980s to the mid 1990s, was the period of rapid catch-up led by big businesses or *chaebols*. It was at this time that Korean firms realized the limitation of licensing and embodied technology transfer, and they began to establish their own in-house R&D centers.[14] With this growth of indigenous R&D capability, the share of domestic inventors increased rapidly. More firms started to apply for US patents because they encountered more IPR-related conflicts, and the Korean government substantially increased the level and scope of IPR protection. The enhancement of in-house R&D activities by firms is reflected in the share of corporate patents which surpassed that of individual patents for the first time in 1986. The average share of corporate patents reached 75 percent at this time, and the ratio of utility patents to invention patents also decreased from 2:1 (in the second period) to 1:1 (in the third period). In this third stage, the number of college students also suddenly doubled, with the enrollment ratio in tertiary education doubling within five years from 14.7 percent in 1980 to 34.1 percent in 1985, surpassing the average level of middle-income developing countries.[15]

  The final period started in the mid 1990s and continues to the present time. The share of domestic inventors in Korea-filed patents indicates that Korean firms have succeeded in catching up. The Korean share surpassed 50 percent in 1993, then reached 62.4 percent in 1999. Since the mid 1990s, Korea's R&D–GDP ratio has exceeded 2 percent, with private R&D accounting for more than 80 percent of the total. The level of productivity of Korean firms also reached 90 percent that of Japanese firms by the late 1990s.[16] Perhaps most tellingly, in 1995, Korea joined the Organization for Economic Co-operation and Development (OECD), which is primarily a grouping of rich countries.

  The previous discussion suggests that an intensification of R&D expenditure and higher education has laid the basis for sustaining catch-up growth. Industries were upgraded, as can be confirmed by the increase in the number of US patents filed by Koreans. In the early 1980s, the number of US patent applications by Koreans was approximately 50, within the range of other middle-income countries such as Brazil or Argentina.[17] In the 1980s and the 1990s, Korean applications increased rapidly to more than ten times the average of other middle-income countries where incomes had remained relatively flat. In 2000, Korea and Taiwan filed about 5,000 US patent applications, whereas other middle- or lower-income countries, including Brazil and Argentina, filed fewer than 500 per year. By the late 1980s, this upgrade in technological capability led Korea into its first ever trade surplus since its independence from colonial rule, and by the mid 1990s trade surpluses were a stable feature of the Korean economy. In this manner,

R&D expenditure
(% of GDP)

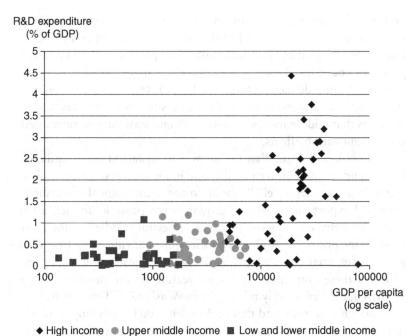

◆ High income ● Upper middle income ■ Low and lower middle income

Figure 1.3 R&D–GDP ratios by country at different income levels (2001–5 averages).

Korea was able to overcome the persistent trap of external imbalances and the stop–go cycle of imbalances and reforms (or devaluations).

In sum, the difference between the more successful Asian economies and the less successful Latin American economies (or the reversal of fortune between these two groups of countries) can be explained by how much priority was given to the enhancement of long-term growth potential, particularly innovation capability. A World Bank assessment of the reform decade of the 1990s observes that growth entails more than just the efficient use of resources. Growth-oriented actions such as technological catch-up and the encouragement of risk-taking may be needed for faster accumulation.[18] Technological innovation is increasingly recognized as one of the most serious bottlenecks of growth in many countries, especially the middle-income countries of Latin America.

Figure 1.3 shows the R&D–GDP ratio of countries at different income levels. Although we would expect a positive correlation between income levels and the R&D–GDP ratio, the ratio suddenly becomes flat among middle-income countries, or countries with per capita incomes of between $1,000 and $10,000. In other words, the ratio does not increase proportionally with per capita income in this group of countries. This suggests that the flat relationship is a root cause of the middle-income trap. The lack of R&D growth along with the growth in income is not a desirable situation, and this finding indicates that middle-income countries should start paying more attention to innovation efforts.

This book will argue that the answer to sustained catch-up lies in building up technological capability and innovation systems at the firm, sector, and country level. Without strong technological capabilities, sustained export and economic growth is not possible. In fact, a key difference between the more and less successful middle-income economies is the priority they give to policies aimed at enhancing long-term growth potential, technology, and higher education in particular. Whereas these emphases are a core feature of the northeast Asian approach, they are starkly missing in the Washington Consensus.

Although this study and that of Amsden (2001) both emphasize the importance of knowledge for economic development, the latter deals with a much broader country group called "the rest." Amsden does not distinguish between those that have moved beyond the middle-income country trap and those that have not. Although both this study and Justin Lin's new structural economics emphasize the importance of structural differences between developed and developing countries, our distinction lies in our focus on middle-income, rather than low-income, countries, and on their building the technological capability required to go beyond the middle-income stage.

1.3 The argument of this book: specializing in shorter-cycle technologies

Lee and Lim (2001) point out that the catch-up paths of countries differ and that an issue exists of strategic choice among alternatives. Lee and Lim identify three different patterns of catch-up (Table 1.4): *(a)* a path-following catch-up, which refers to latecomer firms following the same path taken by forerunners; *(b)* a stage-skipping catch-up, which refers to latecomer firms following the path but skipping some stages, thus saving time; and *(c)* a path-creating catch-up, which refers to latecomer firms exploring their own path of technological development.

Table 1.4 *Three patterns of technological catch-up*

Path of forerunner: stage A –> stage B –> stage C –> stage D
(1) Path-following catch-up
stage A –> stage B –> stage C –> stage D
e.g. consumer electronics in Korea during the analog era, personal computer, and machine tools
(2) Stage-skipping catch-up (leapfrogging 1)
stage A ———> stage C –> stage D
e.g. automobile engine development by Hyundai Motors, D-RAM development by Samsung, and digital telephone switch development by China (Mu and Lee 2005)
(3) Path-creating catch-up (leapfrogging 2)
stage A –> stage B –> stage C' –> stage D'
e.g. CDMA mobile phone and digital TV in Korea

Note: in stage C, the two technologies C and C' represent alternative technologies.
Sources: Lee and Lim (2001), Lee, Lim, and Song (2005), Mu and Lee (2005).

For example, the achievement of Samsung in memory chips (called dynamic random access memory or D-RAM) can be seen as a case of stage-skipping catch-up. Considering the potential of the memory chip business, Samsung decided to enter this new industry as a latecomer and to compete directly with the Americans and Japanese who were the leaders in this industry. They began considering memory chip production seriously during the transition period when the world's D-RAM industry was moving from 16-Kbit to 64-Kbit chips. The Korean government advised its firms to start by producing the 1-Kbit D-RAM, but private firms had the prerogative of skipping from the production of 1- to 16-Kbit D-RAMs, and entering directly into the 64-Kbit D-RAM market. Samsung entered the market directly with 64-Kbit memory chips after purchasing the design technology from Microelectronic Technology and production technology from Japan-based Sharp. This strategy of stage-skipping enabled Samsung to save time, to catch up with the incumbent leader, and to become the market leader in the 2000s.

Another strategy is to execute a bold entry into a not-yet established but emerging industry by taking advantage of a new techno-economic paradigm or new generation of technologies. In this way, a country can create its own different path and diverge from that of its forerunners. This path-creating strategy is consistent with the literature on leapfrogging. Perez and Soete (1988) and Freeman and Soete (1997) propose that some latecomers may be able to leapfrog older technologies, bypass heavy investments in previous technology systems, and adopt new technologies to assume control of the market in competition with the incumbent firms or countries. This strategy of leapfrogging makes most sense during a paradigm shift when every country or firm finds itself faced with the challenge of dealing with a newly emerging techno-economic paradigm. Entry barriers tend to be low at such a time, as some incumbents tend to prefer to ignore the new technologies and maintain the existing technologies in which they are dominant. This idea of leapfrogging is also consistent with the idea of technological discontinuity as proposed by Anderson and Tushman (1990). The authors posit that competence-destroying discontinuity may lead to the rise of new entrants.

The leveling of Korea with Japan would not have been as successful if Korean electronics companies, such as Samsung or LG, had not targeted the emerging digital technology-based products more aggressively than the Japanese companies that preferred to keep the analog products dominant for a longer time.[19] The Japanese companies developed an innovation called the analog-based high definition (HD) TV in the late 1980s, and they offered to transfer technologies related to this new product to Korean firms. Korean companies initially considered the offer to follow the Japanese firms, and to go along the same path as the Japanese had trod in the 1970s and 1980s. However, they decided against this, and instead attempted a leapfrogging strategy by developing digital-technology-based HD TV, which was at the time an alternative and emerging technology. They did this by forming a public–private R&D consortium, and this marked the beginning of a Korean hegemony in the display industry over Japan that remains evident in the world market today. Without such risk-taking and leapfrogging, the leveling of Korea with Japan would have taken much longer or would never have occurred.

We reason that leapfrogging is more likely to occur when changes in technology or product generations occur more frequently, as they do in certain technological sectors. In subsequent chapters, we will demonstrate that such features are closely linked to the length of the cycle time of technologies. Cycle time refers to the speed with which technologies change or become obsolete over time, and the speed and frequency at which new technologies emerge.

We argue then that qualified latecomers can advantageously target such sectors and specialize in them. This venture is risky but sensible because latecomers do not have to rely greatly on the existing technologies dominated by the incumbents, because the short cycle of such technologies implies that the dominance of the incumbent tends more often to be disrupted, and that ever-emerging new technologies always present new opportunities. Therefore we suggest that middle-income countries with some prior experience and technological capability move into shorter-cycle technology-based sectors: a short cycle time means that the sector relies less on existing technologies and can thus leverage the greater opportunities that arise from the emergence of new ones. This property of new opportunities indicates more new growth prospects, and the property of less reliance on existing technologies may lead to the faster localization of a knowledge-creation mechanism. This property also indicates lower entry barriers and the possibility of higher profitability associated with less collision with the technologies of advanced countries, fewer royalty payments, and even first-/fast-mover advantages or product differentiation.

In light of the concept of competence-destroying discontinuity,[20] such discontinuity is more likely to occur in short-cycle technology sectors. Furthermore, even if a sector is prone to competence-destroying discontinuity, that sector is not likely to generate much catch-up by the latecomer if the sector also exhibits a very long cycle time in which discontinuity occurs at very long intervals or very infrequently.

In the empirical analysis of this study, the cycle time of technologies is measured by the mean backward citation, which is the time difference between the application (or grant) year of the *citing* patent and that of the *cited* patents.[21] A long cycle time indicates the greater importance of old or existing knowledge and thus the greater need to study old knowledge from the viewpoint of latecomers. When knowledge in the field changes quickly (i.e. a short cycle time), the disadvantages for the latecomer may not be that great. Therefore, we hypothesize that the shorter the cycle time of a technology is, the higher the possibility of catch-up by the latecomers.

Figure 1.4 presents actual trends in the cycle time of technologies as calculated using US patents held by G5 countries (i.e. the UK, France,

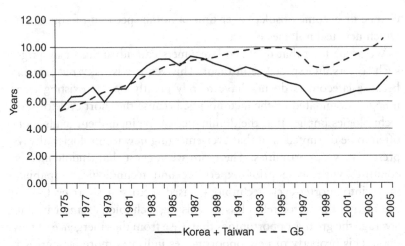

Figure 1.4 Trend of the average cycle time of technologies in the G5 vs. Korea + Taiwan.
Note: G5 comprises UK, France, Germany, Italy, and Canada.
Source: Author's calculation using NBER patent data.

Germany, Italy and Canada) and by Korea and Taiwan. The numbers on the vertical axis represent the average cycle time of patents held by these countries. For example, a value of eight on the vertical axis indicates that an average cycle time of patents is eight years, which means, for instance, that Korea and Taiwan together tend on average to cite eight-year-old patents. The data indicate that the paths of the two catching-up economies of Korea and Taiwan are similar to those of the advanced or G5 countries in the 1970s and the early 1980s. However, beginning in the mid 1980s, the catching-up countries traveled in an opposite direction or took a path toward increasingly shorter-cycle-time technologies. Thus, the average cycle time of the patents held by Korea and Taiwan became shorter in that time, reaching six to seven years by the late 1990s. This is two to three years shorter than the average cycle time of the patents held by the G5 countries, which has ranged from nine to ten years since the late 1980s. As a consequence, Korea and Taiwan have ended up with a completely different patent portfolio from that of the G5 and other advanced countries. Table 1.5 lists the top ten technologies in terms of the number of patents filed by all G5 countries and by Korea and Taiwan together. None of the top ten technological sectors in Korea and Taiwan overlaps with those of G5 countries.

Table 1.5 *Top ten most filed patent classes of G5 and Korea and Taiwan, 1980–95*

	Class	Class name	Patent count
G5			
1	514	Drug, bio-affecting, and body-treating compositions	10,349
2	428	Stock material or miscellaneous articles	3,883
3	73	Measuring and testing	3,789
4	123	Internal combustion engines	3,479
5	424	Drug, bio-affecting, and body-treating compositions	3,389
6	210	Liquid purification or separation	2,853
7	435	Chemistry: molecular biology and microbiology	2,852
8	250	Radiant energy	2,639
9	264	Plastic and nonmetallic article shaping or treating	2,349
10	324	Electricity: measuring and testing	2,325
Korea and Taiwan			
1	438	Semiconductor device manufacturing: process	1,189
2	348	Television	712
3	439	Electrical connectors	408
4	257	Active solid-state devices (e.g. transistors and solid-state diodes)	374
5	362	Illumination	374
6	280	Land vehicles	355
7	365	Static information storage and retrieval	346
8	70	Locks	340
9	360	Dynamic magnetic information storage or retrieval	313
10	482	Exercise devices	311

Note: G5 includes UK, France, Germany, Italy, and Canada.
Source: calculation using the NBER US patent data.

It is for these reasons that we consider the mid 1980s an important turning point that opened a new path for sustained catch-up beyond the middle-income stage. It is in this period when Taiwan and Korea reached the middle-income level: Korea's per capita GDP became 25 percent of that of the USA (Figure 1.2), and Korea and Taiwan began increasing their R&D expenditure, with their R&D/GDP ratio averaging more than 1 percent annually. In other words, when these countries decisively began the journey toward technology-based growth, the cycle time of their technologies tended to move in progressively shorter directions.

Figure 1.4 shows that only since 2000 have their technologies made a turn in the opposite direction toward longer cycles.

This study refers to this strategy of technological specialization in shorter-cycle technologies during the catching-up period as a "detour," because developing countries do not attempt to directly and immediately replicate the path and industries of the advanced economies that specialize in long-cycle technologies. Instead, countries that are successful at catching-up move initially in the opposite direction progressively toward a sector with shorter-cycle technologies, and this gradually results in technological diversification into new sectors. However, as countries reach the point of some technological maturity (as Korea and Taiwan did in the early 2000s), their own success enables them to enter into longer-cycle and other technologies. For instance, the Korean economy began with labor-intensive (long-cycle technology) industries such as apparel or shoes in the 1960s. It then moved toward the shorter- (or medium-) cycle sectors of low-end consumer electronics and automobile assembly in the 1970s and 1980s and then again to even shorter-cycle sectors of telecommunication equipment, memory chips, and digital TVs since the 1990s.[22] Recently, some leading firms have even attempted to enter purely science-based sectors and completely new kinds of long-cycle technology.

One may wonder whether a single variable such as industry cycle time can explain the complex process of technological development, and thus question the explanatory power of this variable. However, cycle time is a key variable because it also reflects changes in other diverse aspects of technological development. Specializing in shorter-cycle time technologies is actually a process of technological diversification. As shown in the curve of the cycle times of Korea and Taiwan, these two economies have exhibited a gradual shortening of their cycle times since the mid 1980s. Such gradual shortening does not mean that these economies have increasingly specialized in a few sectors but that these economies have continued to enter into progressively newer sectors with shorter cycle times, that is, to embark on a process of inter-sector diversification. Simultaneously, the old sectors have not simply given up and ceased to exist, but they have been upgraded into higher-value-added segments in the same industry, which also features shorter-cycle technologies than old or lower-value-added segments. This process is a kind of an intra-sector diversification into higher ends. In sum, a gradual shortening of cycle time occurs when an economy realizes dual diversification, that is, both inter- and intra-sectoral diversification. The economies of Korea and Taiwan have actually experienced these two kinds of diversification and upgrading since the 1980s.

Lee and Mathews (2012) wrote extensively on the outcome of upgrading in the same industry as well as of entry into new industries in East Asia. In a case of intra-sectoral upgrading or diversification, semiconductor firms in Korea and Taiwan began with integrated conductor (IC) packaging or testing (low-value-added activities) before moving into IC fabrication, and eventually to IC design (highest valued-added). Many cases of successive entry into higher-value-added industries are also found in Taiwan and Korea. For instance, the Tatung company in Taiwan has made successive entries into new industries since the 1960s, beginning with black-and-white TVs in 1964, color TVs in 1969, VCRs and PCs in the mid 1980s, hard disk drives in the mid-1980s, TV chips/ASICs (application-specific integrated circuits) in the late 1980s, work-station clones in 1989, and so on.[23] The Samsung group in Korea has also executed successive entries into progressively newer industries over the sixty years of its existence, and its composition of sales by sector has changed dramatically over the decades, with its growth engines shifting from low-end goods to high-end goods.[24] Samsung began with light manufacturing (i.e. long-cycle technology-based) industries such as textiles, but it then entered consumer electronics, followed by semiconductors, telecommunications, flat panel displays, and other industries based on short-cycle technologies.

If a middle-income economy fails to realize these two kinds of upgrading process, it may fall into the middle-income trap, or become a victim of the so-called adding-up problem. Such an economy's early success is often based on its initial comparative advantage in the area of low-wage-labor industries, and it has to move toward higher-value-added activities in order to afford higher wage rates. Moreover, new and cheaper labor sites always emerge in the next-tier countries to replace those currently positioned in the global value-chains, indicating the adding-up problem.[25] Therefore, new industries or activities which the next-tier countries are not yet capable of executing should be started in the middle-income countries, while industries in those countries that become mature would downgrade to lower-value-added activities. Given this situation, an important feature of a successful catch-up is the ability to enter at a progressively earlier stage of the cycle as time passes.[26] Otherwise, an economy is doomed to remain in lower-wage activities or industries, which have few chances for long-term success.

Korea and Taiwan did not set out specifically to target a certain fixed list of short-cycle technologies. Instead, the process of change they underwent indicates that they simply kept moving into shorter-and shorter-cycle technologies, thus achieving technological diversification. Therefore, an interesting measure of a country's catch-up prospects is whether it has experienced such a "technological turning point," and switched from longer cycles to shorter ones along the curve of the cycle time of technologies. This issue will be discussed in relation to other countries, including China and India, in Chapters 8 and 9.

By demonstrating the importance of moving into shorter-cycle-time technologies at three levels (firm, sector, and country), this study suggests that although the transition from low to middle income tends to involve trade-based specialization in sectors inherited from the advanced countries, the next stage of transition from the middle- to high-income level involves technology-based specialization in sectors with short cycle times where there is the frequent emergence of new technologies.

The following chapter provides a theoretical perspective on the issues and discusses the main hypotheses of the study. Chapters 3, 4, and 5 make up the second part of the book in which we analyze catch-up at the country, sector, and firm levels, focussing on the importance of short-cycle technologies in each of these levels. The third part includes Chapters 6, 7, and 8. Chapter 6 synthesizes the findings from the preceding chapters into a tentative theory of knowledge-based catch-up and suggests the concept of "detour" as a development strategy for middle-income countries. Chapter 7 discusses catch-up from a policy perspective and goes into how to implement capability building and industrial upgrading. It maps out also the steps that a country can take to make successive moves into shorter-cycle sectors. Chapter 8 discusses the cases of China and India. The fourth part of the book is the conclusion. Chapter 9 theoretically explores the concept of a technological turning point toward short-cycle technologies and the last chapter provides a summary of the main premises and concerns, and discusses the contributions and limitations of the study.

2 | Knowledge as a key factor for economic catch-up

2.1 Neo-Schumpeterian perspectives on economic catch-up

Since the early work by Gerschenkron (1962) and Abramowitz (1986), numerous studies have followed, but it is the Schumpeterian economists who provide a more theoretical skeleton for the empirical work on the catch-up phenomenon.[1] The work of Nelson and Winter (1982) not only revives evolutionary economics with its explicit linkages to Schumpeter's insight but also stimulates research applying this line of thought to catch-up.[2] A distinctive feature of these studies by neo-Schumpeterians is their emphasis on innovation and technological capabilities as the enabling factors for catch-up. They note that in the 1960s and 1970s, the main factor supporting catch-up is capital accumulation, whereas in the 1980s and 1990s, the accumulation of technological capabilities is more relevant.[3] Currently, only those countries that have invested heavily in the formation of skills and R&D ability seem to be capable of catching up, and those that have not made such investment are falling further behind.

However, while innovation has been the main source of economic progress in the West, learning has also been important for the catch-up of the rest of the non-Western latecomers (Amsden 1989, 2001). Similarly, Jaffe, Trajtenberg, and Henderson (1993) note that, as technological innovation can be regarded as the exploitation of available knowledge stock to generate new knowledge, latecomers tend to reap the benefits arising from the flow of knowledge from advanced economies to facilitate research and invention. Therefore, institutions for local learning and access to the foreign knowledge base are recognized as the critical factors for successful catch-up. Moreover, indigenous technological capabilities have become increasingly important because of the tendency of developed economies to pursue and enforce their IPR in developing countries.

In our attempt to study the phenomenon of sustained catch-up using Schumpeterian economics, we begin with the concept of the technological regime proposed by Nelson and Winter (1982: 258), which is also similar to that of technological paradigm of Dosi (1982).[4] They first introduced the concept of the technological regime as a theoretical framework to interpret a variety of innovative processes observed across technological sectors. They distinguished science-based regimes from the cumulative ones. Breschi, Malerba, and Orsenigo (2000) define technological regimes as a particular combination of key dimensions. They posit four fundamental factors: technological opportunity, appropriability of innovations, cumulativeness of technological advances, and properties of the knowledge base. This neo-Schumpeterian notion of technological regime has been used to explain the specific way in which the innovative activities of a technological sector are organized.[5]

Although the concept of technological regime is formed to express the characteristics of sectors or technologies, we can also consider it in terms of expressing the characteristics of the knowledge bases of countries and firms. Here, we rely on the concept of the national innovation system (NIS) proposed by Freeman and Lundvall in the early 1980s. Lundvall (1992: 2) defines the NIS as the "elements and relationships which interact in the production, diffusion and use of new, and economically useful, knowledge ... and are either located within or rooted inside the borders of a nation state." The NIS deals with the efficiency of a nation in establishing a system for learning and innovation, that is, the acquisition, creation, diffusion, and utilization of knowledge. Specifically, the core idea is how efficiently firms, universities, and research laboratories acquire external knowledge or create new knowledge, and how efficiently this knowledge is diffused and utilized by other institutional actors. Differences in the NIS are hypothesized to affect the direction and speed of a nation's innovation and eventually lead to different levels of competitiveness between nations. Similarly, differences in a corporate innovation system (CIS) affect the direction and/or speed of innovation of a firm and consequently its financial performance, including its values.

In other words, studies on technological development tend to proceed from one of three levels. At the national level, several studies adopting the concept of the NIS are available.[6] At the sectoral level, studies have been based on the concept of sectoral systems of innovation, such as those of Malerba (2004) and Malerba and Nelson (2012). At the firm level, a significant volume of research emphasizes firm-level learning, knowledge, and R&D, which are regarded as sources of inter-firm heterogeneity in the Schumpeterian theory of the firms.[7] Another important study is that of Jensen et al. (2007), which defines the two modes of learning and innovation, namely, the science–technology–innovation (STI) mode and the learning by doing/using/interacting (DUI) mode. This concept of the modes of learning is related to the idea of treating a firm as a learning organization (Senge 1992), that is, an organization that has been designed, developed, and implemented to have the capability to adapt continuously to its environment. The STI mode involves explicit knowledge, whereas the DUI mode involves tacit knowledge. This study is also related to an earlier work by Nonaka and Takeuchi (1995).

Influential scholars in this tradition have recognized the need for multi-dimensional studies on the innovation system. Lundvall et al. (2009) classified the three levels of research and innovation system, namely, NIS as the macro-level, the sectoral or regional innovation system as the meso-level, and the corporate innovation system as the micro-level. They suggest a method to study NIS that moves from the micro- to the macro-level and then returns to micro-level. Therefore, the present study follows this line of integrated study.

At the national level (Chapter 3) we explore the specific features of the national knowledge base that are involved in the national level catch-up and how they evolved. Through these aspects, we will compare the experiences of the advanced countries with those of the more successful (or sustained) catch-up countries in Asia and other less successful (or unsustained) catch-up countries. At the sectoral level (Chapter 4) we will determine which sectors (or technological classes) tend to involve faster catch-up by the latecomers. Again, in this analysis, we will compare the experiences of Korea and Taiwan with those of four other Asian countries (i.e. China, India, Malaysia, and Thailand) and four Latin American countries (i.e. Brazil, Argentina, Mexico, and Chile). At the firm level, a high degree of heterogeneity is expected between firms from catching-up economies and firms from the advanced economies. In Chapter 5 we will verify this hypothesis with focus on knowledge-related aspects, and we will determine which characteristics of the firm-level knowledge base are critical in affecting catch-up performance. We will compare the case of the Korean firms, representing the catch-up firms, with the case of American firms, representing advanced firms.

In sum, whereas the study by Park and Lee (2006) focuses on catch-up at the sector level, the current study proposes not only to extend the sectoral-level study to more countries but also to conduct a comparable study at the firm and country levels. Moreover, the present study introduces not only the traditional characteristic variables but also new and knowledge-related variables as key explanatory variables. This feature marks this study as a work following the tradition of Schumpeter, who emphasizes technical change as the engine of growth. This study is also neo-Schumpeterian in the sense that it recognizes the possibility of predictable regularities in technological change instead of treating technical change as a purely exogenous phenomenon, as in traditional neoclassical economics.[8] Another distinction of the current study is that it begins with the premise that the phenomenon of economic catching-up can also be explained well with a focus on technological capabilities and that this focus will lead to the identification and explanation of certain regularities involved in the catching-up phenomenon.

Recently, economic research in this school of thought has tended to use patent data for the quantitative analysis of innovations and growth. The current study will also use patent data. Therefore, by extending the levels of analysis from sectors to firms and countries, the present study measures the knowledge base of countries, sectors, and firms by primarily using patent data, and investigates the linkages between the characteristics of knowledge bases of latecomer firms and countries and their catch-up performances. This study focusses on the following theoretical issues.

2.2 Knowledge and economic catch-up: overview of the key issues

The premise of this study is that differences in innovation systems across countries affect the catch-up performances of countries and firms. While we attempt to quantify various key aspects of such innovation systems and use patent data in order to empirically explore this idea, there remain a potentially large number of variables that represent different aspects of the innovation system that remain unaccounted for. Given that we cannot deal with all aspects of innovation systems, a good starting point is simply to focus on aspects closely linked to the key ideas discussed in the development literature. This study therefore deals with the four main knowledge variables and measures them consistently at the country, sector, and firm levels. Each variable is supposed to deal with a development idea from the literature.

The first idea concerns technological specialization, or the choice of which technologies or sectors to focus on for catch-up growth. In this regard, we deal with two sub-issues. The first sub-issue is whether latecomers should specialize in short-cycle (emerging) technologies, or in longer-cycle technologies. The second sub-issue is whether a latecomer will do well to target high-quality (original) patents for catch-up growth.

The third idea concerns the learning and creation of knowledge. Here, we deal with the sub-issue of the role of the indigenous creation and diffusion of knowledge versus reliance on a foreign knowledge base. The final idea is that of choosing between an unbalanced (concentrated) and balanced (diversified) growth strategy. These ideas are more fully elaborated and tested in subsequent chapters, but the following section provides a quick overview of the key issues.

Technological specialization 1: short- versus long-cycle technologies

Knowledge base refers to the nature of the knowledge underpinning the innovative activities of firms. Technological knowledge involves various degrees of specificity, tacitness, and complexity, and may differ greatly across technologies. Generic knowledge refers to knowledge of a very broad nature, whereas specific knowledge refers to specialized knowledge targeted on specific applications. Generic and specific knowledge are also related to different sciences: basic sciences tend to produce generic knowledge, whereas applied sciences generate focused knowledge (Breschi et al. 2000). The literature also focusses on the tacitness of knowledge as well as on the conversion of tacit into explicit (codified) knowledge, which is the main theme in the study by Nonaka and Takeuchi (1995). According to Jung and Lee (2010), latecomer firms experience more difficulty in catching up with forerunning firms when a sector involves more tacit knowledge. Latecomers require more time and experience to absorb tacit knowledge.

Moving forward from these efforts, the present study focusses add-
itionally on the life expectancy of knowledge. An important attribute
of knowledge is the fact that it becomes obsolete over time. Knowledge
differs in this respect. Some types of knowledge become obsolete
quickly, while others do not. We can expect the speed of obsolescence
to affect the chance of catching up. Long-cycle technologies place great
importance on old knowledge. From the point of view of latecomers,
more time has to be spent studying old knowledge. However, when the
knowledge in a field changes quickly, the latecomer does not have to
spend a lot of time mastering existing technologies, and can thus be
said to be at less of a disadvantage. Therefore, we hypothesize and
demonstrate that in technology fields with a shorter cycle time, the
latecomer has a greater possibility of catching up. This hypothesis is
consistent with that of Amsden and Chu (2003: 167), who observed
that the competitiveness of a firm engaging in catch-up efforts depends
on its ability to enter new market segments quickly, to manufacture
products with high levels of engineering excellence, and to be first-to-
market through the implementation of the best integrative designs.

Specialization in short-cycle technology implies a specialization in
and reliance on recent technologies. In this sense, our hypothesis on the
advantage of short-cycle technologies contradicts the classical hypotheses of Posner (1961) and Vernon (1966) on the product life cycle.
Posner observed that latecomers tend to inherit old or mature products
or industries, and Vernon subsequently pointed out that the production of goods eventually moves on to developing countries with
cheaper production costs, especially wage rates. However, the authors
did not consider the possibility of local indigenous firms assuming
control of production and winning over business from the multinational corporations (MNCs) of more advanced countries. Vernon
(1966) did not therefore imagine a situation in which not only the
production of standardized goods, but also the innovative or imitative
development of new or existing products, could occur in indigenous
firms in developing countries. Moving forward, we argue that latecomers should in fact explore new opportunities in emerging technologies that rely less on existing technologies that are most likely already
dominated by incumbent advanced countries. After all, inheriting
mature technologies tends to correspond to low-margin (low-wage)
activities that are also not sufficient to sustain the economic growth of
the latecomer beyond the middle-income status. An exception arises

only when the learning and capability building that results from the application of the mature technology can lead at a later stage to an upgrading or leapfrogging into higher-value-added or emerging high-return technologies.

Although the countries most successful at catching up (e.g. Korea and Taiwan) have demonstrated more success in shorter-cycle time technologies, we hypothesize that the same pattern has not been the case in second-tier catch-up countries such as Malaysia, Thailand, Brazil, and Argentina. Rapid technical changes and short cycles present a double-edged sword in that they allow those with a certain level of technological ability to advance, but they also serve as a barrier by interfering with or truncating the learning process (Lall 1992, 2000) for others. Thus, economic growth in second-tier economies may be better served not by short-, but long-cycle technology-based sectors.

This hypothesis is addressed at the country level in Chapter 3 and at the sectoral level in Chapter 4. In Chapter 3 we specifically hypothesize that the countries that are more successful in catching up as measured by their per capita income are those that specialize in technologies with shorter life cycles. Middle-income countries that specialize in longer-cycle technologies tend to present modest growth, or growth that is insufficient for catching up. The firm-level analysis in Chapter 5 looks more specifically at the role of the technology cycle time in producing these differing outcomes. Korean firms in the process of catching up tend to have more patents with shorter cycle times than the more advanced American firms. This feature is hypothesized to be positively associated with the performance of Korean firms in relation to that of American ones.

Technological specialization 2: high-originality versus low-originality technologies

The literature reveals that both the quantity and quality of patents matters to the economic growth of nations. Lee and Kim (2009) stressed the importance of quantity, while Hasan and Tucci (2010) demonstrated the similar importance of both. Although the quality of patents is typically measured by the number of forward citations it receives, quality is in itself more complicated than that and does not lend itself easily to measurement. Acknowledging the importance of qualitative differences, Jaffe and Trajtenberg (2002: 428–9) looked specifically at both the originality and generality of patents. They measured originality based on the number of backward citations, with the measure being higher if a patent cites other preceding patents in a wide range of fields. However, they also measured generality by examining the number of forward citations (citations received), with the measure being higher if a patent had a widespread effect as a result of being cited in subsequent patents in a variety of fields.

Jaffe and Trajtenberg (2002: 428) observe that a high correlation exists between the number of citations received and the measure of generality. Both measures are based on forward citations or the number of citations received after a patent is granted. Thus, quality or generality is not known at the time when a patent is applied for, or at the innovation planning stages. For this reason, then, these two measures are not useful for normative analysis or for the derivation of *ex ante* policy implications because they are essentially unpredictable. In contrast, the measure of originality is based on the number of backward citations, or the number of citations a patent makes of prior existing patents. *Ex ante* planning or targeting thus becomes possible as it is not reliant on an unknown future measure. Backward citations are made by the patents concerned even without intentional targeting or planning, and so they reveal more about the inventors as long as citations are made by inventors other than by the patent examiners in the US Patent Office.

For the above reasons, instead of using more typical quality measures and the measure of generality, we use the measure of originality to analyze catch-up and to present policy implications. Further, because there is a general trend toward technological fusion (Kodama 1992), the implications of specializing in technologies with greater levels of originality (or technologies rooted in knowledge from diverse fields) is interesting to determine.

Through a country-level analysis, we examine further whether specialization in higher-originality technologies tends to foster a faster growth in per capita income. The firm-level analysis in Chapter 5 examines the link between the originality of patents and performance by looking at the difference between firms in advanced and catch-up countries. At the sector level, we examine whether latecomer firms do better (i.e. file more patents) in higher- or lower-originality sectors.

From relying on foreign knowledge to localizing knowledge-creation mechanisms

Technological innovation implies the generation of new knowledge, and requires the exploitation of available knowledge stocks. Given a weak knowledge base, latecomers have to rely on foreign knowledge stocks and go through the sometimes lengthy process of learning from foreigners. Hu and Jaffe (2003) discuss several channels of knowledge transfer, including the transfer of knowledge embodied in imported capital goods, the licensing of foreign-born technology, learning from countries that make foreign direct investment (FDI), and learning from exporting. When the focus is on patenting, citations reflect to a certain extent the flow of knowledge from advanced economies to latecomers through their facilitation of the latter's R&D efforts.[9] However, the knowledge-receiving latecomers eventually have to generate their own knowledge, and this is a question of localization of knowledge creation and diffusion. The latecomer economies are often constrained by the availability of institutional channels for this intranational knowledge diffusion and creation while they learn by international knowledge diffusion in the early stage. Thus, we can hypothesize that the more advanced a country is, the more active its intranational knowledge creation and diffusion. Specifically, successful catch-up coincides with an increase in the localization of knowledge creation and diffusion. Lee and Yoon (2010) verify that Japan, or at least its semiconductor sector, has a higher degree of national-level localization and intranational knowledge creation and diffusion than Korea or Taiwan.

If we consider the process of catch-up to be a long-term phenomenon, the proper sequence would be to start with the international diffusion of knowledge. If this effort is successful, what is likely to follow is an increased level of intranational knowledge creation and diffusion. Given our focus on sustained catch-up, we use in our analysis primarily the variable of intranational knowledge creation and diffusion rather than the international diffusion of knowledge. When measured over the same period, these two measures tend to be inversely related. One measures the share of patent citations going to patents owned by foreigners, whereas the other measures the patents owned by domestic citizens. Therefore, using these two variables in the same regression models may not be a good idea. In Chapter 3, we find a significant difference in the level of localization of knowledge creation between advanced and latecomer countries, and it appears that this difference is related to the difference in the per capita income growth of these countries.

In the firm-level analysis presented in Chapter 5, self-citation at the firm level becomes a counterpart variable of the localization of knowledge creation at the country level. Trajtenberg, Henderson, and Jaffe (1997) see self-citation as a form of appropriability, or a way to protect the innovations of an individual from being copied by another so that the patent holder can then monopolize all profits. However, in the context of firms, self-citations can also be interpreted as a reflection of the degree to which a firm's innovation effort builds upon its own knowledge pool. In general, we hypothesize that the more advanced the firm, the higher its self-citation ratio. Therefore, a firm from a latecomer country that is successful in catching-up would show an increasing trend in this variable. Joo and Lee (2010) show that the self-citation ratio for Samsung Electronics was very low (around 2 percent to 3 percent) compared with that of Sony (15 percent) in the 1980s. However, Samsung has since increased in the proportion of self-cited patents. By the mid-2000s Samsung had caught up to the level of Sony. Given that this is the trend for the Korean firms most successful at catching up, we can deduce that a significant difference generally exists between catching-up (Korean) and advanced (US) firms in terms of their self-citation ratios. This topic is discussed in greater detail in Chapter 5 together with the performance implication of self-citation. If self-citation reflects the degree to which firms are able to consolidate the independent intra-firm mechanism of knowledge generation, we can expect some correlation between the level of self-citation and performance variables. This hypothesis is consistent with the previous country-level hypothesis.

Turning to the level of technological sectors (classes), the self-citation ratios of entire sectors are simply the average of the self-citation ratios of all patents belonging to the same sector (class). Following the original interpretation of Trajtenberg et al. (1997), Park and Lee (2006) use this variable to represent the appropriability of sectors in light of the technological-regime concept. Our sector-level hypothesis suggests that because R&D related resources are limited, latecomer countries and their firms tend to focus on higher appropriability sectors where they can easily and securely enjoy the fruit of their innovations.

Balanced (diversified) or imbalanced (concentrated) growth strategies

Whether a country should consider a balanced or unbalanced app-roach has long been the subject of economic debate. When seeking to balance, a number of factors need to be considered. The first factor is the actors, and it is important to ask, for example, whether the sector is dominated by a few large businesses or a large number of small and medium-sized enterprises (SMEs). A second factor to consider is the sector, for example, whether it is more export oriented, or more concerned with import substitution. The third factor is the region in which the economy operates, for example, whether it is operating in a special economic zone. The idea of unbalanced growth is to focus on only a small number of growth poles, and expect benefits to trickle down to other actors, sectors, or regions. However, opponents of this strategy mention side effects such as inequality and often limited trickle-down effects. Given our focus on the catch-up efforts of late-comers, a degree of initial imbalance seems difficult to avoid because of the high levels of scarcity in human, physical, and financial resources and capabilities. It makes sense then to channel whatever resources are available into a small number of actors, sectors, or regions. However, if growth is to be sustained and upgraded, a certain degree of extension into other actors, sectors, or regions must eventually be expected. This is similar to Kuznets' hypothesis that although initial growth involves increasing inequality or concentration, later stages require rebalancing for sustained growth. Thus, we rationalize that if a country enters the stage of more sustained growth, a positive relationship arises between income growth and economic balance or equity. Consequently, a negative correlation between income growth and concentration also becomes evident.

In the country-level analysis in Chapter 3, we use a measure of concentration of actors or patent holders instead of sectors because the matter of sectoral concentration or specialization is already adequately covered by other measures involving cycle times or origin-ality.[10] The issue of a balanced or unbalanced growth strategy trans-lates in the patent space to a choice between the concentration of innovation by a few inventors or the decentralization of innovation so that there are contributions from a large number of inventors. We compare this measure of concentration in advanced and developing countries, and investigate the relationship between this concentration and economic growth. In the firm-level analysis in Chapter 5, we use a measure of concentration over classes (technological sectors). The analysis involves the comparison of firms from an advanced country with those of a catch-up country in terms of the extent of sectoral concentration of their innovation activities and the effect of this on their performance.

At the sector level, the measurement of concentration should be defined in terms of the actors or patent holders. The concept is similar to that of cumulativeness used in the literature. Originally, cumulativeness referred to the extent to which current technological innovation depends on past innovation. Cumulativeness can thus be defined at the level of organization or technological sector, and captured by the persistent domination of innovation by a few inventors within the technological sector. Therefore, cumulativeness can be measured by the share of total patents in each class held by the persistent innovators in that class. If cumulativeness is low, potential innovators are not at a major disadvantage and the incumbent firms hold no major advantage (Winter 1984). Conversely, we expect that when cumulativeness is high, firms will have a more difficult time catching up. It is the latter hypothesis that we test in this study.

Detour versus direct replication of the forerunner: a recapitulation

The present study investigates the aforementioned ideas at three different levels, namely, those of the country, the sector, and the firm. The main ideas explored include short- versus long-cycle specialization, the localization of knowledge creation (vs. foreign reliance), high- versus low-originality technologies, and balanced or unbalanced growth strategies (concentration over actors or sectors). Unlike other studies in the literature, we measure these ideas using patent data consistently across the three levels. Table 2.1 summarizes our discussion of the four main hypotheses and their application across the three levels. It also shows how the hypotheses will be examined quantitatively using patent data. This is one of the first studies on economic catch-up to be conducted consistently across the three dimensions of firm, sector, and country, and the first to combine this focus with an additional emphasis on the role of knowledge.

Table 2.1 *Four hypotheses at the three levels and their measurement*

Four hypotheses: growth strategies	Country	Sector	Firm
Technological specialization 1 (short vs. long cycle)	Cycle time	Cycle time	Cycle time
Technological specialization 2 (high vs. low originality)	Originality	Originality	Originality
Localization of knowledge creation and diffusion (vs. reliance on foreign sources)	Intranational creation and diffusion (close to self-citation)	Self-citation (appropriability)	Self-citation
Balanced vs. imbalanced	Concentration index over all inventors (HH index)[a]	Concentration over persistent inventors (cumulativeness)	Concentration index over all classes (HH index)[a]

[a] HH = Herfindahl-Hirschman.

2.3 Measuring the catch-up and the data

Measuring the catch-up

Catch-up can be measured by several indicators, including the level and growth of per capita income, productivity, market shares, and technological capability. The selection of the measurement to use should depend on the purpose of research and the dimensions of the catch-up subject, whether country, sector, or firm. For instance, at the country level, the level of per capita income and the size of the economy can be considered a measure of catch-up. More often than not the growth rate of per capita income is important because it determines the change in the level of per capita income over time. In this context, catch-up means that growth rates should be higher than the world average or that of the comparison group.

If we focus more on technological catch-up at the level of technology classes (sectors), various patent-based indicators will be available. Technological catch-up can be defined as the generating of more rapid technological innovations than advanced countries. Therefore, it can be measured by the gap in the average annual growth rate of triadic or US (or other internationally comparable measure) patents. The scope of patenting activities can also be used to measure technological capability and catch-up. Spreading technological activities over a wide range of technological classes represents higher technological capability and functions advantageously toward further technological innovation. Granstrand, Patel, and Pavitt (1997) and Patel and Pavitt (1997) indicate the advantage of implementing innovative activities in a wide range of classes for innovative firms. Park and Lee (2006) show that the average scope of patenting activities, namely technological diversification, in several countries is indicated by the number of classes in which the patents are registered. The difference between groups of countries is considerable. On average, advanced countries are more diversified and tend to register their patents in a much broader range of classes. This finding implies that technological catch-up at the national level can also be considered by the increase in the number of classes with patent registrations.

If the increase in the number of classes with patent registrations is regarded as the *widening* of catch-up, then the rapid increase in the number of patents (annual growth rates) in a specific class can be considered the *deepening* of catch-up. Finally, the *level* of technological catch-up by a firm or a country in a class can be measured as the total number of patents registered by a firm or country divided by the total number of patents in a class.

In our country-level analysis we are interested in the determinants of long-run economic growth. Therefore, we follow typical methodologies used in the literature. We perform cross-country or panel econometric regressions with the growth rate of a country's per capita income as the primary performance variable to measure catch-up. Catch-up in this regard is measured in terms of the catch-up in per capita income levels.

In our firm-level analysis, we use the conventional financial statement of firms listed in stock markets. We adopt various conventional indicators of firm performance, such as growth (measured by sale growth), profitability (return on sales or assets), productivity and firm value (Tobin's Q).

Patent data

In economic research, empirical analysis on innovation and knowledge is challenging because of the difficulty in measuring innovation and knowledge and the lack of data. However, patent data have increasingly become available and used in economics. Patent data, as technological indicators, have advantages and disadvantages.[11]

Patents have the following disadvantages as indicators of innovations. First, not all inventions are technically patentable. Second, not all inventions are patented, especially by firms for strategic and other reasons. Third, firms have a different propensity to patent innovations in their domestic market and in foreign countries, which largely depends on their expectations of exploiting their inventions commercially. Lastly, although there are international patent agreements among most industrial countries, each national patent office has its own institutional characteristics that affect the costs, length, and effectiveness of the protection accorded, in turn affecting the interest of inventors in applying for patent protection.

The advantages of patents are as follows. First, they are a direct outcome of the inventive process, and specifically of those inventions which are expected to have a commercial impact. They are appropriate indicators to capture the proprietary and competitive dimensions of technological change. Second, obtaining patent protection is time consuming and costly. Therefore, patent applications are filed for those inventions which, on average, are expected to provide benefits that outweigh the costs. Third, patents are broken down by technical field. Therefore, they provide information not only on the rate of inventive activity but also on its direction. Fourth, patent statistics are available in large number and for a long time series.

Despite some limitations of patent data, we use these in the present study because of the lack of alternative indicators suitable for our purposes. We need the data on knowledge flows, which are most conveniently available in patent citation data, which are considered as a proxy for the paper trail of knowledge flow. Citations are presumed to be informative links between patented inventions, and knowledge flows leave a paper trail in the form of citations in patents (Jaffe et al. 1993). By conducting a survey of the inventors, Jaffe, Tranjtenberg, and Forgaty (2000) investigate the extent to which citation

actually reflects the knowledge flow and find that a significant proportion of citations reflects knowledge flow.[12] This condition makes it
possible to use the probability of citation as a proxy for the probability
of useful knowledge flow.

However, patent counts from different patent offices are not always
comparable with each other because of different patent breadths,
patenting costs, approval requirements, and enforcement rules for
patenting in different countries. A common remedy is to use patent
data from a single patent-granting country, such as the USA, to standardize the unit of innovation, to make cross-country comparisons
possible. As the USA is the largest and the most technologically
advanced market in the world, any sufficiently large invention being
patented anywhere with a global market in mind is likely to be
patented in the USA as well.[13]

Therefore, we use US patent data to standardize the unit of innovation to make cross-country comparison possible. Specifically, we
use the two different sets of National Bureau of Economic Research
(NBER) patent database. The first one is publicly available at its
website (www.nber.org/patents/) with detailed explanations that are
based on Hall et al. (2001). The same data are available in a CD-ROM
attached to a book by Jaffe and Trajtenberg (2002). However, this
patent database comprises patents registered from 1963 to 1999. The
database also has patent citation data from 1975 to 1999. The data set
extends from January 1, 1963 to December 30, 1999 (thirty-seven
years) and includes all patents granted to all countries during that
period, that is, 2,923,922 patents. Citation data include all citations
made by patents (to other patents and scientific articles) granted from
1975 to 1999, for a total of 16,522,438 citations.

The database includes information such as patent number, grant
year, grant date, application year (starting in 1967), country and state
(if in the USA) of first inventor, assignee identifier if the patent was
assigned (starting in 1969), assignee type (individual, corporate or
government; foreign or domestic), main US patent classes among
417 technological sectors/classes, 6 categories and 36 sub-categories,
and the number of claims (starting in 1975). The patent citation data
also contain the citing patent numbers and the cited patent numbers.
The data contain the address of each inventor's residence. Aside from
this basic information, the NBER data set provides the direct measurement of several knowledge variables and citation data, such as

originality, generality, mean citation lags (which can be used to calculate technology-cycle time), self-citation ratios, and so on. These variables are explained and used in the subsequent chapters.

The second set of patent data used is the updated version of the first. The data period is from 1976 to 2006, and the data are available at the NBER website (https://sites.google.com/site/patentdataproject/Home). However, some variables are missing in the second data set compared with the first. Another difference is that the nationalities of patents are classified by the inventors' address in the first data set, whereas they are classified by the nationality of assignees (or legal owners) in the second or updated data set. Therefore, to obtain more updated information, we use the second data set as in Chapter 8 on China and India or to draw the curve of cycle time up to more recent times. In the regression analyses found in Chapters 3, 4, and 5 on the nature of rapid catching up during the 1980s and 1990s, we use the first data set.

All knowledge-related key variables defined at the firm, sector, and country levels in the previous sections can be calculated using the US patent data, as other scholars have done. Aside from these key variables, in which the present study is keenly interested, we need to have other control variables in regression. Firm-level control variables are obtained from standard firm databases such as the KIS for Korean firm data and Compustat or Value-line for US or global 500 firms. All sector-level variables can be calculated from the patent data alone. County-level data for other control variables are primarily from the World Bank (world development indicators), covering the 1960s to the present.

PART II

Empirical analysis at three levels

3 | *Knowledge and country-level catch-up*

3.1 Introduction

The determinants of economic growth remain an important puzzle in economics. To reflect the depth of this puzzle, debates on these determinants involve several contending factors, such as policies, institutions, and geography, as discussed in the influential articles of Acemoglu et al. (2001, 2002), Glaeser et al. (2004), and Rodrik et al. (2004). Despite the accumulation of knowledge and the increasing amounts of development aid and capital flow, many developing countries remain poor or fail to take off from initial growth momentums (Rodrik 1999; World Bank 2005). Recently, even the concept of the middle-income trap has emerged as an important concern in the development research community. Examples of countries that suffered from the middle-income trap are Brazil and Argentina, where growth stalled during the 1980s and the 1990s. Yusuf and Nabeshima (2009) discuss similar cases in East Asia, particularly those of Malaysia and Thailand. Only a very small number of former middle-income countries have moved beyond middle-income status to join the rich-country club. This growth divergence justifies a growth diagnostic to identify the binding constraints for growth in each country.[1] Bottlenecks or binding constraints may be different not only for each country but also for different groups of countries.

This chapter analyzes the more concrete mechanisms by which innovation is generated at the country level. In other words, this chapter connects the question of growth divergence to the NIS and assumes the view that differences in the NIS lead to different outcomes in innovation and national economic growth. The study focusses on technological specialization, an aspect of the NIS, and determines whether latecomers should specialize in emerging technologies or in mature technologies following the product life-cycle theory. The other focus of the NIS is learning and the creation of knowledge, which is centered on the question of the role of indigenous creation and diffusion of knowledge versus reliance on a foreign knowledge base.

The World Bank classifies countries around the world into four groups, i.e. low-income, lower-middle-income, upper-middle-income, and high-income countries. This study focusses on middle-income countries and compares them with high-income ones and with the successful catching-up economies in Asia such as Korea, Taiwan, Hong Kong, and Singapore.

Section 3.2 provides a short outline of the overall nature of the analysis in the chapter. Section 3.3 measures the different aspects of the NIS of countries treated in this book and derives specific hypotheses about the determinants of sustained catching up. Section 3.4 discusses the results of the regression analysis, while section 3.5 concludes the chapter with a summary.

3.2 From the national innovation system to economic growth

The NIS is composed of elements and relationships involved in the production, diffusion, and use of new and economically useful knowledge that are located within the borders of a nation state (Lundvall 1992). The NIS deals with the question of how efficient a nation is in terms of establishing a system for learning and innovation, particularly in terms of acquisition, creation, diffusion, and utilization of knowledge. Differences in the NIS affect the direction or speed of the innovation of a nation and its national competitiveness. From a catching-up perspective, how firms, universities, and research laboratories acquire external knowledge efficiently, as well as how this knowledge is diffused among national agents, are vital matters.

In this chapter, the NIS of each country is measured using US patent data, and the economic growth of each country is explained in terms of the diverse aspects of the NIS. Regression analysis is conducted with growth of per capita income as the dependent variable, which is conceptualized as a function of the knowledge-related variables (or NIS variables), as well as other traditional control variables. The key NIS variables include the degree of localization of creation and diffusion of knowledge, concentration across inventors, technological cycle time, and originality. In economic growth equations the conventional control variables such as educational attainment, investment to GDP ratio, population growth, and initial level of per capita income are used.

In simple form, model specifications can be conceptualized as follows:

Per capital income growth (economic growth and catch-up)
   = F (innovation = technological catch-up, control variables)   (1)

Technological catch-up
   = F (NIS and other knowledge variables, control variables)   (2)

If the technological catch-up equation (2) is incorporated into equation (1), the reduced form of equation (1) is as follows:

Per capital income growth (economic growth and catch-up)
   = F (NIS variables, other control variables)   (3)

Equation (3) is estimated in a country-panel analysis to determine the impact of NIS variables on economic growth. However, one problem with this kind of analysis is the existence of a potentially large number of variables that may represent different aspects of the NIS. Thus, this study focusses on several variables that seem to be particularly relevant to explain sustained catching up, which occurred from 1980 to 1995. The variables should be those that showed a noticeable change over this period in a group of successful catching-up countries or those that showed some contrasting moves between the more and less successful countries. As the analysis in section 3.3 shows, the variables of localization of knowledge creation and cycle time of technologies are those that showed particularly interesting trends in successful catching-up economies, like Korea and Taiwan.

3.3 Measuring the NIS and the specific hypotheses

Table 3.1 presents the measurement of the key NIS variables, such as localization of knowledge creation and diffusion, concentration of innovation across inventors (i.e. the Herfindahl–Hirschman index of concentration (HHI)), originality of the knowledge base, and technology cycle time, all calculated at the national level. Since this study uses US patent data to describe each country's innovation system, it chooses only those countries that have a sufficient number of US patents or countries that have more than ten patents in every four-year-based sub-period.[2] The NBER database contains only granted patents, and

Table 3.1 (*a*) *Key NIS variables by country group and* (*b*) *test of the significance of the gaps*

(a)

	High-income countries Mean ($\mu 0$)	Middle-income countries Mean ($\mu 1$)	Korea and Taiwan Mean ($\mu 2$)
HHI of concentration	0.105	0.374	0.206
Localization of knowledge creation and diffusion	0.092	0.036	0.041
Technology cycle (years)	9.341	9.946	8.512
Originality index	0.284	0.265	0.217
Number of patents	4,965.2	52.4	920.7
Quality of patent (mean citations received)	17,519.1	73.0	1,583.2

(b)

	High-income countries vs. middle-income countries		High-income countries vs. Korea and Taiwan		Middle-income countries vs. Korea and Taiwan	
	difference $= \mu 0 - \mu 1$	H0: $\mu 0 - \mu 1 = 0$	difference $= \mu 0 - \mu 2$	H0: $\mu 0 - \mu 2 = 0$	difference $= \mu 1 - \mu 2$	H0: $\mu 1 - \mu 2 = 0$
HHI	−0.268	0.0000***	−0.101	0.0005***	0.167	0.0021***
Localization of knowledge creation and diffusion	0.056	0.0000***	0.051	0.0000***	−0.005	0.3291
Technology cycle	−0.606	0.0000***	0.829	0.0051***	1.434	0.0006***
Originality index	0.019	0.0055***	0.067	0.0000***	0.048	0.0220**
Number of patents	4,912.7	0.0000***	4,044.5	0.0446**	−868.3	0.0000***
Quality of patent	17,446.2	0.0000***	15,935.9	0.0369**	−1510.2	0.0000***

Notes: High-income countries are those with GDP per capita in 2000 constant prices that exceed US$ 10,000. In both groups, only those countries that have more than ten US patents in every period are included. A tax-haven country (Bahamas) and countries that have dissolved, such as Yugoslavia and Czechoslovakia, are excluded. ***, **, and * in the cells indicate the levels of significance of 1 percent, 5 percent, and 10 percent, respectively.

patents filed by a country in year t means patents that are applied for in year t and granted afterwards.

Regarding the indicators of the NIS, this study finds many interesting contrasts between the high- and the middle-income groups. In general, high-income countries tend to show higher localization of knowledge creation and diffusion, less concentration of innovation across inventors, a higher degree of originality, and a shorter cycle time of technologies.

Localization of knowledge creation and diffusion

To measure intranational knowledge creation, this study uses the same methodology used by Lee and Yoon (2010), who adopted the methods used in the study by Jaffe et al. (1993). To compare the geographic localization of the citations made by the patents of different countries, Jaffe et al. (1993) suggest an approach to compare the probability of a patent matching the original patent by geographic area, conditional on its citing of the original patent, with the probability of a match not conditioned on the existence of a citation link. The non-citation-conditioned probability makes a baseline or reference value to compare the proportion of citations that match. The basic insight of the approach by Jaffe et al. (1993) is that the probability (or degree) of country A's patents citing (or being cited by) country A's patents has to be compared with a similar probability defined with respect to reasonably comparable reference patents.

Borrowing this insight, this study can measure the degree of localization of knowledge creation and diffusion in a country as the difference between the probability of one country's patents citing its own patents and the probability of the rest of the world's patents citing that country's patents.[3] Formally,

$$\frac{n_{xxt}}{n_{xt}} - \frac{n_{cxt}}{n_{ct}}$$

where n_{xxt} is number of citations made to country x's patents by country x's patents filed in year t, n_{xt} is the number of all citations made by country x's patents filed in year t, n_{cxt} is the number of citations made to country x's patents by all patents except country x's patents filed in year t, and n_{ct} is the number of all citations made by all patents filed in year t except country x's patents.

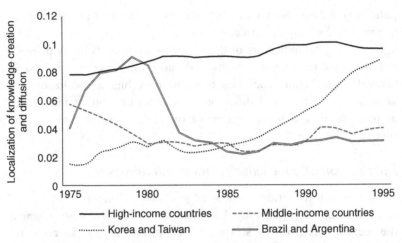

Figure 3.1 Localization of knowledge creation and diffusion.
Note: drawn by the author using the NBER patent data. Five-year moving
averages are taken for smoothing.

Table 3.1(a) shows that the degree of localization of knowledge
creation and diffusion is 9.2 percent for the high-income group
and 3.6 percent for the middle-income group. The test results in
Table 3.1(b) show that this gap is significant. Given that this degree
measures the extent to which patent citations are made within
national boundaries, inventors in middle-income countries tend
to have a lower degree of localization of knowledge creation and
diffusion or an equivalently higher degree of reliance on foreign
knowledge bases, a finding that is not surprising. Figure 3.1, which
also shows this difference in terms of graphs, covers high-income
and middle-income countries, the group of Korea and Taiwan, and
the group of Brazil and Argentina. It indicates that, whereas
the averages for the high-income group range from 8 percent to
10 percent, the average for Korea and Taiwan indicates a steady
and rapid catch-up since the mid 1980s to converge with the level of
the old high-income average by the mid 1990s. By contrast, other
middle-income countries and the two Latin American countries,
Brazil and Argentina, do not demonstrate a similar catch-up in
terms of localization of knowledge creation and diffusion. Given
this contrast between the more and less successful catching-up countries, there is a reason to suspect that localization of knowledge

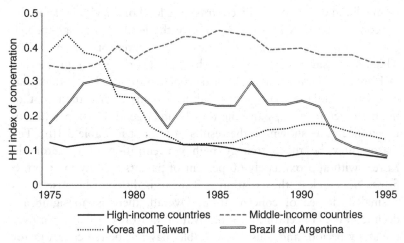

Figure 3.2 HH index of concentration.

creation is one of the key variables that has differentiated countries' economic performance. We will verify this reasoning through a regression analysis.

Patenting concentration across the assignees

Second, this study investigates the degree of inventor concentration, particularly the degree of patent concentration across assignees (excluding unassigned patents), which is measured by the HH. The HH of country x in year t is calculated as follows:

$$\text{HH}_{xt} = \sum_{i \in I_x} \left(\frac{N_{it}}{N^*_{xt}} \right)^2$$

where I_x is the set of assignees, N_{it} is the number of patents filed by assignee i in year t, and N^*_{xt} is the total number of patents filed by country x in year t excluding unassigned patents.

As shown in Table 3.1(a) and Figure 3.2, this index is considerably lower in the high-income group (0.105) than in the middle-income group (0.374). This finding indicates that in higher-income countries, inventions are spread more widely among a larger number of assignees which are typically firms, whereas in the middle-income group, they are dominated by a smaller number of firms. The graph in Figure 3.2 shows that in the case of high-income groups, the HH index ranges from a band of 0.1 to 0.2. By contrast, the level of the HH index in the latecomer countries mostly stays above the level of the high-income group. Brazil and Argentina show a low degree of concentration, which is the same level as that of the high-income group. In the case of Korea and Taiwan, their level of concentration is lower than that of other middle-income countries but remains higher than that of the high-income groups and the Brazil and Argentina group. The gap is significant, as shown by the results of the test in Table 3.1(b). The reason may be the extremely high concentration of inventors in Korea, with approximately 60 percent of patents filed by the top five firms. Nonetheless, the situation in Taiwan is different because it has a smaller degree of concentration. Overall, there is no significant decline in the concentration of innovation in Korea and Taiwan over the study period, and thus this variable may not be the causal factor for the sustained catching up by these Asian countries. This hypothesis will be verified through a regression analysis.

Originality

Third, this study examines the index of originality, which measures the degree to which a patent makes (backward) citations to patents from a wider range of technological classes instead of from a narrow field of technologies. The originality of the knowledge base of a country can be calculated based on the definition of originality in Hall et al. (2001) and Trajtenberg et al. (1997). Conceptually, the originality of a patent is defined as follows for each patent i:

$$\text{Originality}^i = 1 - \sum_{k=1}^{N_i} \left(\frac{Nciting_{ik}}{Nciting_i} \right)^2$$

where k is the technological sector (specifically patent class k), $Nciting_{ik}$ is the number of citations made by the patent i to patents that belong to patent class k, and $Nciting_i$ is the total number of citations made by the patent i. If a patent cites previous patents that belong to a narrow set of technologies, the originality score will be low, whereas citing patents from a wide range of fields will produce a high score. This definition represents the rationale that the broader the technological root of the underlying knowledge or research related to the patents, the higher the originality of a patent.

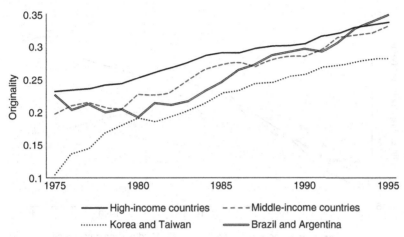

Figure 3.3 Originality.

The synthesis of divergent ideas is probably characteristic of research that has high originality and is thus basic in that sense (Trajtenberg et al. 1997). The variable of originality is directly available from the NBER patent database, and we can simply retrieve the values for all patents held by each country and take their average value for each country.

Table 3.1(a) shows that the level of originality is significantly higher in high-income countries than in middle-income ones. Figure 3.3 seems to confirm this gap, showing the increasing tendency toward originality in all four groups, namely, high-income, middle-income, Korea–Taiwan, and Brazil–Argentina. More interestingly, the two Latin American countries and the other middle-income countries made a significant catch-up, even reaching the level of the high-income countries by the mid 1990s. By contrast, the group of Korea and Taiwan remained consistently lower than that of the Brazil and Argentina group, the middle-income countries, and the high-income countries. This finding may reflect the fact that some middle-income countries, such as India and Brazil, tend to have a relatively stronger foundation in the basic sciences than in the corporate sectors, thus generating more fundamental or original patents. This contrasting pattern suggests that Asian countries achieve sustained economic growth in per capita income without increasing the level of originality of their knowledge base, thus giving rise to the conclusion that

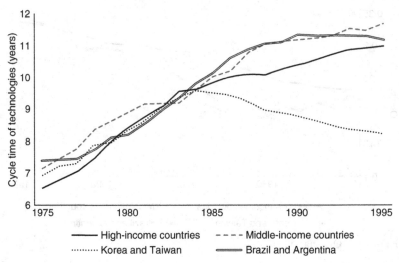

Figure 3.4 Cycle time of technologies.

originality may not be the causal variable that triggers the sustained economic catch-up of some Asian countries. We will verify this reasoning through a regression analysis.

Cycle time of technologies

Fourth, this study investigates the cycle time of technologies, which measures the time lags between the application years of the citing and cited patents or the time span between the predecessor and the successor (Jaffe and Trajtenberg 2002). A long cycle time indicates a greater significance of old knowledge and thus a greater need to study it from the point of view of the latecomers. In the country-level analysis, this variable is the average of technological cycles shown in citations made by a patent by a corresponding country. Computing the technological cycle by application years may be desirable, but this study uses grant years because the NBER database does not provide the application years of patents granted before 1969.

   Table 3.1(a) shows that the average cycle time for higher-income countries lasts 9.3 years, shorter than the 9.9 years for the middle-income countries. Figure 3.4 shows that over the years, the cycle has become increasingly longer. For example, the cycle ran from about six years in the mid 1970s to twelve years in the mid 1990s in the case of high-income countries. An extremely interesting pattern is that of the Korea–Taiwan group, which shows values much lower than the averages for the high- to middle-income groups and the Brazil–Argentina group. A more important pattern is the sustained decline of this value since the mid 1980s, when these two countries started to catch up with the high-income ones. This contrast gives rise to the hypothesis that this variable must be one of those that generates the sustained catch-up of successful Asian countries. In general, we may hypothesize that economic growth in these Asian economies is positively correlated with specialization in short-cycle technologies, whereas growth in other economies is correlated, with specialization in long-cycle technologies.

This lower and ever shortening pattern of the cycle time of the two most successful catching-up countries is highly significant. It is consistent with the fact that the two countries have increasingly specialized in information technology (IT) industries, the cycle times of which are shorter than those of other classes, as discussed in Chapter 4 of this book. Based on the pattern, Park and Lee (2006) argue that sectoral level catch-up tends to occur more easily in short-cycle sectors or technologies. One reason is that when cycle times are short, latecomers do not have to master older technologies.

Summary

Localization of knowledge creation and diffusion and cycle time of technologies may be the variables responsible for the sustained growth of some Asian countries, as only these two variables correspond to the significant change observed in the two countries relative to the other groups from 1980 to 1995. Concentration and originality may contribute to general economic growth, but they are not responsible for the specific episode of catching-up that this study is concerned with. In fact, originality may not be significant for general economic growth, as the results of this study show that this variable consistently increases even among less successful developing countries.

3.4 Catching-up and non-catching-up economic growth: regression results

Table 3.2(a) presents the basic variables such as per capita income growth, human capital and fixed investment ratio, and population growth. In the sample, there are twenty-nine high- and twenty-three

Table 3.2 (a) Basic descriptive data of the country groups; (b) test of the significance of the gaps

(a)

	High-income countries	Middle-income countries	Korea and Taiwan
	Mean (μ0)	Mean (μ1)	Mean (μ2)
Real GDP per capita growth rate (four-year average%)	0.102	0.067	0.260
Initial GDP per capita, each period	15,823	2,883	5,170
Population growth rate (four-year average%)	0.032	0.077	0.054
Fixed investment per GDP (%)	23.5	23.0	27.9
Enrollment rate of secondary education (%)	95.6	58.6	80.7

(b)

	High-income countries vs. middle-income countries		High-income countries vs. Korea and Taiwan		Middle-income countries vs. Korea and Taiwan	
	difference = μ0 − μ1	H0: μ0 − μ1 = 0	difference = μ0 − μ2	H0: μ0 − μ2 = 0	difference = μ1 − μ2	H0: μ1 − μ2 = 0
Real GDP per capita growth rate (four-year)	0.035	0.0000***	−0.170	0.0000***	−0.193	0.0001***
Initial GDP per capita of each period	12,940	0.0000***	11623	0.0000***	−2291	0.0443*
Population growth rate (four-year)	−0.045	0.0000***	−0.024	0.0076***	0.023	0.0533*
Fixed investment per GDP	0.5	0.0656*	−4.4	0.0000***	−4.9	0.0000***
Enrollment rate of secondary education	36.9	0.0000***	14.9	0.0052***	−22.0	0.0000***

Notes: High-income countries are those with a GDP per capita in 2000 constant prices that exceed US$10,000. In both groups, only countries that have more than ten US patents in every period are included. A tax-haven country (Bahamas) and countries that have been dissolved, such as Yugoslavia and Czechoslovakia, are excluded. ***, **, and * in the cells indicate the levels of significance of 1 percent, 5 percent, and 10 percent, respectively.

upper-middle-income countries with a constant per capita GDP in 2000; the former earned more than $10,000, and the latter earned less than that amount. Table 3.2(a) shows that higher-income countries boast income growth rates higher than those of middle-income countries (0.10 percent compared with 0.07 percent) and higher ratio of fixed capital investment to GDP (23.5 percent vs. 23.0 percent). A more stark contrast can be observed in terms of secondary school enrollment ratio, which is 95.6 percent for the higher-income countries and 58.6 percent for the middle-income ones. The *t*-test (Table 3.2(b)) shows that these gaps are all significant. Only in terms of population does the high-income group show a lower growth rate, particularly 0.03 percent compared with 0.07 percent for the middle-income group.

To examine the impact of the components of the NIS on national economic performance or economic growth, we conduct regression analyses using the methods of fixed effect and generalized method of moments (GMM) estimations, which can efficiently deal with small sample, omitted variable, and endogeneity problems.[4] The period of the panel is twenty years (from 1975 to 1995), which is divided into five sub-periods, each lasting four years, namely, 1975 to 1979, 1979 to 1983, 1983 to 1987, 1987 to 1991, and 1991 to 1995. The dependent variable is the GDP per capita growth for each four-year period (constant US$ in 2000).

We will conduct two sets of regression analyses. In the first set (Table 3.3), we will show the general determinants of economic growth in the whole world and in the high-income and middle-income countries. In other words, regressions are conducted for each separate group (high vs. middle) as well as together with a dummy for middle-income countries to test the different effects of the NIS variables at different stages of development. One of the goals is to prove the importance of the variable of localization of knowledge creation and diffusion in high-income countries in contrast to the case of the middle-income countries, which have not consolidated their local knowledge systems. In terms of the cycle time of technologies, we will make a contrast between the successful catching-up economies and the other two groups, high- and middle-income countries. We will first show in Table 3.3 that in both high- and middle-income countries, economic growth is positively correlated with specialization in long-cycle technologies. Then, in the second set of regressions (Table 3.4), which are crucial, we aim to show the difference between successful catching-up

Table 3.3 *The NIS and economic growth*

	Fixed effect panel model			System–GMM model		
	High-income countries	Middle-income countries	Dummy model	High-income countries	Middle-income countries	Dummy model
Log of initial GDP per capita for each period (constant US$ in 2000)	−0.1575	−0.3460	−0.2433	−0.1399	−0.1160	−0.1799
	(−2.57)**	(−4.02)***	(−4.78)***	(−2.81)***	(−3.07)***	(−4.87)***
Growth rate of population for each four-year period	−0.7749	−1.1817	−1.1293	−0.0737	−0.1480	−0.2823
	(−1.71)*	(−1.70)*	(−2.90)***	(−0.09)	(−0.21)	(−0.39)
Fixed capital investment per GDP	0.0030	0.0146	0.0093	0.0089	0.0242	0.0093
	(1.08)	(4.12)***	(4.24)***	(2.58)***	(3.43)***	(2.68)***
Enrollment rate of secondary education	0.0006	0.0009	0.0009	0.0001	−0.0032	−0.0026
	(0.99)	(0.69)	(1.65)	(0.03)	(−1.40)	(−1.38)
HHI: inventor concentration	−0.2254	−0.1494	−0.3355	−0.2189	−0.1867	−0.5009
	(−2.40)**	(−2.14)**	(−3.17)***	(−1.94)*	(−2.85)***	(−2.70)***
Localization of knowledge creation	0.5128	0.3296	0.6397	0.3581	1.0351	0.8361
	(1.87)*	(0.90)	(1.96)**	(1.74)*	(1.07)	(3.32)***
Cycle time of technology	0.0249	0.0145	0.0319	0.0284	0.0274	0.0636
	(3.13)***	(2.30)**	(3.50)***	(2.42)**	(2.01)**	(3.50)***
Originality index	−0.1042	0.1152	0.0239	−0.1778	0.4870	−0.3502
	(−0.52)	(0.73)	(0.10)	(−0.67)	(1.87)*	(−0.90)
Dummy (middle-income country)			(dropped)			−0.3999
						(−2.07)**

Dummy*HHI			0.2059			0.4534
			(1.74)*			(2.19)**
Dummy*localization			−0.2784			0.1565
			(−0.63)			(0.49)
Dummy*cycle time			−0.0183			−0.0337
			(−1.79)*			(−2.04)**
Dummy*originality index			0.0674			0.8946
			(0.26)			(1.73)*
Constant	1.2702	2.2427	1.7257	0.9949	0.2197	1.2895
	(2.41)**	(3.74)***	(4.30)***	(1.95)*	(0.59)	(3.38)***
Number of observations	112	79	191	112	76	191
Number of groups	28	23	51	28	21	51
R^2	0.071	0.367	0.175			
Hausman test	24.28(0.0021)	15.27(0.0541)	26.55			
			(0.0090)			
AR(2)				0.286	0.444	0.800
Hansen test				0.129	0.861	0.260

Notes: Time period: 1975–95 divided into five sub-periods. Dependent variable is GDP per capita growth (%) for each four-year period (constant US$ in 2000). ***, ** and * in the cells indicate the levels of significance of 1 percent, 5 percent, and 10 percent, respectively. Dummy = middle-income country dummy. It takes a value of 0 for countries with a GDP per capita in 2000 exceeding US$10,000. All two-step system GMM analyses are conducted by STATA 10.1 with Windmeijer finite-sample correction. In all of the analyses, the number of groups exceeds the number of instruments.

Table 3.4 *NIS of the four Asian catching-up economies and economic growth*

	High-income group (1)	Middle-income group (2)	Whole world group (3)
Log of initial GDP per capita	−0.3364	−0.3493	−0.2880
for each period	(−4.57)***	(−4.32)***	(−5.48)***
Growth rate of population	−1.1684	−1.1337	−1.0742
for each four-year-period	(−2.26)**	(−1.76)*	(−2.74)***
Fixed investment per GDP	0.0070	0.0140	0.0102
	(2.72)***	(4.36)***	(5.05)***
Enrollment rate of secondary	0.0008	0.0008	0.0012
education	(1.70)*	(0.62)	(2.43)**
HHI	−0.1952	−0.1579	−0.1442
	(−2.42)**	(−2.42)**	(−3.04)***
Localization of knowledge	0.5939	0.3411	0.4261
creation and diffusion	(2.52)**	(0.98)	(2.09)**
Cycle time of technology	0.0381	0.0147	0.0195
	(5.21)***	(2.45)**	(4.49)***
Originality index	0.0200	0.1236	0.0741
	(0.10)	(0.83)	(0.70)
Dummy (Asian 4)	1.2881	1.1123	1.1134
	(4.36)***	(2.37)**	(2.91)***
Dummy*HHI	−0.4630	−0.6132	−0.4820
	(−2.11)**	(−1.87)*	(−1.88)*
Dummy*localization	−0.2715	−0.5187	−0.7163
	(−0.31)	(−0.39)	(−0.68)
Dummy*cycle time	−0.0873	−0.0589	−0.0616
	(−3.16)***	(−1.39)	(−1.78)*
Dummy*originality index	−0.8980	−0.9542	−1.0547
	(−1.53)	(−1.09)	(−1.48)
Constant	2.6933	2.3479	2.1035
	(4.16)***	(4.11)***	(4.97)***
Number of observations	112	95	191
Number of groups	28	27	51
R^2	0.282	0.204	0.118
Hausman test	32.25(0.0013)	20.77(0.0539)	32.44(0.0012)

Note: ***, ** and * in the cells indicate the levels of significance of 1 percent, 5 percent, and 10 percent, respectively. Estimations are made by the fixed effect models. Time period: 1975–95, divided into five sub-periods. The dependent variable is the GDP per capita growth for each four-year-period (constant US$ in 2000). Dummy takes a value of 1 for Korea, Taiwan, Hong Kong, and Singapore from the third period (1983–7), when the catch-up began onward.

countries and other countries. We will show by creating a dummy for the former group that their growth is negatively associated with long-cycle specialization or equivalently positively associated with specialization in short-cycle technologies.

Now turning to regression results in Table 3.3, the variable of localization of knowledge creation and diffusion is positive and significant in the high-income group regressions but not in the middle-income ones. This result suggests that, although knowledge creation and diffusion is one of the determinants of growth in high-income countries, the mechanism of knowledge creation and diffusion is too weak to affect the case of middle-income countries. This finding is consistent with the extremely low degree at 0.04 (Table 3.1(a)) of localization of knowledge creation and diffusion in middle-income countries. The degree of localization of knowledge creation and diffusion in high-income countries is over twice as high at 0.09.

The size of the coefficient ranges from 0.035 to 1.03 in the GMM models. If 1.00 is used as the ballpark figure, the implication is that an increase of one percentage point (e.g. from 0.03 to 0.04) of this variable leads to a 0.01 percent point increase in per capita income growth rates. This magnitude is not small given that the average growth rate of per-capita income is 0.07 percent in the middle-income group and 0.10 percent in the high-income group (Table 3.2(a)). For the Korea–Taiwan group, the level of the intranational diffusion increased from about 0.02 in the early 1980s to 0.09 by 1995, reaching the same level as that of the high-income countries (Figure 3.1).

In Table 3.3, the HHI is negative and significant in the models for both high- and middle-income countries. This finding suggests that the more widespread innovation is across diverse innovators, the more advantageous it is in terms of economic growth. However, this variable does not seem to be the one that triggered catching up by Asian countries because this variable does not show a clear-cut trend from the 1980 to 1995 period, as shown in Figure 3.2. From the beginning of or from the mid 1980s, the level of this index in Korea and Taiwan is between the level of the middle-income and high-income countries.

The originality variable is not significant at all, as shown by the results of the several models tried for both high- and middle-income countries. These results suggest that specializing in technology with higher originality is not necessary for achieving economic growth. These results and observations make sense, given that all country groups, including the high- and middle-income ones and the successful catching-up economies of Korea–Taiwan, show an increasing trend of this variable from 1980 to 1995, although the average level of this variable is shown to be significantly higher in high-income countries (Figure 3.3). Moreover, the successful Asian countries have been doing well even with considerably lower levels of originality than the high- and middle-income groups, as discussed in the preceding sections. By contrast, Latin American countries, such as Brazil and Argentina, seem to have substantially increased their level of originality, as shown in Figure 3.4, but do not seem to have obtained practical gains in growth.

Finally, in Table 3.3 the variable of the cycle time is positive and significant for both groups of countries of high and middle income. This means that in typical middle-income countries economic growth is related to specializing in long-cycle technology-based sectors. However, whether the latecomer countries should keep specializing in longer-cycle technologies remains doubtful, given that this variable becomes shorter among successful Asian countries from 1980 to 1995, as shown in Figure 3.4. This fact raises a significant concern about the role of shorter- or longer-cycle technologies in catching-up growth. Related to this puzzle, an interesting fact is that the coefficient of the cycle time variable is smaller for the middle-income group than for the high-income group. The regression with a middle-income country dummy and its interaction terms (its negative coefficient) also confirms that the impact of the longer cycle is significantly different between the two groups, with a significantly smaller impact in the middle-income group. This observation is consistent with the case of Korea and Taiwan, which have specialized in shorter-cycle technologies and achieved economic growth. Thus, the role of this variable in economic growth, particularly for successful catching-up countries, requires closer examination. Therefore, additional regressions have been run.

Table 3.4 contains the results from the additional set of regression analyses focussing on the differences between the successful catching-up economies of Korea, Taiwan, Hong Kong, and Singapore and those of either high-income or other middle-income countries. In this regression, a dummy variable is created to take a value of 1 for Korea, Taiwan, Hong Kong, and Singapore from the third period (1983 to 1987, when the catch-up began) and onward. Then, this dummy interacts with the NIS variables to reflect the different size/direction of the impact of the variables in these countries during the catching-up period. If the coefficient of the interaction is negative, then the net impact of this cycle time for the four economies could be negative, implying that their growth is negatively associated with long-cycle specialization or equivalently positively associated with specialization in short-cycle technologies. With this specific dummy variable, regressions are run with the three different sample groups, namely, the higher-income, the middle-income and all the groups, to determine whether there is any difference.

Table 3.4 shows that the uniqueness of the technology cycle variable is more clearly indicated when the Asian catching-up economies are compared with the high-income group and all the groups than with the middle-income countries, as the interaction terms are significant and negative in these two cases (columns 1 and 3 in Table 3.4). Although the coefficient of the technology cycle is positive and significant in itself, it becomes negative and significant when interacting with the dummy, thus indicating the possibility of the net effect being negative for the four Asian countries during the post-1983 period. Based on the coefficients in the high-income country column (column 1), the net effects can be estimated as the sum of the coefficient of the cycle time variable (0.038) and the coefficient of the interaction term (−0.087), which is a negative figure or −0.05. Through a separate regression analysis, this net effect is found to be significant and negative.[5] Column 3 (total sample) of the table gives a similar magnitude number of −0.04 as the sum of 0.02 and −0.06 (coefficient of the interaction term).

These estimations suggest that, for successful catching-up economies, there is a positive (negative) correlation between their economic growth and the shorter (longer) cycle of their knowledge base, which is exactly opposite to the case of other middle-income countries or high-income countries. In other words, these results confirm that they became successful by specializing in shorter-cycle technologies. As shown in Figure 3.4, the growth of these four countries during the earlier stage (from the 1970s to the early 1980s) is accompanied by the slightly increasing trend of the cycle time. Then, this pattern reverses in the mid 1980s or the period when these countries started to upgrade to higher-value-added industries and segments, that is, the cycle times of their knowledge base became significantly shorter. By contrast, the positive coefficient of the cycle time variable for other middle-income countries is consistent with the reasoning of Lall (2000) that, for those relying on FDI and low-tech-based manufacturing and exports, disruptive technological change (which is common in short-cycle sectors) may lead to the truncation of learning and harmful for growth, and thus it is safer for them to pursue economic growth by specializing in long-cycle technologies.

Table 3.5 shows the list of technological classes generating the largest number of US patents by Korea and Taiwan together as well as the actual years in the cycle time of these technologies. It shows that these two economies have generated more patents in IT technologies including extremely short-cycle technologies (5.5 to 7.5 years) of semiconductors, TV/displays, information storage, telecommunications, and computer graphics as well as some medium-cycle technologies (about 8.0 to 9.0 years) such as electronic connectors, electrical lighting, land transportation, and electrical heating. The table also shows that the weighted average of cycle time of these top thirty technologies for the 1980 to 1995 period is 7.69.

By contrast, in other middle-income countries, such upgrading or moving to shorter-cycle technologies has not yet occurred, which may be one of the reasons for their failure to reach the status of high-income countries. Table 3.6 shows the list of top thirty technologies in terms of the US patents held by Brazil and Argentina. The top thirty fields include longer-cycle technologies (longer than nine years) such as wells, pumps, hydraulic engineering, food and beverages, surgery, metal-working, and fluid-handling technologies as well as medium-cycle technologies (8.0 to 9.0 years) such as drugs, surgical devices, prostheses/dental devices, stocking materials, and bearings. Their weighted average cycle time is long at 9.26 in the 1980 to 1995 period.

The fact that both middle- and higher-income countries have the same long-cycle technologies is consistent with the reasoning that the former group seem to be in charge of the low-end segments of the same industry (for instance, medicine and pharmaceuticals), whereas the high-income countries take the high-end part of the industry, as pointed out in the trade literature.[6] This finding is consistent with the image of specialization shown in Table 3.7, which lists the top ten technologies of the G5 countries, eight middle-income countries, and Korea–Taiwan. The top ten technologies of the eight middle-income countries overlap more with the G5 countries than

Table 3.5 *Top thirty technology classes by the US patents held by Korea and Taiwan and their cycle times (1980–95)*

Class	Count	Cycle time (years)	Class name (out of 417 classes)	Sub-cat	Sub-categories (36)
438	1189	6.07	Semiconductor manufacturing	46	Semiconductor devices
348	712	5.91	Television	49	Miscellaneous elec
439	408	7.98	Electrical connectors	41	Electrical devices
257	374	7.02	Transistors, solid-state diodes	46	Semiconductor devices
362	374	7.76	Illumination	42	Electrical lighting
280	355	8.21	Land vehicles	55	Transportation
365	346	5.74	Static information storage	24	Information storage
70	340	9.20	Locks	65	Furniture, house fixtures
360	313	6.47	Dynamic information storage	24	Information storage
482	311	8.82	Exercise devices	59	Miscellaneous mechanical
340	237	8.07	Communications: electrical	21	Communications
219	232	8.96	Electric heating	49	Miscellaneous electrical
361	228	8.04	Electrical power systems	45	Power systems
369	227	5.53	Information storage or retrieval	24	Information storage
313	213	8.81	Electric lamp and devices	42	Electrical lighting
359	208	7.53	Optics: systems and elements	54	Optics
473	204	10.01	Games using tangible projectile	62	Amusement devices
74	194	8.72	Machine element or mechanism	59	Miscellaneous mechanical
62	193	9.66	Refrigeration	69	Miscellaneous others

Table 3.5 (*cont.*)

Class	Count	Cycle time (years)	Class name (out of 417 classes)	Sub-cat	Sub-categories (36)
206	193	10.21	Special receptacle or package	68	Receptacles
248	187	9.16	Supports	69	Miscellaneous others
345	183	6.42	Computer graphics processing	23	Computer peripherals
386	183	6.01	Television signal processing	49	Miscellaneous electrical
327	182	7.54	Electrical nonlinear devices, circuits	41	Electrical devices
315	162	8.28	Electric lamp and devices	42	Electrical lighting
137	158	10.85	Fluid-handling	69	Miscellaneous others
318	157	7.65	Electricity: motive power systems	45	Power systems
428	157	8.36	Stock material or miscellaneous articles	69	Miscellaneous others
81	155	10.10	Tools	59	Miscellaneous mechanical
15	154	10.73	Brushing, scrubbing, and cleaning	69	Miscellaneous others
135	154	10.15	Tent, canopy, umbrella, or cane	69	Miscellaneous others
Top 30 sum	8683	7.69	(weighted average cycle time)		
% of top 30	43.4		(two country total patent count = 19,984)		

with Korea–Taiwan; out of the top ten technological sectors of the eight middle-income countries, five classes shown in bold fonts are also in the top ten list of the G5 countries. In striking contrast, none of the top ten technological sectors of Korea–Taiwan overlaps with those of G5 countries.

Table 3.6 *Top thirty technology classes by the US patents held by Brazil and Argentina and their cycle times (1980–95)*

Class	Counts	Cycle time	Class names (out of 417 classes)	Subcat	Sub-categories
604	30	8.73	Surgery	32	Surgery and medical instruments
514	25	8.20	Drug, bio-affecting/ body treating compositions	31	Drugs
166	23	10.10	Wells	64	Earth working and wells
417	23	9.25	Pumps	53	Motors and engines and parts
424	20	8.52	Drug, bio-affecting/ body treating compositions	31	Drugs
405	17	10.05	Hydraulic and earth engineering	64	Earth working and wells
99	16	10.34	Foods and beverages: apparatus	61	Agriculture, husbandry, food
128	15	10.20	Surgery	32	Surgery and medical instruments
623	14	8.35	Prostheses (parts, aids and accessories	39	Miscellaneous drugs and medical
29	13	9.43	Metal-working	52	Metal-working
137	13	10.85	Fluid-handling	69	Miscellaneous others
92	12	9.93	Expansible chamber devices	53	Motors and engines and parts
123	12	6.36	Internal combustion engines	53	Motors and engines and parts
210	12	9.90	Liquid purification or separation	19	Miscellaneous chemical

Table 3.6 (*cont.*)

Class	Counts	Cycle time	Class names (out of 417 classes)	Subcat	Sub-categories
220	12	10.48	Receptacles	68	Receptacles
428	12	8.36	Stock material or miscellaneous articles	69	Miscellaneous others
62	11	9.66	Refrigeration	69	Miscellaneous others
418	11	9.36	Rotary expansible chamber devices	53	Motors and engines and parts
52	10	11.06	Static structures (e.g. buildings)	69	Miscellaneous others
206	10	10.21	Special receptacles or packaging	68	Receptacles
379	10	6.47	Telephonic communications	21	Communications
384	10	8.86	Bearings	59	Miscellaneous mechanical
426	10	10.28	Food material and products	61	Agriculture, husbandry, food
607	10	8.14	Surgery: light, thermal, and electrical application	32	Surgery and medical instruments
73	9	9.13	Measuring and testing	43	Measuring and testing
75	9	9.29	Metallurgical processes, metal powder compositions	52	Metal working
222	9	10.42	Dispensing	19	Miscellaneous chemical
261	9	10.68	Gas and liquid contact apparatus	19	Miscellaneous chemical
318	9	7.65	Electricity: motive power systems	45	Power systems

Table 3.6 (*cont.*)

Class	Counts	Cycle time	Class names (out of 417 classes)	Subcat	Sub-categories
425	9	10.34	Plastic articles and apparatus	51	Material processing and handling
435	9	8.22	Molecular biology and microbiology	33	Biotechnology
606	9	8.17	Surgery	32	Surgery and medical instruments
Top 30 summary	423	9.26	(= weighted average cycle time of technologies)		(our of 36 sub-categories)
Share, top 30 (%)	41.50		(two-country total count = 1,019)		

3.5 Summary

Compared with middle-income countries, high-income countries are those with higher per capita income growth rates, a higher ratio of investment, and considerably higher school enrollment ratios but with lower population growth. In some of the key aspects of the NIS, rich countries tend to show a more even distribution of innovators and a higher rate of localization of knowledge creation and diffusion, as well as a knowledge base having a higher rate of originality and medium-short time of the technology cycle.

A regression analysis of the determinants of per capita income growth in the high-income group shows that all the variables, except originality, are significantly related to growth. This finding shows the importance of promoting the localization of knowledge creation and diffusion and spreading the base of the national inventors. But a country does not have to be overly concerned about moving toward higher-originality technologies. While the balanced distribution of innovation across inventors is related to economic growth in high-income countries, this does not seem to be a variable that triggers the catching up of Asian countries because no clear-cut trend of a decline in this variable is observed in these countries from 1980 to

Table 3.7 *Top ten classes of G5, Korea–Taiwan, and eight middle-income countries, 1980–95*

	Class	Class name	Patent count
G5			
1	514	Drug, bio-affecting and body treating compositions	10,349
2	428	Stock material or miscellaneous articles	3,883
3	73	Measuring and testing	3,789
4	123	Internal combustion engines	3,479
5	424	Drug, bio-affecting and body treating compositions	3,389
6	210	Liquid purification or separation	2,853
7	435	Chemistry: molecular biology and microbiology	2,852
8	250	Radiant energy	2,639
9	264	Plastic and nonmetallic article shaping or treating	2,349
10	324	Electricity: measuring and testing	2,325
8 middle-income countries			
1	514	Drug, bio-affecting and body treating compositions	120
2	424	Drug, bio-affecting and body treating compositions	76
3	435	Chemistry: molecular biology and microbiology	54
4	75	Metallurgical compositions, metal mixtures	52
5	65	Glass manufacturing	44
6	604	Surgery	44
7	210	Liquid purification or separation	40
8	423	Chemistry of inorganic compounds	40
9	502	Catalyst, solid sorbent, or product	40
10	123	Internal combustion engines	38
Korea–Taiwan			
1	438	Semiconductor device manufacturing: process	1,189
2	348	Television	712
3	439	Electrical connectors	408
4	257	Active solid-state devices (e.g. transistors and solid-state diodes)	374
5	362	Illumination	374
6	280	Land vehicles	355
7	365	Static information storage and retrieval	346
8	70	Locks	340
9	360	Dynamic magnetic information storage or retrieval	313
10	482	Exercise devices	311

Notes: G5 includes the UK, France, Germany, Italy, and Canada.
Source: calculation using the NBER data mentioned in the text.

1995. By contrast, the localization of knowledge creation and diffusion variable may be a factor because a significant increase (i.e. three times) exists in the degree of intranational diffusion in Korea and Taiwan, although these countries have yet to further consolidate their own mechanisms of knowledge creation and diffusion to have the impact of the variable realized.

The most tricky and essential variable is the technology cycle time. Whereas the longer cycle time is positively related to economic growth for both high- and middle-income countries, it is negatively (and thus shorter time is positively) related to economic growth in the most successful catching-up countries, namely, Korea, Taiwan, Hong Kong, and Singapore in the catching-up period of the late 1980s. Moreover, the level of the technology cycle time for these countries is considerably shorter than that of the high-income groups. These four economies used to have longer or similar degrees of cycle time technologies to those of the high- and other middle-income countries until the mid 1980s, but they have since started to move into sectors with a shorter cycle time of technologies. This finding suggests that these economies became successful by specializing in shorter-cycle technologies, which has been confirmed by regression analyses in this chapter.

This strategy of technological specialization (in shorter-cycle technologies and against high-originality technologies) can be regarded as a detour strategy in the sense that the catching-up countries did not directly replicate the high-originality and long-cycle technologies of the advanced economies, as shown in Table 3.7. Instead, the successful catching-up countries initially moved to the opposite direction of pursuing shorter-cycle and low-originality technologies. The direct replication strategy focussing on high-originality and longer-cycle technologies, as in some Latin American economies, may lead to continuing reliance on foreign and advanced countries, and thus to a lower chance of consolidating indigenous knowledge bases.

The policy implications for other middle-income countries are that these countries could also consider initiating such an upgrade or moving into shorter-cycle technologies instead of into high-originality technologies if they want to join the club of high-income countries. The experience of Korea and Taiwan suggests that, to join the high-income group, countries have to upgrade to higher-value segments of the same industries and/or to the new, higher-value-added industries, as discussed in Chapter 1 and in the work of Lee and Mathews (2012).

4 | Knowledge and sector-level catch-up: Asia versus Latin America

4.1 Introduction

The analysis of technological catch-up at the sector level in this chapter relies on the concept of the technological regime by Nelson and Winter (1982: 258).[1] Technological regimes are perceived as a combination of several dimensions, such as technological opportunity, appropriability of innovations, cumulativeness of technological advances, and properties of the knowledge base. Although this notion of technological regime has been used to explain the specific way in which the innovative activities of a technological sector are organized in many advanced economies, Lee and Lim (2001) use this concept in the context of catching up by latecomers in technological capability building. The econometric study of Park and Lee (2006) is one of the first attempts to generalize the finding from many case studies of catch-up.[2] Their study finds that different elements of technological regimes of sectors affect the catching-up performance of a country differently. Their study and this study analyze the patent data at the levels of technological classes, so using the term "classes" to refer to the analysis is more precise. However, the term "sector" is more commonly used than classes, and using "technological sectors" in place of classes is appropriate as long as we place the word "technological" before "sectors" to distinguish them from industrial sectors. Hereafter, we will use the term "technological sectors" in place of the more precise term "technological classes."

Although Park and Lee (2006) examine the case of the two most successful economies of Korea and Taiwan, this chapter aims to encompass more countries to determine whether differences exist between these next-tier countries and the first-tier countries of Korea and Taiwan. The focus will be on four Asian (i.e. China, India, Malaysia, and Thailand) and four Latin American countries (i.e. Brazil, Argentina, Mexico, and Chile), because some of them are perceived as innovative developing countries by the literature (Morel et al. 2005). This comparison will determine whether the variable of cycle time of technologies, which is most important in the cases of Korea and Taiwan, has the same or a different degree of explanatory power as the determinants of catch-up across different groups of latecomer economies.

In this comparison, an interesting issue is the possible double-edged-sword nature of the technological regime featured by rapid technical change or short technical cycles. The short cycle time of technologies can serve as a window for catch-up only for latecomers that have already accumulated certain technological capabilities. Otherwise, frequent changes in technology can become additional barriers against catch-up. The double nature of technological changes has also been analyzed in the contrasting cases of the telecom industries in the more successful China and Korea versus the less successful Brazil and India.[3] This nature is consistent with the so-called truncation of the FDI-based learning process noted in Lall (1992, 2000), which shows that frequent technological changes interfere with learning and accumulation by latecomers. In this case, short cycles cause them additional hardship.

Therefore, we address the phenomenon in which the latecomers achieve remarkable catch-up in some technological sectors, whereas they do not in other sectors. We ask how the difference between the technological sectors can be explained. What are the conditions affecting the occurrence and the degree of technological catch-up? In answering these questions, we examine the phenomenon of technological catch-up by distinguishing between the *occurrence* of catch-up and the *speed* of catch-up. We then conduct regression analyses to find the determinants of each of these two aspects of technological catch-up. Furthermore, we analyze the determinants of the levels of technological capability in catching-up economies and compare them with those in advanced countries.

We use the same proxy variables to represent diverse aspects of the technological regimes using US patent data and patent citation data. We use quantitative patent-based expressions of the technological regimes for the four original regime variables of Breschi et al. (2000) and for the four additional variables proposed in Park and Lee (2006). The latter four include accessibility to the external knowledge base, the initial stock of knowledge in the field, the cycle time of technologies, and the uncertainty (fluidity) of the trajectory of technologies.[4] We examine how far these factors affect the occurrence and speed of technological catch-up.

This chapter proceeds as follows. Section 4.2 examines the literature, constructs a theoretical framework for analysis, and suggests hypotheses for empirical verification. Section 4.3 provides a review of the record of the technological catch-up by country groups worldwide using US patent data. Section 4.4 discusses the structure of regression models and the regression results. Section 4.5 provides the summary and concluding remarks.

4.2 Theoretical framework and hypotheses

Technological regime and the catch-up: two main hypotheses

The notion of technological regime defines the nature of technology according to a knowledge-based theory of production. Innovation is regarded as a problem-solving activity drawing upon knowledge bases that are stored in routines (Nelson and Winter, 1982: 258). Technological regimes are important because they constrain the pattern of innovation emerging in an industry. Some econometric studies have been conducted on the relationship between technological regimes and technological specialization and/or trade specialization in the context of advanced economies, the most notable of which are Breschi et al. (2000) and Malerba and Orsenigo (1996).[5] The current study can be considered an extension of these empirical analyses of technological regime; the difference is that we try to link the technological regime to technological catch-up by latecomer countries or firms.

The implication of technological regimes for catching-up countries differs from that of advanced countries. For example, latecomer economies suffer from innovation impossibility when the regime of a technology has high cumulativeness because they do not command a good mass of R&D and a sound institutional basis for IPR. Malerba and Orsenigo (1996) assert that as long as the dimensions of technological regimes are similar across countries, each pattern of innovation should be invariant across countries. However, the ability to generate and exploit opportunity is less similar among countries, even among advanced countries. Therefore, even though patterns of innovation may be invariant across advanced economies, this relation may not hold between advanced economies and catching-up economies. Malerba and Orsenigo (1996) acknowledge that country-specific patterns of innovation possibly exist and are related to the major differences between countries in terms of historical industrial development, in the competence and organization of their firms, and in the architecture and policies of their specific national innovation. They argue that technological imperatives and technology-related factors such as technological regimes have a major role in determining the specific pattern of innovative activities of a technological class across countries. Among these major constraints identified by technological regimes, country-specific factors introduce differences across countries in the pattern of innovative activities for specific technological classes.

Lee and Lim (2001) posit that technological capability is determined as a function of technological effort and existing knowledge base. They examine the technological regimes of the sectors as determinants of technological effort. They analyze such elements of technological regimes as the cumulativeness of technical advances, the uncertainty (fluidity) of the technological trajectory, and properties of the knowledge base as determinants of technological effort. Using this framework, they argue that when the technological regime of an industry has higher cumulativeness and a more unpredictable technological trajectory, catching up is more difficult, especially in large conglomerate-style firms.

Based on the foregoing, we put forward the main hypothesis of the research, that is that the technological regime is essential in technological catch-up. As a close relationship exists between the different elements of the regime of technological fields and the occurrence and speed of technological catch-up, we will identify which factors are significant. From this main hypothesis, we can derive many sub-hypotheses that will be discussed later. One sub-hypothesis that we want to emphasize is related to the leapfrogging argument that shifts in technological trajectory or the emergence of new technologies often serve as a window of opportunity for latecomers. The disadvantages of the latecomers are not tremendous during this time as everyone is a beginner. In the regression analysis, we will test a related version of this argument by determining whether technologies with shorter cycle times yield better chances for catch-up.

Park and Lee (2006) find that technologies with shorter cycle times yield better chances for catch-up in Korea and Taiwan. However, this finding may be true only in countries with a certain level of technological capability. Other latecomer countries with less capability may face more difficulties when more frequent changes in technology occur. Therefore, one of the main focusses of this chapter is to ascertain whether differences exist between next-tier countries and the first-tier countries of Korea and Taiwan. This comparison will determine whether the variable of cycle time of technologies, which is most important in the cases of Korea and Taiwan, has the same or a different degree of explanatory power as the determinants of catch-up across different groups of latecomer economies. Specifically, we hypothesize that, although shorter cycle times are positively related to catching-up performance in first-tier countries, they may be negatively or insignificantly related to it in second-tier countries.

The regime variables and the related sub-hypotheses

In this subsection,[6] we devise a proxy variable for each element constituting the regime of the technologies. Two sets of variables serve as explanatory variables in the regressions. The first set includes variables often discussed in the context of advanced countries by other researchers: technological opportunities, the appropriability of innovations, the cumulativeness of technical advances, and the property of the knowledge base. Conversely, the other set of variables are those first proposed by Park and Lee (2006), which are more relevant in the context of catch-up, namely, accessibility to external knowledge flows, the uncertainty of the technological trajectory, the initial stock of knowledge, and the technological cycle time.

Technological opportunity

Technological opportunity refers to the likelihood of successful innovation for any given amount of money invested for innovation activities. High opportunities provide powerful incentives to undertake innovative activities and denote an economic environment that is not functionally constrained by scarcity (Breschi et al. 2000).[7] In this case, potential innovators may come up with frequent and important technological innovations. We measure technological opportunity by the annual average growth rate of patents registered in each sector in the application year base as follows:

$$\text{Technological opportunity of } i \text{ sector} = \sum_{t=1980}^{1995} G_{it}/16$$

where G_{it} is the growth rate of the US patent registrations in application year t in i sector, and 16 is the number of years in the period (e.g. from 1980 to 1995 in our case).

This variable is a good measure of technological opportunity to the extent that the patent registrations of each sector reflect innovation outcomes. The higher the technological opportunity, the more competition exists and consequently there is a low possibility of technological catch-up by latecomers. However, more ambitious latecomer firms also want to join in these potentially profitable technologies. The regression analysis ascertains which reasoning is correct.

Cumulativeness of technological innovation

Cumulativeness refers to the extent to which today's technological innovation depends on past innovation. Innovation generates a stream of subsequent innovations that are a gradual improvement on the original or create new knowledge for use in other innovations in related areas. High levels of cumulativeness are typical of economic environments characterized by continuities in innovative activity and increasing returns (Breschi et al. 2000). Generally, cumulativeness can be defined at several levels: (1) at the level of organization (at the laboratory or at the firm level); (2) at the level of the market (market success breeds further success); and (3) at the level of technological sector. In this chapter, given our focus on sectoral analysis, we measure cumulativeness at the technological-sector level. At the sector level, cumulativeness can be captured by the persistence of innovation within the technological sector. Therefore, we measure the cumulativeness of a class by the share of the patents held by persistent innovators in that class. In a measure (i.e. Cumul1), persistent innovators are patent assignees that have continuously (at least one patent every year) registered patents throughout the period (1980–95). A less strict measure (i.e. Cumul2) uses the definition of persistent innovators as those who have registered at least four patents in the first and second eight-year periods during the sixteen-year period from 1980 to 1995.[8] Therefore, we have

$$\text{Cumulativeness of sector} = \sum_{t=1980}^{1995} \sum_{j=1}^{n} P_{ijt} \bigg/ \sum_{t=1980}^{1995} P_{it}$$

where P_{it} is the number of patents registered in i class in application year t, and P_{ijt} is the number of patents registered in i class in application year t by persistent innovator j.

If cumulativeness is low, would-be innovators will not be at a major disadvantage with respect to incumbent firms (Winter 1984). Thus, the higher the cumulativeness, the more difficult it will be for catching-up countries to catch up advanced incumbent firms.

Appropriability of technological innovation

Appropriability of innovations refers to the possibility of protecting innovations from imitation and of reaping profits from innovative activities. High appropriability refers to the existing ways to success-fully protect innovation from imitation. Low appropriability conditions denote an economic environment characterized by the widespread existence of externalities (Breschi et al. 2000). With this meaning, the degree of appropriability cannot be represented by patent data because patent data have little to do with financial returns. Therefore, some researchers such as Levin et al. (1987) tend to use the questionnaire survey to measure appropriability. However, several studies, such as Jaffe et al. (1993) and Stolpe (2002) use a high proportion of self-citations as an indicator of appropriability.

The rationale for the ratio of self-citations is that subsequent patents are likely to reflect the follow-up developments of the original invention and that these developments are the conduit that leads to the appropri-ation of returns. Thus, the higher the proportion of these later develop-ments that take place in house, the larger is the fraction of the benefits captured by the original inventor (Trajtenberg et al. 1997). On the one hand, citations to patent that belong to the same assignee represent transfers of knowledge that are mostly internalized within the innov-ators. On the other hand, citations to patents of others are closer to the pure notion of diffused spillovers (Hall et al. 2001). Therefore, self-citations represent a positive externality used by the same innovators.

Considering the intrinsic limit and some rationales, we follow the literature and represent appropriability by the proportion of a patent's subsequent citations by other patents that have been assigned to the same owner as the cited patent or simply by the ratio of self-citations received to total citations received. This ratio of self-citation can be computed using the US patent citation data as follows:

$$\text{Appropriability in } i \text{ class} = \sum_{t=1980}^{1995} SC_{it} \Bigg/ \sum_{t=1980}^{1995} TC_{it}$$

where SC_{it} is the number of self-citations received in i class in applica-tion year t, and TC_{it} is the number of citation received in i class in application year t.

On one hand, whenever possible, most inventors would focus on high-appropriability sectors. This premise holds true even for latecomer firms with limited or scarce R&D resources. Moreover, higher appropriability is defined as having more self-citations, implying a smaller need for reliance on knowledge from other firms or agencies so that the latecomer firms may feel that focussing on such technologies is advantageous. Therefore, firms from developing countries may want to focus on high-appropriability technologies. On the other hand, appropriability of innovations will have less importance or no relevance to catching up if catching-up countries, especially those at lower levels of catch-up, are merely trying to emulate preexisting technologies instead of achieving real innovations. In sum, hypothesizing a positive or negative coefficient for this variable is not easy.

Property of the knowledge base: originality
The property of the knowledge base relates to the nature of the knowledge underpinning firms' innovative activities. Technological knowledge involves various degrees of specificity, tacitness, complexity, and independence, and it may greatly differ across technologies. Previous literature has mainly focussed on specificity. Generic knowledge refers to knowledge of a very broad nature, whereas specific knowledge refers to knowledge specialized and targeted to specific applications. Generic or focussed knowledge is also related to different types of science: that is, basic sciences generate generic knowledge, whereas applied sciences generate focussed knowledge (Breschi et al. 2000).

Given our interest in catch-up, we focus on the originality of the knowledge base, hypothesizing that the degree of originality may affect the easiness or difficulty of catch-up more than other properties of the knowledge base, such as specificity. Originality can be calculated as suggested by Trajtenberg et al. (1997) and Hall et al. (2001):

$$\text{Originality}^i = 1 - \sum_{k=1}^{Ni} \left(\frac{Nciting_{ik}}{Nciting_i} \right)^2$$

where k is the technological sector (more precisely patent class k), $Nciting_{ik}$ is the number of citations made by patent i to patents that belong to patent class k, and $Nciting_i$ is the total number of citations made by patent i.

This definition represents the rationale that the broader the techno-logical root of the underlying knowledge or research related to the patents, the higher the originality of a patent. The synthesis of diver-gent ideas may be a characteristic of research that has high originality and is thus basic in that sense (Trajtenberg et al. 1997). If a patent cites previous patents that belong to a narrow set of technologies, the originality score will be low, whereas citing patents from a wide range of fields will result in a high score. We calculate the mean originality of each technological sector as a proxy for the nature of technological knowledge.

In terms of the nature of technological knowledge, latecomers or catching-up countries experience more difficulty in acquiring know-ledge based on very broad sources. Conversely, gaining knowledge that is specialized and targeted to specific applications is easy. How-ever, in some technological sectors, these factors do not always function against technological catch-up. Aggregation from diverse sources is often not a task that catching-up economies have to achieve directly. In many cases, catching-up economies simply acquire and emulate the result of innovation based on aggregation from diverse sources.

Relative technological cycle time (speed of obsolescence of knowledge)

One important attribute of knowledge is obsolescence over time, and knowledge differs in this respect. Some knowledge becomes quickly obsolete, whereas some does not. The speed of obsolescence affects the chances of catch-up. If the life expectancy of knowledge is long, mastering knowledge and technology in that field requires more time. However, if knowledge is short lived, catching-up countries can acquire technology in a time that is similar to that taken by advanced countries, enabling them to specialize in an area according to their technological capability at that time. This factor can be expressed as the technological cycle time.[9] Technological cycle time is measured by the time span between the predecessor and the successor, and is calcu-lated as the time difference between the application year of the citing patent and that of the cited patents (Park and Lee 2006). To normalize or compare across classes, we define the relative technological cycle time as the ratio of technological cycle time of patents in a class to the average of all patents as follows:

Technological cycle time of i class = Average(TCT_{it})/Average(TCT_t),
$t = 1980 \ldots 1995$

where TCT_{it} is the technological cycle time of patents in i class applied year t, and TCT_t is the technological cycle time of all patents applied in year t.

A value greater than one represents a longer cycle time and thus a slower speed of change in the knowledge base of a technology. A value less than one represents high speed. Long cycle time indicates a greater importance of old knowledge, and thus more time is needed to study old knowledge from the latecomers' point of view. However, when knowledge in the field changes quickly, the disadvantages for the latecomer may not be that great. Therefore, we hypothesize that the shorter the cycle time of a technology, the higher the possibility of catch-up. This hypothesis is also consistent with the observation by Amsden and Chu that the catching-up firm's task is to source its high-tech inputs from overseas and create scarcities in other inputs, designs, or functions when a "new" mature product is still in demand. Therefore, the competitiveness of a catching-up firm depends on its ability to enter new market segments quickly, to manufacture with high levels of engineering excellence, and to be first-to-market through the best integrative designs.

Accessibility to external knowledge flows

The existing literature on developed economies tends to focus on the technological opportunity and the nature of knowledge itself, with some exceptions such as Bell and Pavitt (1993) and Laursen and Meliciani (2002), who examine the impact of spillovers and learning. However, when the situation of the catching-up economies is considered, accessibility to external (foreign) knowledge flows can be more important. As asserted by Hu and Jaffe (2003), although advanced economies naturally create most of this knowledge stock, non-advanced economies try to tap into it, constrained by the limited channels of knowledge diffusion and their ability to absorb and adapt new knowledge. In this way, the knowledge from advanced countries has the function of facilitating technological development in catching-up economies. Therefore, the extent of spillover from advanced countries to catching-up economies in each technology is important for catch-up.

Access to the knowledge base or spillovers from the core is measured by the proportion of citations by non-G7 held patents to G7-held patents out of the total citations in a class as follows:

$$\text{Accessibility to external knowledge flows in } i \text{ class} = \sum_{t=1980}^{1995} \sum_{j=1}^{n} P_{ict} \Big/ \sum_{t=1980}^{1995} P_{it}$$

where P_{it} is the number of all citations in i class in application year t, and P_{ict} is the number of citations G7-held patents received from the non-G7 held patents in i class in application year t.

Catching-up economies need to be connected with a knowledge base abroad and to have access to the international knowledge frontier. Therefore, this variable of accessibility is positively related to the possibility and speed of catch-up and the level of technological capability to be achieved by latecomer firms.

Initial stock of knowledge

Previous literature focusses on the cumulativeness of technology and the possibility of appropriability of technology innovation. However, when the situation of the catching-up economies is considered, their knowledge gap with advanced countries for every technological sector must also be addressed. The larger the gap, the more difficult the catch-up process, which militates against technological effort. In this light, we introduce the variable of the initial stock of accumulative knowledge as one explanatory variable because it also represents the amount of knowledge in each technological class that catching-up economies have to master to conduct innovation in that class. This factor can act as a barrier to catch-up and functions as the environment that affects the decision of which technology is selected and targeted for catch-up. However, a possibility also exists for a stock of accumulative knowledge to function as a pool of knowledge to be utilized by catching-up firms and countries.

We measure this variable as the total number of US patents in each class normalized by the total number of US patents in all classes as follows:

$$\text{Initial stock of accumulative knowledge in } i \text{ sector} = \sum_{t=1975}^{1979} P_{it} \Big/ \sum_{t-1975}^{1979} P_t$$

where P_{it} is the total number of patents registered in i class in application year t, and P_t is the total number of patent registered in application year t.

Uncertainty (fluidity) of a technological trajectory
Each technology is different in terms of the degree of uncertainty that firms encounter in the sectors. Uncertainty is often associated with the age of the technologies. In technologies at their early stage, predicting how they will evolve in the future is difficult and the level of uncertainty is greater. By contrast, in a mature technology sector, firms generally face a more stable environment. This element can be described as the uncertainty or fluidity of technological trajectory, which may have implications for technological catch-up. We measure the uncertainty of a technological trajectory of a technology as follows:

Uncertainty of class $i = (Max_i - Min_i)/AVG_i$ for each class i

where Max_i is the number of patents in a class i in the year when the largest number of patents was recorded during the 1980 to 1995 period, Min_i is the number of patents in a class i in the year when the smallest number of patents was recorded during the 1980 to 1995 period, and AVG_i is the average number of patents in a class i per year during the 1980 to 1995 period.

The larger value of this variable identifies the technologies that show larger variations in the number of patents each year during the specified period. Although no firm wishes to live in an uncertain environment, firms of different organizational characteristics show different degrees of fitness in such an environment. Suppose that two types of firms, namely, small specialized firms and large diversified firms, exist. Under a high-uncertainty environment, large conglomerate firms experience more difficulty in devising a stable catch-up strategy focussing on targeted R&D projects. Conversely, SMEs in another catch-up country such as Taiwan will not be at a disadvantage in an uncertain environment because they tend to be more flexible than Korean *chaebols*.[10]

Using patents to measure technological regimes

Despite the limitations of patent data as output data of innovations, we have no choice but to use patent data in this study given the lack of alternative indicators suitable for our purposes. However, our results are partly free from the limitation of patent data. First, differences in patenting activities across classes are equally applicable to any country. In other words, we can assume that a given number of innovation outcomes in each class will lead to a similar number of patent applications across countries, or assume that the propensity to apply patents in a class is the same across countries. Therefore, comparing the growth rates of patents in each class and the share of each country in patent classes across countries, or between those of catching-up economies of Korea and Taiwan and those of advanced economies, is rational.

Second, as discussed in Chapter 2, we use US Patent and Trademark Office (USPTO) patent data. Specifically, in this chapter we use the NBER patent database or the first data set explained in Chapter 2. The data contain the residential address of each inventor. The country is identified by the addresses of the inventors in the first data set.[11] For patents involving multiple inventors, the country is identified by the address of the first inventor, which can be a source of problem since some Korean inventors are hired by US companies to work in the USA. Our results are not affected by this issue.

Finally, considering the nature of patent citation data, the so-called truncation problem, and the actual situation of catching-up countries, we confine our analysis up to the year 1995 or the period of 1980 to 1995, when the successful catch-up by Korea and Taiwan occurred.

Table 4.1 shows some examples of measurement of elements of the technological regimes using US patent data for nine technologies or nine different US patent classes, from apparel to computer hardware and software. For example, in terms of the cycle time of technologies, communication technologies have the shortest cycle among the nine classes, whereas apparel has the longest-cycle technology. Biotechnology represented by class number 435 has the lowest degree of appropriability and a medium cycle time of technologies. Solar power technologies classified as belonging to class 136 have cycle times lower than average. By reading the cycle times of each class from the table, we can see that the leading sectors of the Korean economy have moved from the long-cycle technology of apparel (1.18) in the 1970s to the medium cycle of autos (0.89) and PCs (0.84) in the 1980s, and finally to the short-cycle technologies of memory chips (0.79) and mobile telecommunications (0.74) in the 1990s.

Table 4.1 *Technological regimes of nine technologies*

USPTO class	Name of technology	Opportunity	Cumulativeness1	Cumulativeness2	Appropriability	Originality	Uncertainty	Initial stock	Cycle time	Accessibility
2	Apparel	0.08	0.00	0.51	0.46	0.23	1.04	0.12	1.18	0.04
136	Batteries (including thermo and PV)	0.16	0.00	0.34	0.13	0.31	1.09	0.07	0.92	0.03
180	Transportation (auto)	0.05	0.30	0.66	0.19	0.33	0.98	0.46	0.89	0.05
290	Prime mover dynamo plants (wind power)	0.11	0.00	0.49	0.30	0.42	1.59	0.08	0.90	0.06
435	Biotechnology	0.13	0.13	0.39	0.11	0.25	2.48	0.67	0.98	0.06
455	Communications	0.13	0.25	0.57	0.12	0.36	2.66	0.39	0.74	0.07
424	Drugs	0.13	0.09	0.40	0.15	0.36	2.45	0.67	1.02	0.05
711	Information storage (memory chips)	0.19	0.50	0.63	0.12	0.44	2.38	0.08	0.79	0.02
712	Computer hardware and software (PC)	0.16	0.28	0.67	0.12	0.46	2.32	0.05	0.84	0.02
	All sector average	0.10	0.10	0.46	0.21	0.33	1.19	0.27	1.10	0.06

Source: author's calculations using the NBER patent data classified into 417 classes following the method explained in the text. See the text for the definitions of variables.

4.3 Divergence in technological catch-up: first- versus second-tier countries

Defining and measuring technological catch-up at the sector level

Many late-industrializing countries have attempted to use technological innovation to achieve economic growth despite the unfavorable environment of innovation. Although the majority of them have not made much progress, a few developing countries show rapid technological catch-up. To reduce the technological gap with advanced countries, developing countries must generate technological innovation more rapidly than advanced countries. In this regard, we define catching-up economies as those that generate more rapid technological innovation than advanced countries. We regard advanced countries as those belonging to the G7, namely, the USA, Japan, Germany, the UK, France, Italy, and Canada. However, we will exclude the USA (and Japan as a giant) from the reference group because we will use US patents to measure and compare the technological capabilities of countries.

Tables 4.2 and 4.3 show the numbers and average annual growth rate of the US patents from 1975 to 1995 in countries around the world categorized into G6 (G7 minus Japan), the first-tier (Korea and Taiwan), the four Asian second-tier, and four Latin American second-tier economies.

A huge difference exists between advanced countries and the latecomers. Whereas the G6 countries filed on average 7,885 patents in the USA in 1995, the two first-tier economies filed only 2,164, which is less than one-third of the former. However, the gap between the first- and second-tier economies is even greater in terms of the ratios. The second-tier countries file fewer than 40 patents per year, which is about one-fiftieth that of the first tier. On the other hand, the gap is not that great during the early years. In 1985, second-tier countries file about 15 US patents per year, and Korea and Taiwan file about 160 patents, which is ten times greater than that of the second-tier economies. Up to the year of 1975, the Latin American countries file more patents than the first-tier countries of Korea and Taiwan, and in 1985, the second-tier Latin American countries file more than the second-tier Asian countries. These findings imply that a reversal of fortunes between

Table 4.2 *Number of US patents registered by selected countries*

| Country | Average number of the US patents | | | |
	Until 1975	1985	1995	1975–95 (period sum)
G6	29,203.2	4,707.7	7,885.7	113,706.3
Korea and Taiwan	67	161	2,163.5	10,155.5
Second-tier (Asia plus Latin America)	163.5	15.1	37.4	415.6
Asia (second-tier)	68	8.5	36.3	282.5
Latin America (second-tier)	259	21.75	38.5	548.8
Korea	53	70	2,092	8,048
Taiwan	81	252	2,235	12,263
China	88	13	63	557
India	166	14	51	406
Malaysia	11	3	19	106
Thailand	7	4	12	61
Argentina	241	15	35	466
Brazil	182	31	60	789
Chile	46	3	9	91
Mexico	567	38	50	849

Note: Calculations using the US patents. The numbers are the compound annual growth rate (CAGR).

the Latin American and Asian countries occurred in the decades of the 1980s and the 1990s.

Table 4.3 confirms this implication. In the period of 1975 to 1995, the first-tier countries of Korea and Taiwan record an annual growth rate of 27.4 percent. By contrast, the Latin American countries record growth at only less than 4 percent, which is much lower than that of the second-tier Asian countries at 11 percent.

As capitalism develops and competition becomes fiercer, there is an increasing trend to fuse technology into making one product. Technological diversification, or spreading technological resources over a wider range of technological classes, represents higher technological capability, and it functions in favor of further technological innovation. Granstrand et al. (1997) and Patel and Pavitt

Table 4.3 *Average annual growth rate of the US patents registered by selected countries*

Country	Average annual growth rate (%)		
	1975–85	1985–95	1975–95
G6	2.40	4.13	3.25
Korea and Taiwan	21.29	34.07	27.44
Second-tier (Asia plus Latin America)	3.71	11.43	7.42
Asia (second-tier)	6.96	15.69	11.11
Latin America (second-tier)	0.46	7.18	3.73
Korea	21.23	43.27	31.79
Taiwan	21.34	24.87	23.09
China	23.45	9.35	16.19
India	0.00	13.76	6.66
Malaysia	1.34	20.81	10.65
Thailand	9.6	20.02	14.69
Argentina	−4.25	9.50	2.40
Brazil	3.84	9.95	6.85
Chile	7.18	6.49	6.83
Mexico	−2.98	3	−0.03

(1997) indicate the advantage of having innovation activities in a wide range of classes in the case of innovating firms.

Table 4.4 shows the average scope of patenting activities of several countries marked by the number of classes where the patents are registered. The difference between groups of countries is considerable. On average, the G6 countries register patents in 331 out of 417 classes in 1995, and the first-tier and second-tier countries record only 249 and 32 classes, respectively. As expected, the advanced countries register their patents in a much broader range of classes.[12] This fact implies that technological catch-up at the national level can also be considered in terms of the increase in the number of classes with patent registration or simply technological diversification. In this regard, the notable countries are again Korea and Taiwan. For instance, these two countries on average register patents only in 21 classes in 1975 and in 90 classes in 1985, but in 1995, they register in 249 classes (Table 4.4).

Table 4.4 *Number of classes with patents registered by country*

Name	1975	1985	1995	1976–85	1986–95
G6	308.7	318.7	330.7	316.2	328.5
Korea and Taiwan	20.5	90	249	44.5	220.6
Second-tier	13.4	12.9	31.5	10.8	21.9
(Asia plus Latin America)					
Asia (second-tier)	4.5	7.25	30.5	4.6	18.7
Latin America (second-tier)	22.25	18.5	32.5	17.1	25.0
Korea	9	52	232	22.8	186.4
Taiwan	32	128	266	66.2	254.7
China	3	13	63	4.3	42.9
India	10	9	30	9.3	19.2
Malaysia	4	3	17	2.4	7.8
Thailand	1	4	12	2.2	4.9
Argentina	20	14	25	15.8	20.5
Brazil	20	30	60	21.9	40.3
Chile	2	3	8	2.5	5.9
Mexico	47	27	37	28.3	33.4

Note: The numbers indicate in how many classes the patents have been registered. The total number of the classes in the USPTO system is 417.

4.4 Structure of the regression models and their result

Structure of the models

In this section,[13] we build an empirical model to analyze the phenomenon of the technological catch-up in relation to the notion of the technological regimes. Technological catch-up is defined as the faster increase in technological capability measured against comparable groups. Technological capability is measured by the share of a country in the total patents in a specific technological sector. Our investigation of the catch-up process is conducted in terms of the following three steps:

First, as emphasized in Section 4.3, technological catch-up does not occur in every technological class. In other words, there are some classes in which catching-up economies do not register any patents or the number of registered patents never increases. Therefore, we examine what determines the probability of the occurrence of technological catch-up after defining "occurrence" as the increase in the share of a country from zero to positive or from a positive number to a larger number. The reason we pay attention to this occurrence is that one important aspect of catch-up is registering patents in diverse classes, thus increasing the diversity of their technological capabilities. Therefore, the specific question is in which classes featured by which technological regimes there is more possibility of technological catch-up. For this question, the specification of the regression model is as follows:

Occurrence of technological catch-up = F (technological regimes)

For this regression specification, we estimate a Probit model appropriate for a qualitative binary dependent variable and determine the contributions of different elements of the technological regimes to the probability of technological catch-up.

Second, we select only those classes in which technological catch-up occurs, and then see what determines its speed. The speed of catch-up is defined as the change in the patent shares of a country (i.e. Korea and Taiwan, or either of the two, depending on the regressions) measured as a percentage point between the year 1980 and 1995. For this question, the regression specification is as follows and is run as an ordinary least squares (OLS) regression:

Speed of technological catch-up in each class
= F (technological regimes)

Finally, the occurrence and speed of catch-up determine the level of technological capability of economies in each class. In other words, in some technological fields, latecomer economies will achieve higher technological capabilities (i.e. higher share of their patents in sector) because some technological fields correspond to the higher probability of the occurrence of catch-up and/or higher speed of catch-up, whereas in other technologies, their achievement will be lower because these technologies have a number of intrinsic difficulties associated with their technological regimes. For this question, the regression specification is as follows and is run as an OLS regression:

Level of technological capability = F (technological regimes)

Different elements of the technological regimes are represented by the factors of technological regimes suggested by Breschi et al. (2000) and also by other elements we find appropriate for catching-up economies. To test this hypothesis, we measure each element of a technological

Table 4.5 *Descriptive statistics of the variables*

Country	Occurrence Mean	Speed Mean	Level Mean
G5	0.348	−2.246	8.804
Korea and Taiwan	0.814	3.677	2.164
Second-tier (Asia plus Latin America)	0.151	0.030	0.080
Asia (second-tier)	0.140	0.059	0.041
Latin America (second-tier)	0.162	0.000	0.120
China	0.226	0.106	0.061
India	0.170	0.066	0.059
Malaysia	0.096	0.035	0.024
Thailand	0.066	0.028	0.019
Argentina	0.130	−0.015	0.078
Brazil	0.276	−0.008	0.211
Chile	0.059	0.023	0.020
Mexico	0.181	0.002	0.170

regime and use econometric analysis to determine which elements have a close relationship with the building of technological capability and thus the degree of catch-up. We posit the period of 1980 to 1995 as the appropriate time period considering the characteristics of the database and the history of innovation in catching-up economies.

Determinants of technological catch-up

First, we conduct a Probit analysis of the occurrence of technological catch-up in relation to the technological regimes. A Probit analysis is used for analyzing a qualitative binary dependent variable. Here, the dependent variable measures whether there is an occurrence of technological catch-up. The occurrence of technological catch-up is defined as a positive change between the patent share of a country at the beginning year of 1980 (i.e. the average of the 1979, 1980, and 1981 shares) and the patent share of that country at the end year of 1995 (i.e. the average of the 1994, 1995, and 1996 shares). If an occurrence or a positive change exists, the value of the dependent variable is set to 1; otherwise, it is set to 0. Based on this criterion, the first-tier countries achieve catch-up in 81 percent of sectors, but the second-tier countries achieve catch-up in only 15 percent of sectors (Table 4.5).[14]

Table 4.6 *Determinants of technological capability and catch-up: catching-up vs. advanced economies*

Variable	Occurrence of technological catch-up (first time registering of a patent)		Speed of technological catch-up (%P change in share)		Technological capability (shares in patent counts by class)		
	Two catch-up countries	One virtual catch-up country	Two catch-up countries	One virtual catch-up country	Advanced countries	Two catch-up countries	One virtual catch-up country
Oppor							
Cumul1					(−)**	(−)**	(−)**
Appro		(+)***	(+)***	(+)***		(+)***	(+)***
Originality							
Fluid							
Initial stock	(+)***	(+)***					
Cycle time	(−)***	(−)**		(−)**	(+)***	(−)***	(−)***
Access			(+)***	(+)***		(+)**	(+)**

Notes: A simplified tabulation of the regression results reported as Table 5 in Park and Lee (2006). One virtual catch-up country is produced by pooling the patent data of the two catch-up economies of Korea and Taiwan. Empty cells indicate that the regression coefficients are not significant. Levels of statistical significance: *** (1 percent), ** (5 percent), * (10 percent).

In terms of occurrence, the Latin American countries are doing slightly better than their Asian counterparts. However, in terms of speed, the former are doing much worse than the latter. Whereas the second-tier Asian countries record a 4 percent level of catch-up speed (annual growth rates), the second-tier Latin American countries record only almost 0 percent of catch-up speed.

Tables 4.6 and 4.7 show the regression results for the first-tier catching-up economies (Korea and Taiwan) and the two groups of the second-tier countries in Asia and Latin America, respectively. The basic correlation tables can be found in the appendix (Table 4.1). In the regressions, the usual multicollinearity problem is checked by the variance inflation factor option in the SAS program, which turns out to be not serious.[15] In the two-country regression, the number of observations is 752 (2 countries * 376 sectors), and in the one virtual catching-up country regression, the number of observation is 376 because the virtual catch-up economy is defined as having a patent share in each class as the sum of those of Korea and Taiwan. In other words, a virtual catch-up economy is a hypothetical country formed by the combination of Korea and Taiwan.[16]

Two factors of the technological regimes show a consistent pattern across the regressions for both the first- and second-tier countries to find the determinants of the occurrence of catch-up: initial stock of accumulated knowledge (Initial stock) and technological cycle time (Cycle time). In a technology featured by a shorter technological cycle time, catch-up is more likely to occur as expected and the more initial stock of knowledge there is in a class, the more likely it is that catch-up will occur. These results imply that faster change in technological knowledge allows technological niches and room for catching up, thus promoting the possibility of technological catch-up, and that pre-accumulative knowledge functions as a pool to be utilized by the catching-up countries and contributes to the widening of the scope of technological innovation in those countries.[17] Albert (1998: 20–1) also finds from his study on patenting trends in the USA that Taiwan and Korea emphasize fast commercialization of information technology, as the patents by these countries show a much shorter technology cycle time than those by Japan and cite less scientific literature. Mathews (2005) also argues that technologies that show business cycles offer more chances for new entrants to jump in.

Now we select only those technological classes that have shown the occurrence of catch-up and analyze what determines the speed of technological catch-up in these classes. In the regressions, the dependent variable of the speed of technological catch-up is measured by the change between the year 1980 and the year 1995 in the patent shares by the latecomers. The regression results are presented in the center columns of Tables 4.6 and 4.7. In these regressions, we find strikingly different results for the first- and second-tier latecomers in determining the technologies that show greater speed of catch-up.

First, whereas the first-tier countries of Korea and Taiwan do well in sectors with shorter cycle times (negative signs), the second-tier countries in Asia and Latin America do worse in short-cycle sectors. This finding implies that, although frequent technical changes allow room

Table 4.7 *Determinants of technological catch-up and capability: second-tier countries in Asia and Latin America*

Variable	Occurrence of technological catch-up			Speed of technological catch-up			Level of technological capability		
	8 catch-up	4 Asia	4 LA	8 catch-up	4 Asia	4 LA	8 catch-up	4 Asia	4 LA
Oppor	-0.979*	-0.576	-1.560**	1.160**	0.405	2.900**	-0.078	-0.004	-0.152
Cumul1	-0.589**	-0.454	-0.727*	0.078	-0.058	0.165	-0.134**	-0.022	-0.246**
Appro	0.252	0.198	0.323	1.204**	2.917***	0.135	0.210***	0.181***	0.239*
Originality	0.249	0.340	0.164	0.874*	1.210**	0.577	0.034	0.089*	-0.020
Fluidity	0.120	0.102	0.149	0.079	-0.040	0.072	-0.001	-0.014	0.011
Initial stock	1.084***	1.019***	1.154***	-0.375***	-0.289***	-0.410***	0.000	0.016	-0.015
Cycle time	-0.469**	-0.755**	-0.186	1.519***	0.280	2.321***	0.015	-0.042	0.071
Accessibility	-1.123	-2.180	-0.310	2.068	0.795	3.765	0.307	0.037	0.577
India	-0.216*	-0.217**		0.004	0.012		-0.002	-0.002	
Malaysia	-0.587***	-0.581***		-0.179	-0.148		-0.037	-0.037***	
Thailand	-0.796***	-0.791***		-0.170	-0.134		-0.042*	-0.042***	
Argentina	-0.394***			-0.189			0.017		
Brazil	0.169*		0.567***	0.049		0.226	0.151***		0.134***
Chile	-0.869***		-0.478***	0.023		0.199	-0.041*		-0.058*
Mexico	-0.168		0.227**	0.153		0.334**	0.109***		0.092***
LR ratio /adj. R²	275.492	125.915	155.578	0.189	0.224	0.217	0.045	0.021	0.039
F-statistics	0.108	0.104	0.117	8.010	6.481	7.100	10.517	3.863	6.601
No. of observations	3008	1504	1504	453	210	243	3008	1504	1504

Note: Cumul1 = share of the inventors with more than one patent in every year.

for new entries and catch-up for some, such changes give others additional difficulties and act as barriers that prevent them from catching up. This implication confirms one of the key hypotheses of this research.

Second, we find that, whereas the first-tier countries do well in sectors with easy access, that is, registering a faster increase in patents, second-tier countries do not do well in these sectors. This result is consistent with the interpretation that, although some are able to take advantage of higher accessibility of knowledge in achieving some progress on the road to catch-up, others fail to utilize such access. This result may be due to some difference in access strategies, in that some access strategies are better than others. For example, Koreans are known to rely more on licensing than on FDI as a means of gaining access to foreign technologies, whereas in Latin America, FDI is more utilized.

One common pattern across the two groups of latecomers is the positive sign of the appropriability variable. However, interpreting this positive sign is not easy.[18] Given that appropriability is defined in terms of self-citations, more self-citations mean less need for reliance on external knowledge from other firms or agencies, thus allowing latecomer firms to catch up easily. Another interpretation is that given the limited resources for R&D, latecomer firms tend to focus on the technologies in which they enjoy the fruit of innovations more easily and securely. This result is consistent with the survey finding that SMEs tend to be concerned about the possibility that their own innovation outputs are taken and commercialized by large firms (Lee, Lim, and Park 2003: 65). Such comparison between large and small firms can be made similarly between firms from advanced countries and those from catching-up economies. The same survey on Korean firms also reveals that SMEs are more successful than large firms in commercializing R&D outcomes because they are more constrained in R&D resources and are thus more sensitive to commercial viability of their R&D projects. Therefore, they tend to select only those projects that have better chance of success and appropriability. In the catch-up regressions conducted separately for Korea and Taiwan, the appropriability variable is significant only in the regressions for Taiwan (Table 7 of Park and Lee 2006).

These two sets of regression results imply that catching-up is more likely to occur in classes with a greater initial stock of knowledge and shorter cycle time. However, the determinants of the actual speed of catch-up are different between the first- and second-tier latecomers. This finding is consistent with the finding of Park and Lee (2006) that the factors that determine the occurrence (0 or 1) of catch-up and the speed of catch-up are different. This finding is interesting, important, and somewhat expected. Our interpretation is that catch-up can occur in certain technological sectors, and it can be a slow or a fast catch-up, depending on other factors. For example, catch-up is likely to occur in classes for which more patents have been registered in the past, but this expectation may not assist in shortening the time of catch-up. Instead, it shows a negative sign for the second-tier countries, indicating that additional difficulty will face them in these sectors. In other words, more stock of accumulated knowledge indicates a lower barrier of entry (positive sign in the occurrence regressions), but it may adversely affect the actual speed of catch-up (negative signs in the speed regressions) once entry occurs in those classes, unless a stable access is set up in the continuously increasing stock of knowledge.

Other variables, for example, uncertainty and originality, do not seem to play a consistent role in the regressions. Cumulativeness seems to be negatively related to catch-up as shown by the significantly negative coefficient in the occurrence regressions for the second-tier countries.

So far, we have discussed which elements of the technological regimes determine the probability and degree of catch-up. Now, we focus on the levels of technological capabilities realized as a result of cross-class differences in the occurrence and speed of catch-up. Therefore, we posit the following relationship:

Levels of technological capability achieved by catch-up
economies in each class = F (occurrence of catch-up,
speed of catch-up)

where the period average shares in each class's patents by the country concerned measure the levels of technological capabilities in the period 1980 to 1995.

This relationship suggests that in some classes, catch-up has never occurred, and thus the levels of technological capability achieved by the catch-up economies are low. A difference also exists among the technological sectors that have experienced catch-up. The reason is that these technologies are subject to different speeds of catch-up after the initial occurrence. We have to conduct this regression to determine the across-class differences in terms of the level of technological capability achieved by the catching-up economies.

As expected, the result is like a synthesis of the "two" results on the determinants of the occurrence and degree of catch-up. As indicated previously, we focus on the variables that are shown to be significant in the regressions. To make our study more comparable and persuasive, we also present the results of advanced countries in Table 4.6. In the regressions, advanced countries include the G5 excluding the USA and Japan from the G7. The USA is excluded because all the patent data are US patents, and thus the USA is not strictly comparable with other countries. Japan is excluded as an outlier because of its peculiarity of having an extraordinarily high propensity to patent in the USPTO. Therefore, in this regression, Germany, France, the UK, Canada, and Italy comprise the advanced countries.

The variables having a significant impact on the levels of technological capability of the first-tier catching-up economies are cumulativeness (−), technological cycle time (−), appropriability (+), and accessibility (+), and for the second-tier countries, the variables are cumulativeness (−) and appropriability (+). In the case of advanced countries, the significant variables are cumulativeness (−), uncertainty (−), and cycle time (+).

One of the most interesting and important findings has to do with the opposite impact of cycle time variable on the advanced and catching-up countries. Some (first-tier) catch-up economies achieve higher levels of technological capability in such classes, as featured by the short cycle time of technology, whereas advanced countries do significantly better in classes with a longer cycle time. The cycle time variable is significant as a determinant of occurrence and speed of catch-up. Shorter cycle time or faster change in technological knowledge allows technological niches to emerge for catching-up economies, thus promoting the building of technological capability by latecomers.[19] This point is similar to the variance of the leapfrogging argument that frequent changes in technology can serve as a window of opportunity for the latecomers and allow leapfrogging by developing countries, as verified in the case of code division multiple access (CDMA) wireless technology and digital TV.[20]

However, the insignificance of this cycle variable for the second-tier countries is consistent with the reality that leapfrogging has not occurred there. This finding implies that frequent changes in technology may serve as an additional barrier to catch-up. The observation of Park and Lee (2006) that short cycles give latecomers a better chance to catch up is true only when the latecomers have already accumulated a certain technological capability. The role of an additional barrier comes from the so-called truncation of FDI-based learning process, that is, frequent technological changes interfere with the learning and accumulation of latecomers. The results also imply that the reasons for the difference may have to do with access strategies, which are the major difference between the first- and second-tier groups, especially in the speed of catch-up regressions. The second-tier countries are also shown to have difficulty in sectors with a higher stock of knowledge.

One great difference between the latecomers and the advanced countries is the role of appropriability. The appropriability variable is not significant in the case of advanced countries but is significant and positive in the case of the catching-up economies. It is also significant and positive in the speed of catch-up regressions. As discussed above, it may imply that higher appropriability, defined as the occurrence of more self-citations, means less need for reliance on knowledge from other firms or agencies, thus allowing latecomer firms to catch up easily. Another possibility is that given the limited resources for R&D, latecomer firms from the catching-up economies tend to focus on the technologies in which they enjoy the fruit of innovations more easily and securely.

Another difference is observed in terms of uncertainty. Uncertainty negatively affects advanced countries but not the latecomers. This finding is associated with the fact that latecomers are not on the technology frontier and do not have to be affected by uncertain R&D projects that aim at new and radical technologies. One policy implication is that the policy intervention by the government targeting specific R&D goals may work in these countries.

4.5 Summary

Using US patent data, this chapter attempts to link the technological regime to the technological catch-up by latecomer economies. Using patent data and patent citation data, it examines in which technological class catch-up tends to occur or not, and what affects the speed of technological catch-up. To analyze the phenomenon of techno-logical catch-up, this study decomposes the phenomenon into the occurrence of catch-up and the speed of catch-up. Then it explains the across-class differences in the levels of technological capability achieved by catching-up economies in terms of the combined effects of the occurrence and speed of catch-up.

With this method, this chapter analyzes the determinants of techno-logical catch-up in the second-tier countries in Asia and Latin America and compares the results with those of the first-tier countries (i.e. Korea and Taiwan) and advanced countries. The following are the main findings.

We have examined whether the shorter cycle time of a technology implies a higher occurrence and speed of technological catch-up, and thus a higher level of technological capability attained by catching-up economies. This question is consistent with the notion of "window of opportunity" brought about by rapid technological change, as asserted by the leapfrogging argument. One of the most interesting and import-ant findings has to do with the opposite impact of the cycle-time variable on the advanced and catching-up countries. We also find that whereas some (first-tier) catch-up economies achieve higher levels of technological capability in classes characterized by a short cycle time of technology, others fail to do so. Therefore, the insignificance of this cycle variable for the second-tier countries is consistent with the reality that leapfrogging has not occurred in these countries. The results also imply that the reasons correlate with access strategies, which are the major difference between the first- and second-tier groups, especially in the speed of catch-up regressions. The second-tier countries also face difficulty in sectors with a higher stock of knowledge.

This difference between the first- and second-tier countries can also explain the reversal of fortune between the Asian and Latin American countries. As noted in section 4.3, although Latin American countries used to have more patents in the early 1980s than their Asian counter-parts, they failed to file more patents continuously in the 1980s and 1990s, with their patents having lower growth rates than those of Asian countries. In the speed of catch-up regressions, the positive coefficient for the cycle variable is significant only in the four Latin America country regressions but it is not significant in the four Asian country regressions. Moreover, the absolute value of the negative sign of the variable of initial knowledge stock is much larger in the cases in

Latin America than in Asian countries, implying that Latin American countries are affected more seriously by the burden of mastering a large knowledge stock.

The sources of the difference between East Asia and Latin America can be explained in terms of many factors, including historical and political factors. However, one of the most directly related variables is the amount of R&D expenses by these groups of countries. Another factor is the difference in enrollment between high school and colleges and training systems. In East Asia, a strong unit of well-trained engineers and a broadly skillful and competent workforce in general has been created to a much greater degree than in Brazil, which used to have highly trained and talented scientists and engineers. They were, however, operative in ivory towers somewhat isolated from the general economy and society.[21]

5 | Knowledge and firm-level catch-up: Korean versus US firms

5.1 Introduction

Given that economic growth is driven by firms in the private sector, what determines firm performance is an important issue in the study of economic catch-up. In the analysis of firm performance, our starting point is that firms in advanced countries and latecomer countries differ in many respects, including the level of capability and behavior. In Mathews (2002a), a latecomer firm is defined as a late entrant to an industry that is resource poor but has some initial competitive advantages, such as low cost. We take the second condition of being resource poor as one of the most distinguishing aspects of latecomer firms. We consider that the main task of firms in developing economies is not only to utilize existing resources efficiently but, more importantly, to acquire the resources they lack and improve the availability of these resources over time.

We can then reason that firms from latecomer or catching-up countries will pursue growth rather than short-run profitability, as compared with firms in advanced economies that are more pressured to pursue profits to be redistributed to shareholders. Although the growth versus profitability comparison is one of the basic characterizations of firms in the catching-up and advanced economies, other distinctive dimensions of firms in the catching-up context are available. This chapter explores such dimensions, focussing on the aspect of the knowledge bases of firms.

The concept of knowledge and inter-firm heterogeneity is at the heart of the Schumpeterian theory of the firm. Nelson (1991, 2008c) and Winter (2006) emphasize the heterogeneity of firms and consider knowledge and imperfect learning as the source of inter-firm heterogeneity. Nelson (1991, 2008c) points out that the typical firm-characteristic variables available as accounting information may not be enough to explain the behavior and performance of firms. We hope that several quantitative expressions of various aspects of the know-ledge base of the firms will do a better job of predicting the different behaviors and performances of the two kinds of firm that should be heterogeneous, namely Korean and US firms, with the former repre-senting catching-up firms and the latter representing advanced or mature firms.

Some studies have compared firms from different countries.[1] How-ever, few of these studies have an explicit concern with how firms from developing countries differ from those from more mature economies. Although Lee and Temesgen (2009) focus on firms from several developing countries and compare them in terms of the availability and impact of diverse resources, such as human capital, managerial capital, and R&D capital, their study is not about comparing them with firms from advanced economies.

This chapter compares firms from latecomer countries and those from mature and advanced countries. This aspect is distinctive to the current study. Nevertheless, the study is also different from the existing literature in that it focusses on the comparison of the knowledge-related aspects of firms, such as the originality of their knowledge base, the cycle times of their technology, technological diversity, and the quality of their patents. We derive the measures of these aspects from the US patent data and compare firms in the USA and Korea to show their differences in these knowledge-related aspects and their impacts on firm performance (i.e. growth, profitability, and firm values).

5.2 Theoretical framework and hypotheses

Literature on the catching-up firms and advanced firms

The theoretical basis of our work goes back to the earlier work of Penrose (1995, first published 1959), in which she proposes a resource-based view of firm growth. Her theory has greatly influenced later works in the study of firms, with it further developing several vari-ations such as the capability-based theory of the firm, the knowledge-based theory of the firm, and the evolutionary theory of the firm.[2] In her original work, Penrose (1995/1959: xi) sees the function of the firm as "acquiring and organizing human and other resources in order to profitably supply goods and services to markets," and defines the firm as "a collection of resources bound together in an administrative framework, the boundary of which is determined by the area of administrative coordination and authoritative communication." Here, the resource-based theory of the firm is labeled. One of the key ideas of this theory is that firm performance and growth depend on the kinds, and how much, of these diverse resources the firm commands and can utilize for its growth.

If we apply the resource-based view to the case of firms from latecomer economies, we will discover their fundamental differences, such as that many critical resources are not easily available either within the firm itself or from neighboring firms. Thus, the main task of firms in developing economies is not only to utilize existing resources but also to acquire the resources lacking and sustain the availability of these resources. As a result, profit is sought not merely for redistribution to shareholders but more importantly for use in the further expansion of firm's resources. In other words, accounting profitability may be lower because of the additional "growth costs" borne by firms from developing countries. Growth costs include the costs of increasing the capabilities of workers, managers, R&D team, and brand power. Although these costs are borne by all firms, including those from advanced economies, they are heavier in firms from developing countries because they are faced with more market imperfections and other constraints in the business environment or investment climate (Tybout 2000).

Based on the above discussion, we can first hypothesize and verify that (Korean) firms from latecomer or catching-up countries pursue growth rather than short-term profitability compared with (US) firms in advanced economies, which are more pressured to pursue profit in order to redistribute it to shareholders. Although the comparison of growth and profitability is a basic characterization of firms in catching-up and advanced economies, other dimensions can characterize firms in catching-up contexts. The literature tends to look at other diverse resources that can affect firm performance and growth, including social (network and connections), physical, human (employees), managerial, R&D (capability to conduct it independently), and brand capital.

Theoretically, the relative importance of human capital and learning by doing has been recognized as a factor of economic growth in developing economies since the study of Lucas (1988). In this tradition, Kim and Kim (2000) point out the need to distinguish between general and specific human capital in economic growth. Among the empirical studies, Jensen and McGuckin (1997) find, using US data, that the majority of variations in firm performance are associated not with traditional observables, such as location, industry, size, age, and financial capital, but with unobservable and relatively permanent firm attributes, such as managerial capital and the skill composition of the workforce. Griffith, Redding, and van Reenen (2004) cite R&D and human capital as statistically important for firm performance or productivity. Moreover, Lee and Temesgen (2009) use the data from an investment climate survey, which was conducted by the World Bank in eight developing countries covering approximately 6,600 manufacturing firms, to examine the four endowments available in firms, namely, human, physical, managerial, and R&D capital, and interpret their importance in terms of the level of economic development and/or capabilities of countries and their firms. Lee and Temesgen report that in relatively low-capability firms, firm growth is contributed mainly by what can be called the relatively basic resources, such as physical and human capital, whereas in high-capability firms growth is driven more by higher-level resources, such as managerial and R&D capital. Their study further indicates that the difference between low- and high-growth firms has more to do with the different levels of effectiveness of the use of relevant resources and less with the difference in the absolute amount of resources.

The current study can also be considered broadly as a variant of these studies on firm-level resources. However, our distinctiveness lies in the emphasis on the firm-level innovation system and knowledge-related variables as its elements, which are not dealt with in the literature and can be expressed with patent and citation data.

Group-affiliated Korean firms versus stand-alone US firms: first aspect

With regard to firms from latecomer economies, an important strand of research has focussed on business groups. Defined as a collection of firms bound by equity ties and often under centralized family ownership and control, business groups are more common in latecomer economies, albeit they are a reflection of a higher degree of market failure in such economies (Goto 1982; Leff 1978). The existence and performance of business groups have become important issues in economic and business studies, and there seems to have been a surge of related literature, including a survey article in the *Journal of Economic Literature* (Khanna and Yafeh 2007).[3] The phenomenon is associated with the observation that business groups exist in many countries with some variations. In Korea and Japan the *chaebol* and the *keiretsu* are symbols of economic growth. Business groups play an important role in many other economies as well.[4] Although earlier research on business groups tends to revolve around more traditional questions, such as why they exist at all and how they perform in relation to stand-alone companies, more recent studies have attempted to come up with a more theoretical or systematic identification of and explanation for their behavioral characteristics. For instance, Ferris, Kim, and Kitsabunnarat (2003) report that group-affiliated firms are valued at a discount relative to comparable stand-alone firms and associate such a discount with several behavioral hypotheses of profit stability over absolute profitability, overinvestment, cross-subsidization, and related/ unrelated diversification in an empirical analysis of Korean business groups (*chaebols*) in the 1990s. According to Lee, Kim, and Lee (2010), whereas Korean *chaebols* in the 1990s prioritized profit stability over profit maximization, overinvested in low-return businesses, cross-subsidized low-performing affiliates of their group, possessed greater debt capacity, and consequently enjoyed lower tax burdens, they now (in the 2000s) tend to show higher profitability by refraining from excessive investment and cross-subsidizing and to be less indebted and pay comparable taxes.

Cheong, Choo, and Lee (2010) perform formal modeling to derive predictions on the behavior of business group firms and verify these predictions using data from Korea. Their model draws upon the resource-based theory of firm growth originally proposed by Penrose, and its key idea is that some important resources are lumpy or indivisible and thus must be purchased or installed only in certain sizes. The model suggests that business groups have certain advantages because affiliate firms can share the costs of acquiring such input. This so-called resource-sharing advantage (Chang and Hong 2000) can be considered valid and not subject to market failure. The disadvantage of a stand-alone firm stems not from its incapacity to obtain external financing but from its inability to fully utilize the asset. The model predicts that compared with stand-alone firms, business group firms invest more to achieve higher sales and have a fixed asset-to-labor ratio, which leads to faster growth and a higher profit margin on sales but lower profits on investment.

Cheong et al. (2010) confirm these predictions only with data from Korean firms. The current study revisits these predictions by comparing Korean and US firms. Our data on Korean firms are limited to those that applied for and obtained US patents from 1992 to 1995. Given that the application of Korean firms for US patents is dominated by large businesses, the behavior of these sample firms is likely to reflect that of business group-affiliated firms. By contrast, US firms listed in the stock market tend to be stand-alone companies with a dispersed ownership structure. Therefore, the comparison between Korean and US firms in this chapter equates to a comparison not only between firms in the catching-up and advanced stages but also between group-affiliated and stand-alone firms. The latter aspect makes sense to the extent that group-affiliated firms tend to dominate latecomer economies, and advanced economies tend to be populated by stand-alone companies.

Different knowledge bases of catching-up and advanced firms: second aspect

With the emergence of knowledge-based economies, knowledge has become a new key factor input of firms. The Schumpeterian theory of firms, such as in Winter (2006) and Nelson (1991, 2008c), emphasizes the heterogeneity of firms and regards knowledge and imperfect learning as one source of inter-firm heterogeneity. Given the emphasis on the black box linking the input and output of a firm, this study examines the knowledge base of firms. We hope that several quantitative expressions of various aspects of this knowledge base will do a better and new job of predicting the different behavior and performance of two kinds of firm (i.e. Korean and US firms).

We can consider several variables to express this knowledge base. Knowledge-related variables are indicators of the nature of the knowledge base of a firm, that is, the knowledge pool that each firm utilizes for its innovation and other activities. The property of the knowledge base relates to the firm-level innovation system underpinning the innovative activities of a firm. Technological knowledge involves various degrees of specificity, tacitness, and complexity and may differ significantly across technologies. This distinctiveness of knowledge matters more among firms in different sectors, and the same is true with regard to tacitness. In the current study, which focusses on catching-up firms, we deal with the aspects of knowledge where there are marked differences between advanced and catching-up firms.

First, we are especially interested in the technology cycle time variable. Our interest is stimulated by Park and Lee (2006), who observe that catch-up tends to occur in sectors with a shorter cycle time and that advanced countries file more patents in sectors with a longer cycle time. In terms of firm-level study, the modified reasoning is that successful catching-up firms tend to specialize more in short-cycle technologies. In terms of performance, we can hypothesize that firms specializing in knowledge fields with a shorter cycle time tend to be better in terms of catching up. Thus, the competitiveness of catching-up firms depends on their ability to enter new market segments quickly, to manufacture with high levels of engineering excellence, and to be first-to-market using the best integrative designs. Although this observation is very interesting, no research has confirmed this view at the firm level. The present research intends to fill this gap.

Second, we compare the self-citation ratio in patent citations between catching-up and advanced firms. In the literature, as in Trajtenberg et al. (1997), self-citation represents appropriability, the capability to protect one's innovations from being copied by others and thus to monopolize profits from the innovations. However, self-citation is a poor measure of appropriability because appropriability ultimately should involve some measure of protected commercialization. A more straightforward interpretation of self-citation is the degree to which the innovation of a firm builds upon its accumulated knowledge pool. In general, we can reason that the more advanced or older the firm is, the higher its patent self-citation ratio.

For instance, the proportion of self-citation in patent citations by Samsung Electronics used to be very low compared with the 15 percent of Sony.[5] However, since the late 1980s, Samsung has shown an increasing trend in its proportion of self-cited patents, catching up with Sony in the mid-2000s. Given that Samsung is one of the most successful catching-up firms in Korea, we can infer that generally a significant difference exists between catching-up (Korean) and advanced (US) firms in terms of self-citation ratio. We can also examine the implication of self-citation for performance. If self-citation reflects the degree to which firms have consolidated the independent intra-firm mechanism of knowledge creation, we can expect some correlation between self-citations and performance variables. This hypothesis is consistent with the country-level finding in Chapter 3 that localization of knowledge creation (country-level self-citations) is significantly related to per capita income growth in advanced countries but insignificantly in developing countries.

For consistency with the country-level analysis, we also examine the impact of the originality of the knowledge base of a firm and the degree of concentration (i.e. inverse diversification) across technological classes. Given that US firms listed in the stock market are in the frontier of technology, we can deduce that their knowledge base/pool is abundant in highly original ideas. Therefore, we can hypothesize that originality is higher in US firms than in Korean firms. We also examine the effect of originality on performance. No study has confirmed the significance of this variable, although the literature tends to strongly emphasize the importance of "being creative or original" in this era of knowledge-based economy. However, we cannot be sure whether originality is significantly related to typical performance indicators, such as return on asset (ROA) or Tobin's Q, which measure the financial success of firms. This notion holds especially because the country-level regressions performed in Chapter 3 find no significance of originality.

In sum, in a firm-level analysis of catch-up, we try to explain firm performance as a function of knowledge-related firm characteristics and other traditional control variables as follows:

Firm performance (catch-up)

= F (knowledge-related variables, other control variables)

The model specification in our regression models is consistent with the neo-Schumpeterian idea of firm innovation performance depending on the intra-firm innovation system or on the knowledge base. Within the knowledge base of each firm lie both codified and tacit knowledge. However, given the intrinsic difficulty in capturing tacit knowledge, the present study utilizes patent data as proxy for the codified (i.e. explicit) knowledge of each firm. We show some contrast between catching-up firms (i.e. from Korea) and firms from advanced countries (i.e. the USA) by indicating the more important variables affecting firm performance.

5.3 Measurement and data

Dependent variables

Defining and measuring firm-level catch-up is not easy. The first measure of catch-up performance is sales and/or market share growth. Market share is most closely related to the idea of catch-up; several studies on catch-up have measured it in these terms. However, in many cases, the boundaries of the markets of firm products are hard to define, the more so with firms from two or more countries. In this case, one alternative is to focus on sales growth rates, which have been used often in empirical literature on firm growth. Using sales growth is logical because sales growth is mostly related closely to market share, that is, firm sales divided by the sum of sales by all firms in the same sector. Another merit of using sales growth is that firms from latecomer countries pursue growth rather than profitability during their catch-up stages, as compared with firms from advanced countries with active shareholderism. In the current study, the sales growth of a firm is measured as follows:

$$\text{Sales growth}_t = (\text{Sales}_t - \text{Sales}_{t-1})/\text{Sales}_{t-1}$$
for each firm i

The second measure of catch-up is sales per worker or labor productivity. Labor productivity is a good alternative because it is measured easily and clearly across different countries. Moreover, catch-up is perceived often as moving up the ladder of value chains toward increasingly high value-added activities, and performance is shown in terms of the increasing labor productivity of firms (Rabellotti, 2006).

We also use other conventional measures, such as return on asset (ROA = net income over total asset), return on sales (ROS = net income over sales), profitability, and Tobin's Q as a measure of firm value. A simplified measure of Tobin's Q is used in the current study, defined for each firm as (market value of equity stock + book value of total debt)/book value of total assets.

Independent variables

We used both basic control variables and variables representing various aspects of the knowledge base of firms as regressors.

The basic control variables include firm size (i.e. size of employment), the debt–equity ratio (i.e. total debt over equity), the capital–labor ratio, and the investment ratio (i.e. the growth propensity of firms). For Korean firms, the capital–labor ratio is measured by the ratio of total tangible assets except those under construction to the number of employees, whereas the ratio for US firms is the value of property, plant, and equipment divided by the number of employees. The investment ratio or propensity is measured by the increase in the value of total tangible assets during the period (one year) divided by the value of total tangible assets at the beginning of the year or at the end of the previous year. For US firms, the investment ratio is the change in the value of the property, plant, and equipment during the given year divided by the value of the property, plant, and equipment at the beginning of the year. For sector dummies, three-digit KSIC (Korea Standard Industrial Classification) codes are used for Korean firms and two-digit SIC codes are used for US firms.

Next, our key interest variables include the cycle time of technologies, originality, diversity of the knowledge base (i.e. the number of diverse fields in which each firm has patents), and the self-citation ratio. Although these are the main interest variables, we also examine basic variables such as the number of patents held by each firm (i.e. the number of patents each firm i applied for in year t) and their quality measured by the average impact factor (i.e. the average number of times its patent is cited by others relative to the average of patents in the same class and weighted by the share of each class in the patent portfolio of the firm).

First, originality is the same variable used in Chapter 3 and 4, calculated based on the definition of Hall et al. (2001) and Trajtenberg et al. (1997). This definition represents the rationale that the broader the technological root of the underlying knowledge or research related to patents, the higher is the patent originality. The variable is directly available from the NBER US patent database, and we retrieve this value for all patents held by each firm and take their average for each firm for each year.

Second, the average cycle time of firm patents is measured by taking the average of the mean backward citation lag of each patent over all patents held by each firm. The mean backward citation lag refers to the time difference between the application or grant year of the *citing* patent and that of the *cited* patents. This variable is also directly available for each patent from the NBER patent data explained in Jaffe and Trajtenberg (2002: 421). Therefore, we simply have to take the average of the patents for each firm for the period (up to 1995) covered by the first version of the NBER patent database. A longer cycle time means a slower speed of change in the knowledge base of a technology, whereas a shorter cycle time means higher speed.

The diversity of the knowledge base of each firm can be measured in two ways. One way is to simply use the number of technological sectors (classes) where each firm has applied its patents. The other way is one minus the HHI of concentration. HHI can be measured for firm i at time t as follows:

$$\text{HHI} = \text{HHI}_{jt} = \sum_{j} \left(\frac{P_{ijt}}{P_{it}}\right)^2$$

where P_{ijt} is the number of patents that company i applied in year t in class j, and P_{it} is the number of patents that company i applied for in year t.

Data

The US company financial data are from Compustat North America, and the data on Korean companies are from KIS Value, both of which have been used widely in the literature. Patent data for both countries are taken from (the book and CD-ROM of) Jaffe and Trajtenberg (2002) based on the NBER database ("The NBER Patent Citations Data File: Lessons, Insights and Methodological Tools," NBER working paper, 2001 (www.nber.org/papers/w8498)) that is also available on the website. This NBER data set conveniently provides the Compustat firm ID for each patent matched with each firm to which it belongs. For the Korean data, matching the assignee of each item patent data from the NBER data set to the name of the Korean companies has taken us some time, as some assignee names needed to be cleaned up.

The year span for the analysis here is from 1988 to 1995. The number of companies each year and the patent counts and citations are shown in Table 5.1. For example, for 1995, we analyze 1,863 patents held by ninety-four Korean firms as well as 8,614 citations by these firms. For the US firms, the numbers are much larger. The companies used in the analysis are those that have applied for at least

Table 5.1 *Number of firms, patent counts, and number of backward citations*

	Number of companies		Total number of patents		Average number of patents per firm		Total number of backward citations	
Year	Korea	USA	Korea	USA	Korea	USA	Korea	USA
1988	23	623	114	13,835	4.96	22.21	623	117,401
1989	37	576	317	15,044	8.57	26.12	1,494	126,565
1990	31	550	400	14,706	12.90	26.74	1,932	124,971
1991	41	561	656	16,308	16.00	29.07	3,113	147,914
1992	45	539	779	17,600	17.31	32.65	4,209	169,636
1993	57	533	904	18,020	15.86	33.81	4,476	194,877
1994	78	516	1,330	19,324	17.05	37.45	6,600	211,304
1995	94	509	1,863	22,581	19.82	44.36	8,614	267,054

Source: the author.

one patent in the corresponding year and are publicly traded. We merge patent data with financial data by company name and year. Therefore, the number of Korean firms included in the sample is limited. Thus, we cannot regard them as good representatives of typical Korean firms but only as a representative of successful innovative or catching-up firms, which is acceptable given our focus on the catching-up phenomenon. Tables of descriptive statistics and correlations are available as Appendix Tables A5.1 and A5.2 respectively.

5.4 Knowledge and firm-level performance

Basic comparison of firms in the USA and Korea

In terms of general characteristics, US firms are much larger and hire more than twice as many workers as Korean firms (Table 5.2). Interestingly, Korean firms keep a much higher capital–labor ratio than US firms, probably because the leading large Korean firms represented in this sample tend to grow rapidly based on their aggressive investment in typically capital-intensive sectors. This difference in the capital–labor ratio is also translated into higher sales per worker in Korean firms.

Hiring more capital and being more indebted relative to size, Korean firms have lower ROA (8 percent) and lower firm values measured by Tobin's Q (1.01) than US firms, which have an ROA of 9 percent and

Table **5.2** *Basic characteristics of firms: means and median comparison*

(a): comparison of sample means

Variables	USA	Korea	Difference (US–KOR)	t–value
Number of employees (person)	13,719.57	6,857.53	6,862.04	7.634**
Sales per employee (thousand dollars)	187.11	294.47	−107.35	−7.445**
ROA (%)	9.3	8.2	1.1	3.232**
ROS (%)	4.7	9.9	−5.2	−5.228**
Firm value: Tobin's Q	1.76	1.01	0.74	34.171**
Sales growth rate (%)	8.8	12.1	−3.3	−2.788**
Investment propensity (%)	1.0	2.6	−1.6	−3.356**
Debt–equity ratio (%)	266.1	302.7	−36.6	−0.342
Capital–labor ratio (thousand dollars)	60.24	153.91	−93.67	−7.251**

(b): comparison of sample medians

Variables	USA	Korea	Difference (US–KOR)
Number of employees (person)	3,499	3,323	176
Sales per employee (thousand dollars)	158.97	232.36	−73.4
ROA	0.1	0.08	0.02
ROS	0.08	0.09	−0.01
Firm values: Tobin's Q	1.39	0.99	0.4
Sales growth rate	0.05	0.09	−0.04
Investment propensity	0.01	0.01	0
Debt–equity ratio	0.99	2.78	−1.8
Capital–labor ratio (thousand dollars)	35.86	86.71	−50.85

Note: All values calculated by the author. Current values are deflated by the 2000 constant gross domestic price index; values in Korean currency are converted by the average market exchange rate. Investment propensity is measured by (increases in total tangible assets except construction in progress)/(total capital); capital–labor ratio is measured by (tangible assets except construction in progress)/(number of employees). Level of significance: ** $p < 0.01$; * $p < 0.05$, + $p < 0.1$.

Tobin's Q of 1.76. However, Korean firms show a higher ROS (10 percent) than US firms (5 percent) and pursue more growth, as evidenced by their higher investment propensity (3 percent vs. 1 percent) and sales growth rates (12 percent vs. 9 percent).

Table 5.3 *Comparison of knowledge variable: means and medians*

(a): sample means

Variable	USA	Korea	US–KOR gap	*t*-value
Patent count	18.5	9.56	8.94	4.592**
Relative patent quality (citations received)	1.14	0.73	0.41	6.821**
Number of sectors with patents	6.9	4.15	2.75	5.044**
HHI (degree of sector concentration)	0.51	0.71	–0.2	–8.808**
Originality	0.42	0.3	0.12	7.662**
Technology cycle (years)	14.05	11.91	2.15	4.39**
Intra-firm diffusion (self-citation)	0.12	0.03	0.09	18.001**

(b): median comparison

Variables	USA	Korea	US–KOR gap
Patent count	4	1	3
Relative patent quality (citations received)	1.02	0.48	0.51
Number of sectors with patents	3	1	2
HHI (degree of sector concentration)	0.44	1	–0.56
Originality	0.43	0.31	0.12
Technology cycle (years)	12.69	10.35	2.34
Intra-firm diffusion (self-citation)	0.09	0	0.09

Source: the author.

In sum, this comparison is consistent with the hypothesis in the preceding section based on Cheong et al. (2010): the commonly held perception that catching-up country firms led by business groups tend to pursue growth, whereas advanced country or Anglo-Saxon firms tend to pursue profitability or firm values in stock markets.

In terms of the characteristics related to knowledge, US firms are superior to Korean firms in many aspects of the knowledge base or the corporate innovation system (Table 5.3). US firms have a number of patents larger or twice as large (18.5 vs. 9.6), higher quality (1.14 times cited vs. 0.73 times cited), and higher originality (0.42 vs. 0.30) of patents in more diverse classes (lower HHI) than their Korean counterparts (0.51 vs. 0.71) (Table 5.3(a)). US firms also tend to show a higher rate of self-citation than Korean firms

(12 percent vs. 3 percent). Higher self-citation means that US firms rely relatively more on their own pool of knowledge accumulated over time, which can be treated as an attribute of advanced firms. In terms of the technology cycle time of patents, US firms have a longer patent cycle (fourteen years) than Korean firms (twelve years), which is what we hypothesized.

All these differences in means are statistically significant as determined by *t*-tests (Table 5.3(a)). The comparison of medians is consistent with the differences in terms of means (Table 5.3(b)). Therefore, a significant difference exists between firms in advanced and latecomer catching-up countries. Figures 5.1(a) to 5.1(c) represent the graphical trends of these variables from 1988 to 1995. These figures are consistent with the significant gap between the firms of the two countries and suggest some catching-up record by Korean firms in terms of self-citation ratio, increasing from nil to over 2 percent over the period.

From knowledge to performance: regression results

We run several regressions to reveal the differences between US and Korean firms. For the US regressions, the data period is from 1988 to 1995, and for the Korean regressions, the data period consists of four years (1992 to 1995) to obtain a sufficient number of firms for regression analysis. Moreover, among the three results of the OLS, fixed effect, and random effect models, we use for interpretation either the fixed or the random effect results based on the results of the Hausman test.[6] Table 5.4 presents the summary of the main results.

In Table 5.4, we inserted only the number of US patents held by each firm as the key interest variable aside from other typical control variables. In general, patent counts are important variables affecting firm performance in diverse dimensions. Consistent with the literature, patent counts are a significant determinant of productivity (value-added per worker) in the regressions for both countries. Patent counts are also significant in profitability indicators such as ROA and/or ROS. Interestingly, more technologically active firms seem to be better valued by the stock market only in the US context, as shown by the significance of the patent count variable in the Tobin's Q regression.

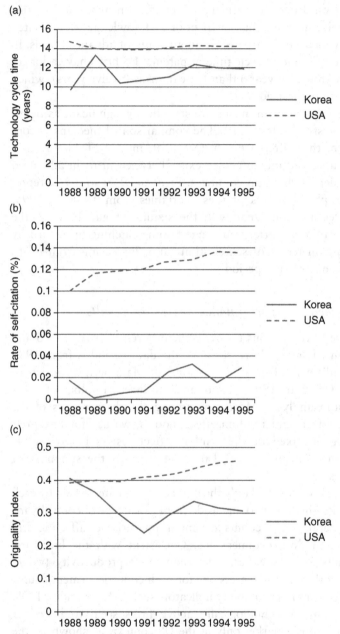

Figure 5.1 (a) Cycle time, (b) self-citation ratio, and (c) originality of US and Korean firms (1988–95).

Note: drawn by the author.

Table 5.4 *Summary of the regression results: benchmark results (with patent count only)*

Dependent variables	US firms				
	Growth	ROA	ROS	Sales/Emp	Tobin's Q
Independent variables					
Patent count	(−)	(+)*	(+)	(+)**	(+)**
No. of workers	(+)	(+)*	(−)	(−)**	(−)*
Investment propensity	(+)**	(+)**	(+)**	(−)**	(+)**
Debt to equity ratio	(−)	(+)	(−)	(−)	(+)
Capital–labor ratio	(−)**	(+)**	(−)**	(+)**	(−)**
No. of observations	3,475	3,479	3,478	3,479	3,362
Dependent variables	Korean firms				
	Growth	ROA	ROS	Sales/Emp	Tobin's Q
Independent variables					
Patent count	(+)**	(+)*	(+)+	(+)**	(+)
No. of workers	(−)	(−)	(−)	(−)	(−)
Investment propensity	(+)+	(−)	(+)	(−)	(−)*
Debt to equity ratio	(+)	(−)+	(−)**	(−)	(+)
Capital–labor ratio	(+)	(−)**	(−)**	(−)+	(−)**
No. of observations	239	240	240	240	127

Notes: significance level: + (10 percent), *(5 percent), **(1 percent). We conduct the Hausman tests between random and fixed effects, and report only the results selected by the test. Sectoral dummies are used but not shown. An outlier of Samsung Electronics is excluded.

This linkage is not present in the Korean context, which seems to reflect the degree of stock market development in the mid 1990s. The Korean stock market became globalized with more foreign investors and became more transparent only after the major opening and restructuring of the economy after the 1997 financial crisis (Choo et al. 2009).

Other than the patent count variable, the variable of fixed investment turns out to be very important among all the performance indicators of US firms. In Korean firms, fixed investment matters only in growth regressions but not in the profitability or firm-value model, consistent with the fact that Korean firms pursued growth in the 1990s by conducting aggressive and often excessive investment, which did not help in terms of firm efficiency or value (Lee, Kim, and Lee 2010). Ferris et al. (2003) and Lee et al. (2010) confirm the tendency of overinvestment by Korean firms in the 1990s, but this tendency was corrected in the 2000s or after the restructuring following the 1997 Asian crisis.

In general, these benchmark results on patent counts only are not surprising and do not reveal much difference between catching-up and advanced firms, as patents are similarly important determinants of sales growth, profitability, or productivity, justifying our further search for the different aspects of the two types of firms by replacing simple patent counts with other knowledge variables. Given a somewhat higher degree of correlation of the patent count variables with other variables, such as firm size and the HHI of concentration over classes (see Table A5.2 for the correlations), this variable should be replaced by other variables that are free from such relations.

For the identification of a possible important variable from the designated pool of knowledge variables, we first run many regressions to replace patent count by each of the knowledge variables in separate regressions, that is, with each knowledge variable included in each regression model of various performance measures, to identify the significant knowledge variable in a particular model. The results in Table 5.5 are striking. First, the cycle time variable is not significant at all in all the US firm regression models, but self-citation is significant in several models, such as in productivity and growth. By contrast, self-citation does not matter at all in any of Korean firm model specifications, but the cycle time variable is significant in the two models of profitability (i.e. ROS and ROA). The other two variables of originality and concentration are significant in some models.

Therefore, we run regressions with relevant (potentially significant) knowledge variables only. For US firms, we do not use the cycle time variable because it is not significant at all in all models, but we include the other three variables; for Korean firms, we do not use self-citation because it is not significant at all in all models, but we include the remaining three variables. The final results with relevant variables in Table 5.6 are mostly consistent with the results in Table 5.5. The main results are summarized as follows.

First, in US firms, self-citations are significant and positive in growth, productivity, and firm value (Tobin's Q) models. Originality matters in

Table 5.5 Summary of the regression results (with one knowledge variable in each model)

US firms

Dependent variable	Growth	ROA	ROS	Sales/Emp	Tobin's Q
Independent variable					
HHI	(+)*	(−)	(+)	(−)**	(−)
Originality	(+)	(+)	(+)	(+)**	(+)
Technology cycle	(−)	(−)	(+)	(−)	(+)
Self-citation	(+)+	(−)	(−)	(+)*	(+)
Number of employees	(+)	(−)+	(−)	(−)**	(−)+
Investment propensity	(+)**	(+)**	(+)**	(+)**	(+)**
Debt-equity ratio	(−)	(−)	(−)	(−)	(+)
Capital-labor ratio	(−)**	(−)**	(−)**	(+)**	(−)**
No. of observations	3,482 / 3,475 / 3,475	3,480 / 3,486 / 3,484	3,485 / 3,478 / 3,479	3,483 / 3,486 / 3,479	3,484 / 3,479 / 3,369 / 3,362 / 3,362 / 3,367

Korean firms

Dependent variable	Growth	ROA	ROS	Sales/Emp	Tobin's Q
Independent variable					
HHI	(−)	(+)	(+)	(−)+	(−)
Originality	(−)	(+)	(+)+	(−)	(+)*
Technology cycle	(+)	(+)+	(−)*	(−)	(+)*
Self-citation	(−)	(−)	(+)	(−)	(−)
Number of employees	(−)	(+)	(+)	(−)	(−)
Investment propensity	(+)	(+)	(+)	(−)	(−)*
Debt-equity ratio	(+)	(−)**	(−)**	(−)	(+)
Capital-labor ratio	(+)	(−)*	(−)**	(−)+	(−)**
No. of observations	239 / 239 / 231	217 / 240 / 240	240 / 232 / 218	240 / 240 / 232	218 / 127 / 127 / 122 / 114

Note: Significance levels: +(10 percent), *(5 percent), **(1 percent). Those reported are selected by the Hausman tests. Sectoral dummies are used. Samsung Electronics is excluded.

Table 5.6 *Summary of the regression results (with relevant knowledge variables)*

Dependent	US firms				
	Growth	ROA	ROS	Sales/Emp	Tobin's Q
Independent					
HHI: concentration	(+)*	(−)	(+)	(−)**	(−)
Originality	(+)	(+)	(+)	(+)**	(+)
Self-citation	(+)+	(−)	(−)	(+)*	(+)+
Number of workers	(+)	(−)+	(−)	(−)**	(−)+
Investment propensity	(+)**	(+)**	(+)**	(−)**	(+)**
Debt–equity ratio	(−)	(−)	(−)	(−)	(+)
Capital–labor ratio	(−)**	(−)**	(−)**	(+)**	(−)**
No. of observations	3,468	3,472	3,471	3,472	3,355

Dependent	Korean firms				
	Growth	ROA	ROS	Sales/Emp	Tobin's Q
Independent					
HHI: concentration	(−)	(+)	(+)	(−)+	(−)
Originality	(−)	(+)	(+)+	(−)	(+)
Technology cycle	(+)	(−)*	(−)*	(+)	(−)
Number of workers	(−)	(−)	(+)	(−)	(−)
Investment propensity	(+)+	(−)+	(+)	(−)	(−)
Debt–equity ratio	(+)	(−)**	(−)**	(−)+	(+)
Capital–labor ratio	(+)	(−)+	(−)**	(−)	(−)+
No. of observations	231	232	232	232	122

Note: significance level: +(10 percent), *(5 percent), **(1 percent). We conduct Hausman tests between random and fixed effects and report only those results selected by the tests. Sectoral dummies are used but not shown. An outlier of Samsung Electronics is excluded.

productivity only. Concentration matters positively in growth but negatively in productivity.

Second, in Korean firms, shorter cycle time positively affects profitability (i.e. ROA and ROS). Originality matters in profitability (ROS). Concentration is negatively linked to productivity.

Third, fixed investment matters for growth, profitability, and firm values in US firms, but it matters for growth and profitability only in

Korean firms. The three knowledge variables are significant as determinants of productivity in US firms, but not in Korean firms. None of the knowledge variables is important for the firm values of Korean firms; self-citation matters in the firm values of US firms.

In sum, the series of regressions shows that for US firms, one of the most important variables representing the knowledge base is self-citation, whereas cycle time is the most important variable for Korean firms. In other words, in US firms, all three knowledge variables of self-citation, originality, and diversity matter in one or more performance measures, whereas in Korean firms, only the cycle time variable matters, especially if we apply the 5 percent significance rule. Therefore, the results on sectoral data in Chapter 4 of this book, that is, catching-up countries are strong in short-cycle sectors, seem to have been replicated in firm-level regressions.

Although we do not prove rigorous causality, a significant correlation between self-citation and performance is a very new and interesting finding for US firms, and the same condition is true for the correlation between short cycle time and some performance indicators in Korean firms. The sectoral distribution of Korean firms shown in Appendix Table A5.3 indicates that the sample firms are distributed widely over diverse sectors, with the chemical sector representing the biggest share. Therefore, the results are not driven by firms in short-cycle technology-based sectors, such as IT. An outlier of Samsung Electronics is also excluded in the regressions.

5.5 Summary

The comparison of the basic profile of catching-up firms (Korean firms) and advanced firms (US firms) confirms the commonly held perception that catching-up firms tend to pursue sales growth by borrowing and investing more, whereas advanced country firms pursue profitability and firm values in stock markets.

In terms of the basic profiles of knowledge bases, catching-up or Korean firms are inferior to US firms in many respects: patent counts, quality, originality, and diversity. The final and interesting difference is that Korean firms tend to have patents with shorter cycle times than with US firms.

The regression analysis of firm performance (i.e. growth, profitability, firm value, and productivity) reveals an interesting finding:

although intra-firm knowledge creation and diffusion or self-citation is significantly correlated with these performance variables, cycle time is not important at all in US firms. By contrast, specializing in short-cycle time technologies is closely linked to performance variables in Korean firms, but intra-firm knowledge diffusion (self-citation) is insignificant. Moreover, the weak or marginal importance of originality in both US and Korean firms is consistent with the finding at the country level (Chapter 3).

The importance of short cycle time at the firm level in the catching-up context is consistent with the results at the sector level (Chapter 4) and country level (Chapter 3) of this book. The contrasting significance of intra-firm knowledge creation and diffusion (self-citation) in the USA and Korea is also comparable with the country-panel regression results (Chapter 3), as intranational creation and diffusion of knowledge (localization of knowledge creation) is significant only in the case of developed countries. Therefore, the insignificance in Korean firms still indicates a weak level of the mechanism of in-house knowledge creation, as the ratio of self-citation is only 3 percent in Korean firms compared with the 12 percent (four times higher) in US firms (Table 5.3). The median is zero for Korean firms but 9 percent for US firms.

Specialization in short-cycle technologies may promote the possibility of raising the level of self-citation (self-production of knowledge) at a later period because specializing in such technologies means less reliance on the knowledge base of other (advanced) firms and thus a higher probability of a faster increase in the self-citation ratio. Samsung has shown a fast increase in the self-citation ratio over time. Korean firms in this sample have also attained catching up in their self-citation over time (Figure 5.1(b)). The results imply that the ultimate task for the catching-up firm is to consolidate its in-house knowledge-creation and diffusion mechanism, given that this remains one of the most important performance variables in advanced firms.

Finally, the fact that a shorter cycle does not affect sales growth, but only profitability, and that sales growth is primarily linked to fixed investment, deserve some attention and interpretation. If specialization in a shorter cycle time is confirmed to affect growth, it will be a more straightforward verification of the growth-over-profitability hypothesis proposed for catching-up firms. However, as noted by Penrose in her book, growth cannot be separated from profit or equivalently firms cannot grow without making a profit. Therefore, although we emphasize that catching-up firms pursue more growth than profitability, catching-up firms still cannot grow without profit, but they can use profit not for redistribution but for reinvestment. In this regard, earning profit is more critical for firm growth in emerging economies which often have less developed capital markets. Thus, specializing in shorter-cycle technologies for less reliance on existing dominant technologies means that latecomer firms find a niche for profitability in such technical fields. Moreover, such fields with shorter cycles tend to be where they feel less disadvantaged in competition against incumbent firms because they may rely less on existing dominant technologies. In sum, catching-up firms pursue growth with profitability by conducting fixed investment in fields with shorter cycle times. This interpretation is also consistent with the notion of dynamic capabilities (Teece 2000, 1986; Nelson 1991), indicating not only innovation capability but also profit-making out of innovation. Therefore, Korean firms have been successfully developing dynamic capabilities in their catching-up period.

PART III

Toward a theory and how to escape the trap

6 | *Toward a knowledge-based theory of economic catch-up*

6.1 Introduction

This chapter synthesizes the findings on catching up at the firm, sector, and country levels, with a view to presenting a comprehensive, knowledge-based theory of catching-up growth that takes a neo-Schumpeterian perspective. We have defined a number of key variables that capture different aspects of innovation systems adopted in catching-up efforts, and have measured these at the firm, sector, and country levels. We have also found that catching-up can be analyzed and explained well using these variables across those levels, and that there is a level of consistency in the three levels. One of the main contributions of this study is the examination of the most important details of innovation systems adopted in each country and firm, and the determination of which aspects of technology are significant or insignificant at the firm, sector, and national levels.

This chapter is organized as follows. First, we provide a summary of the findings of each chapter at the firm, sector, and country levels in section 6.2. Then, we synthesize these findings to suggest a theory of knowledge-based catching up in sections 6.3 and 6.4. Section 6.5 discusses the policy implications of the theoretical arguments in the preceding sections.

6.2 Summary of the findings in part II

Country level

Compared with middle-income countries, high-income countries generally have lower population growth, but higher per capita income growth rates, higher investment ratios, and markedly higher school enrollment rates. Looking more specifically at NIS-related factors, high-income countries tend to possess a balanced distribution of innovators, a high rate of localization of knowledge creation and diffusion, a patent port-folio of greater originality and medium to short technology cycle times. A regression analysis of the determinants of per capita income growth indicates that these variables are all significantly related to growth, except the originality variable. Therefore, while promoting localization of knowledge creation and spreading the base of national inventors is important, a country does not have to be overly concerned with moving toward more original technologies. Similarly, although it was significant in the regression analysis of high-income countries, having a balanced distribution of innovation across inventors does not appear to be a key variable in enabling sustained growth among Asian developing countries because we do not observe a clear-cut trend of this variable increasing in these countries between 1980 and 1995. In contrast, the variable of localization of knowledge creation seems to carry greater weight in enabling catching-up performance. Since the 1980s, Korea and Taiwan have exhibited a threefold increase in knowledge localization.

The most important variable we found was also the most tricky, namely the cycle time of technologies. Although having more long-cycle technologies in the patent portfolio was found to be positively related to economic growth in both high- and middle-income coun-tries, this condition was actually negatively related to economic growth in the most successful catching-up countries, namely, Korea, Taiwan, Hong Kong, and Singapore during the catching-up period that began in the mid 1980s. Moreover, the average cycle time for technologies in these countries has become increasingly shorter over that period and is thus now remarkably shorter than that of high-income and other middle-income country groups. Until the mid 1980s these four econ-omies used to hold patents with cycle times similar to those of the high- and middle-income countries, but their cycle times have begun to shorten significantly since then. These findings further suggest that short-cycle technologies were a key to the success in these countries and that specialization in highly original technologies, as was the focus in the Latin American economies, is not an effective catch-up strategy.

Sector level

We have determined which technological classes tend to promote economic catch-up, and what factor most affects the speed of technological catch-up across technological fields. Using patent data and patent citation data, we have examined in which technological class catch-up tends to occur or not, and what affects the speed of technological catch-up. In other words, this study has decomposed the phenomenon into the occurrence of catch-up and the speed of catch-up. Then it explains the across-class differences in the levels of technological capability achieved by catching-up economies in terms of the combined effects of the occurrence and speed of catch-up. In doing so, we have measured the relative technological capability of the countries by looking at their share of each class of US patent. Using this method, we have looked at the determinants of technological catch-up in second-tier countries in Asia and Latin America and compared the results with those in first-tier (i.e. Korea and Taiwan) nations and advanced countries.

In the case of the first-tier countries, a short technological cycle time implies the potential for a greater degree of technological catch-up and, consequently, the attainment of a greater level of technological capability by successful catch-up economies. This finding is consistent with the notion of the "window of opportunity" that is enabled by rapid technological change, and with that asserted by the leapfrogging argument. However, another interesting finding is that cycle time has the opposite effect in the advanced and catching-up countries. More importantly, although first-tier catching-up economies achieved higher levels of technological capability in classes with short technology cycle times, second-tier countries failed to accomplish this. In other words, the positive coefficient of cycle time for second-tier countries is consistent with the reality that leapfrogging has not occurred in these countries. Although short cycles imply a greater opportunity for catch-up for countries that command a certain degree of technological capability, frequent changes in technology may present an additional barrier to catching up because these changes interfere with learning, leading to a truncation of the learning process.

These results also imply that the divergence in performance across economies attempting to catch up may be related to the different access strategies. These strategies mark the major difference between the first- and second-tier groups, and this is especially apparent in the speed of catch-up. Second-tier countries experienced particular difficulties in sectors with higher stocks of knowledge. This difference between the first- and second-tier countries in their ability to overcome the problem of mastering entrenched knowledge can explain the rise of the Asian countries, and the fall of the Latin American countries. Although Latin American countries obtained more patents in the early 1980s than their Asian counterparts, the former failed to continue their lead in the 1980s and 1990s and recorded much lower patent growth rates. In terms of the speed of catch-up, the positive coefficient for the cycle variable is significant only in four of the Latin American country regressions (implying that they obtained more patents in long-cycle technologies) but not in the four Asian country regressions. Moreover, the absolute value of the negative sign of the variable of initial knowledge stock is significantly larger for Latin American countries than Asian countries. Thus, Latin American countries are affected more seriously by the burden of mastering the existing stock of knowledge.

One significant difference between latecomers (both first and second tiers) and the advanced countries is the role of appropriability (i.e. average self-citation at the sector level). The appropriability variable is not significant in the case of the advanced countries, but is significant and positive in the case of all the catching-up economies. This variable is also significant and positive in the speed of catch-up regressions. Higher appropriability, defined as more instances of self-citation, indicates less reliance on knowledge from other firms or agencies, which enables latecomer firms to catch up in a more independent manner. Alternatively, given limited R&D resources, latecomer firms from the catching-up economies tend to focus on the technologies that enable them to protect and more easily secure and enjoy the fruit of their innovations. Another aspect of the difference between latecomer and advanced economies is the level of uncertainty or the level of the fluidity variable. Uncertainty negatively affects advanced countries, but not latecomers because latecomers are not positioned at the technology frontier and are less involved with new R&D projects aimed at new and more radical technologies.

Firm level

A comparison of the basic profile of catching-up (Korean) and advanced (US) firms confirms the common perception that catching-up firms tend to pursue sales growth by borrowing and investing more, whereas firms in advanced countries pursue greater profitability and firm values in stock markets. In terms of their basic knowledge base, firms playing catch-up (such as Korean firms) are inferior to US firms in many respects, including patent counts, quality, originality, and diversity. A final, interesting difference observed between the two classes of firms is that the latecomer Korean firms tend to obtain more patents with short cycle times than do the more established US firms.

A regression analysis of US firms indicates that the intra-firm localization of knowledge creation and diffusion (measured by firm-level self-citation) is significantly correlated with performance variables (sales growth, firm value, labor productivity, and especially profitability), and that the cycle times of technologies are not at all important. In contrast, specializing in short-cycle-time technologies is closely linked to the outcome variables indicative of performance, especially profitability, in Korean firms, while the intra-firm localization of knowledge creation and diffusion is insignificant. Moreover, the weak or marginal importance of originality in both US and Korean firms is consistent with the finding at the country level. The insignificance of self-citation in Korean firms still indicates the weak level of the mechanism of self-production of knowledge. In Korean firms, a short cycle does not affect sales growth, but it does affect profitability, and growth is primarily linked to fixed investment. Therefore, it implies that catching-up firms tend to pursue growth under a certain level of profitability by conducting more fixed investment in fields with short cycle times.

6.3 Specializing in short-cycle technologies for sustained catch-up

Korea and Taiwan acquired a level of per capita GDP similar to that of Latin American countries in the early 1980s. However, in contrast to the stagnation experienced by Latin American countries over the next two decades, the Asian countries more than tripled their per capita real incomes over the 1980 to 2000 period, joining the ranks of the rich countries. This achievement should be considered an important historical event, and how this phenomenon became possible is the important economic question that the current study attempts to elucidate. Having analyzed this catch-up phenomenon at the firm, sector, and country levels, we now propose a relevant theory.

The changes in the innovation systems adopted by latecomer countries since the 1980s should provide us with an important indicator on which to base our theory. In the early 1980s, Korea and Taiwan were similar to other middle-income countries in terms of their NIS, specifically the number of US patents they registered, the level of localization in their knowledge creation, the concentration of invention activities among their firms, and the cycle time and originality of their patented technologies. However, since the mid 1980s, the number of US patents that these countries registered has rapidly increased. More importantly, these countries have gradually moved into sectors with shorter cycle times than those of the advanced countries, and their level of localization of knowledge creation has increased accordingly.

The increased level of innovation as measured by patent counts has been identified in the literature as a causal factor for long-term economic growth. This study has outlined and differentiated other factors responsible for either the catching up or falling behind of developing countries. A close link exists between the nature of the innovation system (knowledge base) and catching-up performance at the firm, sector, and national levels. In this three-dimensional linkage, the most critical variables are the cycle time of technologies and self-citation instances as measured across the three levels. A short cycle time indicates the lesser importance of old knowledge that is dominated by the advanced countries and a reduced need for latecomers to master old and existing knowledge. Therefore, we have hypothesized in Chapter 2 that the shorter the cycle time of a technology, the greater the possibility of catch-up. This study has confirmed this hypothesis at the three levels concerned.

The results of the current study also lead us to observe that firms that are successful in catching-up tend to specialize increasingly in technologies with short cycle times. Such specialization does not occur in less successful developing countries and their firms. Although most developing countries tend to begin with and attain success in the low-wage-based, low-value-added activities or segments of the global production network, continuing to focus in this area will not enable them to rise above the ranks of the middle-income nations. There is a tendency for the countries in the next tier of economic development to offer lower wage rates and thus emerge as new production sites. Also, the initial success based on cost advantages will push wage rates upward, and erode price competitiveness. This phenomenon was observed in Korea and Taiwan in the 1980s, and in China since the mid 2000s. In this scenario, self-defeating competition is inevitable among the developing countries, leading to the adding-up problem.

This study demonstrates that the gradual specialization in shorter-cycle technologies since the mid 1980s was instrumental in bringing about a progressive upgrading from low-wage production in the successful catch-up economies.

Thus, to be free from the adding-up problem, a firm or country should enter a higher-value segment in the same industry, or enter an entirely new industry which presents a higher added value. Such intra- and inter-sector upgrades present a process of technological diversification. The advantage of specialization in short-cycle technologies is consistent with the concept of leapfrogging, in which emerging generations of technology serve as windows of opportunity for the catching-up countries that are not locked into the old technologies, and allow them to thrive in emerging industries.

A window of opportunity can be said to be open at the time of the emergence of a new generation or paradigm of technologies. The leapfrogging argument can be considered at different levels, with two different types of leapfrogging being possible, namely *intra*- and *inter*-sector leapfrogging. If a country enters a totally new and emerging industry, this is a case of inter-sector leapfrogging. If a country or its firms skip an old vintage or generation of technologies in a given sector and adopt new or emerging generations of technologies, this is a case of *intra*-sector leapfrogging.

The replacement of analog with digital technologies seems to have served as a critical window of opportunity for some latecomers. Many products, such as calculators, watches, fixed line telephones, mobile phones, cameras, and TVs, were digitized after the mid 1980s. Korea especially benefitted from this opportunity to catch up with Japan. The digitization of these products and their production processes implied that latecomers were not badly disadvantaged by their lack of prior knowledge, as the function and quality of the products was determined more by electronic chips and less by the skills of the engineers, whose experience is critical in the production of analog products.

This study also reveals the double-edged nature of the short cycle time or the frequent generation change in technologies. Although the successful catching-up countries of Korea and Taiwan performed well in the short-cycle sectors, other lower-tier countries did not fare as well. This phenomenon is related to the notion of truncated learning, which posits that frequent changes in technology interfere with the effectiveness of learning, which ceases or becomes useless with the advent of new technologies. As discussed in Chapter 4, Latin American countries were not successful in registering more patents in the short-cycle sectors.

The impact of technology cycle time deserves further discussion in light of the following three seemingly conflicting findings. First, in the cross-country regressions, a long cycle time is positively related to growth in both high- and middle-income countries. Second, however, the patents obtained by high-income countries tend to be of shorter cycle times than those obtained by the middle-income countries, and the patents held by Korea and Taiwan tend to be of even shorter cycle time than those held by high-income countries. Third, a short cycle time is positively related to growth in the successful catching-up economies.

These patterns seem to imply the existence of a high equilibrium (in the high-income countries), a low equilibrium (in the low- or middle-income countries), and a transition path between these two equilibra (in the catching-up countries). Although the long cycle time of technologies tends to be correlated with stable income growth in both high- and middle-income groups, high-income countries tend to specialize in high value-added activities in relatively medium- to long-cycle sectors (high equilibrium). Conversely, middle-income countries tend to specialize in low-value-added activities in long-cycle sectors (low equilibrium). Fast-growing countries, such as Korea and Taiwan, catch up by specializing in short-cycle sectors over time. However, as their patents spread and become more balanced, there comes a time when these countries converge toward a high-equilibrium pattern, approaching the level of the existing high-income countries.

This concept of high versus low equilibrium is consistent with the idea of Hidalgo et al. (2007), who wrote about the division of core versus peripheral product spaces, categorized by the sophistication of their products. They argued that most countries can reach the core only by traversing "empirically infrequent distances." This may help explain why poor countries have trouble developing more competitive exports, and why they fail to match the income levels of rich countries. However, their study does not discuss how to traverse the space. The present study suggests a transition strategy from low equilibrium to high equilibrium, which involves the adoption of shorter-cycle technologies, exemplified by the precedents of several Asian economies.

This move into short-cycle technologies can be gradual, but countries may sometimes adopt a leapfrogging strategy. The idea of leapfrogging is consistent with Hidalgo's concept of the "long jumps" (Hidalgo et al. 2007), which are required to make a shift to products distant from the current position, and to generate subsequent structural transformation.

However, we cannot rule out the possibility of an alternative transition path or a direct replication strategy. For example, a latecomer country may decide to adopt a strategy of specializing in high-originality technologies, considering that high-income countries tend to obtain more patents in these classes. This path seems to characterize the patenting activities of the Latin American countries, which have a more advanced grasp of the pure sciences and thus generate more original patents than Korea or Taiwan. Figure 3.4 illustrates the greater originality of Brazil and Argentinian patents compared with those of Korea and Taiwan. Unfortunately, however, originality is not a significant factor in the country-level regressions and in the sector-level level analysis. Moreover, the performance of catching-up firms (i.e. Korean firms as in Chapter 5) is not significantly related to such originality. This discussion implies that, although originality may be characteristic of high equilibrium levels, aiming for more original technologies is not warranted as a transition strategy.

Although originality is not significantly related to better performance at the firm, sector, and country levels, in the context of developing countries, self-citation or appropriability at the sector level is of equal importance to Korea and Taiwan as it is to other latecomer countries. One interpretation of this finding is that given the limited resources for R&D, latecomer firms tend to focus on technologies that enable higher appropriability. This result is consistent with the survey finding that small- and medium-sized firms tend to be concerned with the possibility that the outcome of their innovation efforts will be stolen and quickly commercialized by large firms (Lee, Lim, and Park 2003: 65). Moreover, given that appropriability is defined in terms of self-citations, or the lesser need for reliance on external knowledge from other firms, high-appropriability technologies would be the technologies that latecomer firms would consider it more comfortable or safer to pursue.

Higher self-citation indicates that a country relies on its own existing knowledge base. This concept is equivalent to the localization of knowledge creation and diffusion at the country level. Interestingly, the country-level regressions in Chapter 3 demonstrate that this is a significant and positive factor for advanced economies, but not for developing countries. This suggests that the mechanism of indigenous creation and diffusion of knowledge is not yet consolidated in developing countries. These results are replicated in the firm-level regressions of US and Korean firms: the variable of self-citation is significantly higher in the US firms, but not high enough in the Korean firms to be a significant determinant of performance.

6.4 Technological turning point and high, middle, and low roads for development

The previous discussion explores the possibility of three alternative strategies for catching up, namely, the high, low, and middle roads. The three roads are summarized in Table 6.1.

The low road refers to the situation of typical low- or lower-middle-income countries that specialize in low-value-added activities or

Table 6.1 *Three alternative roads for development*

	Strategy	Technology cycle time	Originality	Example countries
Low road	Existing comparative advantage	Long	Low	Typical low-income countries: Bangladesh; Sri Lanka; Korea and Taiwan in the 1960s and 1970s; China in the early 1980s
High road	Direct replication	Long	High	Some middle-income countries: Brazil and Argentina in the 1980s and 1990s
Middle road	Detour	Short	Low	Successful middle-income countries: Korea and Taiwan since the mid 1980s; China at present

Source: the author.

low-end goods in fields with a longer technological cycle. This is likely the rational choice, as it follows from the comparative advantages dictated by a country's initial resource endowment. Countries adopting this strategy tend to achieve a certain degree of economic growth, as indicated by the positive coefficient of long cycle time in the country panel regressions in Chapter 3. This achievement was evident in Korea and Taiwan in the 1960s and 1970s, in China in the early 1980s, and continues to be evident in today's lower-income economies, such as Bangladesh and Sri Lanka. However, these countries will experience difficulty in continuing their growth beyond the middle-income levels unless they can initiate an upgrade and establish a different specialization or diversification.

The high road strategy is one in which a low-income country attempts to directly replicate the knowledge base of the high-income countries by specializing in high-quality and highly original technologies. Several relatively advanced Latin American countries, such as Brazil and Argentina, seem to have attained positions close to this road as they boast an advanced level of academic research in science. However, as our analysis indicates, specialization in highly original technology is not significantly related to economic growth. The chance of localizing knowledge creation and diffusion may also be low because highly original technologies tend to be dominated by advanced countries; therefore, countries on this trajectory must continue to rely on the patents held by the advanced economies. Consequently, we observe that countries on the high road failed to catch up in the 1980s and 1990s.

The middle road is exemplified by Taiwan and Korea in the 1980s, and China today, with their specialization in short-cycle technologies and their promotion of a localization of knowledge creation (or indigenous innovation). Several second-tier catching-up countries in East Asia, such as Malaysia and Thailand, have also tapped into short-cycle time technologies such as IT, but they have not made decisive moves toward upgrading (Rasiah 2006). In this sense, these countries are experiencing the so-called middle-income country trap, as discussed by Yusuf and Nabeshima (2009), because they are still muddling through the middle road. This observation is confirmed in Chapter 4 in the sectoral analysis which shows that second-tier catch-up economies have failed to achieve the higher levels of technological capabilities in classes featured by short-cycle time technologies. The positive coefficient of this cycle variable for second-tier countries as well as for high-income countries is consistent with the reality of the non-occurrence of leapfrogging. In this light, some studies use trade data in a cross-country panel setting and observe no evidence of leapfrogging, although they define it differently.[1] Therefore, although short cycles provide some opportunity for catching up for those that command a certain degree of technological capability, frequent changes in technology may serve as an additional barrier against catching up because these changes interfere with learning and lead to a truncation of the learning process.

The aforementioned realities and findings imply that the middle road is not smooth and easy. Selecting the road of short-cycle technologies requires a certain threshold level of technological capability not only at the firm level but also in national-level institutions and policies. However, taking risks does not guarantee success, and refusing to take risks means a continuation of the old "low" equilibrium. In this sense, the middle road is not a sufficient condition for eventual upgrading, and should instead be seen as a necessary condition.

The three roads can also be discussed in relation to the three technological catch-up strategies or patterns (Table 1.4), specifically path-following, stage-skipping, and path-creating. The low road is similar to the path-following strategy, which may be a safe choice but cannot ensure the reduction of the gap with the forerunners. The high road may appear similar to the stage-skipping strategy but it essentially targets long-cycle technologies or pure science-based technologies instead of short-cycle technologies. Commercial viability is not certain under this strategy. The third strategy is the middle road or detour strategy, and it also involves a stage-skipping or leapfrogging stage but targets short-cycle technologies, especially during the time of paradigm or generation shift, thus avoiding an over-reliance on existing or dominant technologies.

The three roads are not necessarily mutually exclusive alternatives, because a mixed or sequential strategy as a combination of the three ways is possible. Many developing countries will initially begin on the low road by selecting industries according to their initial comparative advantages, which is driven usually by their initial endowment conditions. In many cases, such industries will involve labor-intensive manufacturing using low-cost labor in the own equipment manufacturing (OEM) arrangement. Lin (2012a: 91; 2012c: 205) cited Mauritius since the mid 1970s and 1980s as an example similar to that of Korea, Taiwan, and China in their early stages of development. Mauritius achieved some success by specializing in sectors in which it had some initial comparative advantage. However, Lin reiterated also that developing countries eventually have to upgrade to higher-value-added industries and technologies if they intend to join the ranks of rich countries. They need to take the middle road or take a detour toward short-cycle technologies instead of remaining on the low road, or instead of directly replicating the high-quality or highly original technologies of rich countries. When such countries begin the journey toward higher-level technologies, their experience on the low road will not be without use as they will have benefitted from their acquisition of greater absorption capacity (Cohen and Levinthal 1990) and design capability (Hobday 1995: 37–8; Lee 2005). After they build a certain degree of design capability, such countries can then attempt to enter new and emerging industries or the higher-value segments of existing industries. Acquiring these capabilities requires a combination of access to foreign knowledge bases and learning opportunities (e.g. OEMs, FDIs, licensing, technology imports, and on-site training, among others) with firms' own in-house R&D efforts.[2]

Toward the end of this detour, the successful latecomers will arrive at the entrance to the high road where technological deepening and diversification into high-quality and highly original technologies can occur. Therefore, the best way to navigate the catch-up process is not to choose exclusively between one route and the other, but to move in proper sequence, beginning at the low road, moving into the middle road or detour route, and finally embarking on a journey on the high road. Less successful or failed cases of catching up will either be a result of remaining too long on the low road, or taking a wrong turn from the low road directly to the high road.

This scenario is complementary to the new structural economics of Lin (Lin 2012a, 2012c), who is concerned primarily with low- or lower-middle-income countries (e.g. China in the early 1980s) and their choice between the right and wrong latent comparative advantage sectors. The current study focusses on the choice facing the upper-middle-income countries (e.g. today's China) between short-cycle (and low originality) and long-cycle (and high originality) technologies. In contrast to the comparative advantage in trade (trade specialization) that is determined by initial endowment conditions, this study focusses on the dynamic comparative advantages in technology (technological specialization) determined not by natural resource endowments, but by the R&D and technological capabilities accumulated over time in human bodies and minds.

Although the middle road means adopting a different route from the incumbent high-income countries, countries employing the middle-road strategy will acquire a greater chance of building a knowledge base that is eventually similar to that of the high-income countries. Furthermore, short-cycle technologies are in a sense a niche for late-comers, ensuring a higher rate of profitability, as presented by the firm-level analysis in Chapter 5.

Therefore, the strategy of technological specialization (toward short-cycle technologies and away from highly original technologies) can be regarded as a "detour" strategy, in which latecomer countries do not attempt to replicate directly the advanced economies featuring highly original and long-cycle technologies. Instead, catching-up countries initially move in the opposite direction toward shorter and less original technologies. This turning point in technological specialization occurred in the mid 1980s in Korea and Taiwan. Subsequently, the success of these firms in technological development enabled them to move into longer and more original (or diverse) technologies. As shown in Figure 6.1,

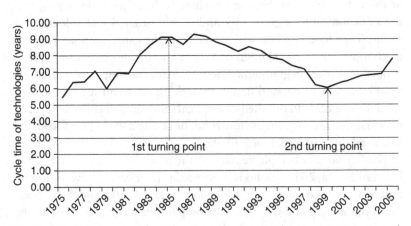

Figure 6.1 Turning points in technological specialization in Korea and Taiwan, 1975–2005.

Note: Average cycle time of technologies from US patents held by Korea and Taiwan. Drawn by the author using the updated NBER patent database. Based on annual figures, not five-year moving averages as in some other tables.

Korea and Taiwan have been moving into technologies with long cycle times since the 2000s, reversing the earlier shift toward technologies with short cycle times. The detour they took at the start of their journey became a shortcut and contributed to their ability to catch up quickly. While the move to technologies with short cycle times can be seen as the first turning point, the reversal to long cycle times since the 2000s can be regarded as the second turning point, signaling that their technological specialization has reached a level of maturity in the post-catch-up era.

In contrast, direct replication, or the high-road strategy focussing on highly original and long-cycle technologies may lead to the continuing reliance on foreign advanced countries and forestall the consolidation of indigenous knowledge bases. To test this assertion, we examine whether such a technological turning point occurs in other economies that have the potential for successful catch-up such as China or India. We address this issue in Chapter 8.

6.5 From trade-based specialization to technological specialization

We now suggest a sketch roadmap for developing countries. In this roadmap, trade-based specialization is assigned to low-income countries, and technology-based specialization is assigned to the middle-income countries, as summarized in Table 6.2.

In the low-income stages, a country tends to follow trade-based specialization in order to exploit the comparative advantages associated with its natural resource endowments. In this way, low-income countries can command international competitiveness in the factor-intensive industries that they tend to inherit from high-income countries. This effect is predicted by the product life-cycle theory of Vernon (1966). Although these countries can grow to reach the status of middle-income countries, the medium-term risk is that their own success with the initial comparative advantage industries that are based on low-wage-based labor industries tends to cause their own wage rates to increase accordingly. At the same time, cheaper labor sites are always emerging in the next-tier countries to replace their position in the global value chain. In these scenarios, after reaching the status of a middle-income country, the economy may fall into the middle-income country trap. A longer-term challenge and task for low-income countries is then to move upward to higher value-added activities in the

Table 6.2 *From trade specialization to technology specialization*

Stages	Low or low middle income	Upper middle income toward high income
Type of specialization	Trade specialization	Technology specialization
Source of specialization	Comparative advantages from resource endowment	Technological capability from learning/R&D effort
Type of sector	Labor-intensive/mature/resource industries	Short-cycle/emerging technologies
End goal	Competitive export industries	Localizing knowledge creation and diffusion
Source of competitiveness	Low costs (wage or natural resources)	Product differentiation/fast-mover advantages
	Low risk from adopting existing equipment	Less need to rely on existing technologies
Risk	Middle-income trap due to competition as low-wage sites	Design capability difficult to acquire
	Growth slowdown after exhaustion of initial advantages	Correct technologies/standards that are not easy to target
Policy tools	Industrial policy (tariffs, undervaluation of currency, entry control)	Technology policy (public–private R&D consortia, exclusive standards, subsidies for early adopter)
Background theory	Product life cycle (inheriting)	Catch-up cycle (leapfrogging)
Medium-term trajectory	A long and difficult road	Detour but may become an *ex post* shortcut
Long-term challenge	Moving up the value chains	Rebalancing toward long-cycle and high-originality technology
	Switching to technology specialization	

Source: the author.

same industries and/or to enter newly emerging industries that may withstand higher wage rates.

Therefore, for a developing country to surpass the middle-income stage, technological specialization in short-cycle technologies can be implemented to identify a new upgraded niche in a higher-value segment or industry. This transition requires technological capabilities based on learning and in-house R&D effort. Although difficult, this process can allow the attainment of higher profitability and the status of high-income countries. Specializing in emerging fields indicates a lesser need to rely on existing and dominant technologies, and as such, it becomes a "detour via niche" strategy, which may be a viable shortcut. Along this road, the economy of a latecomer will eventually become similar to that of the current high-income country which features both long- and short-cycle technologies and higher-originality technologies.

The idea of specializing in the short-cycle sector does not imply the maintenance of a fixed list of technologies or business, but instead, a constant entry into new areas. Therefore, as we will show in the next chapter, the constant transfer to newer (not new to the world, but new to a latecomer economy or firm) and shorter-cycle technology sectors results in a gradual technological diversification and causes a movement away from a concentrated specialization in a few fields. The continuous emergence of new technologies suggests that new windows of opportunity are always available for new entrants that are not locked into existing technologies. This idea is exactly the opposite of that of the product life cycle, which states that latecomers only inherit old or mature industries or segments from the incumbent economies. This process can be termed a catch-up cycle, in which latecomers equipped with new emerging technologies make a competing entry into industries to catch up with the incumbent economies that are often locked into their existing technologies.

Windows of opportunity make up a key variable for latecomers that can trigger a positive catch-up cycle and bring about successive changes in industrial leadership. However, the flipside of the latecomer's opportunity is the incumbent's trap.[3] Specifically, the rise of a new techno-economic paradigm or radical innovation serves as a window of opportunity for late entrants, while the incumbents may fall into a trap of sticking to existing technologies and products to avoid the greater uncertainty associated with new technologies with often lower productivity in the initial years. Moreover, the incumbents tend to wait until they fully recover their sunk investment into existing technologies and products before moving into the development of new technology products. In doing so, they can end up being late entrants in new technologies, and fall into the perils of the incumbents' trap.

Such changes in industrial hegemony or meaningful catch-up by latecomers occur in both the IT and non-IT industries, such as in semiconductor chips (USA->Japan->Korea/Taiwan), TVs (USA-> Japan->Korea), mobile phones (Motorola->Nokia->Samsung), and steel (USA->Japan->Korea Pohang Steel Corporation->China?). We observe that a change in the technical paradigm or generation plays a key role in many such incidents of catch-up. Examples of this include frequent generation changes in the memory size of chips (Kim and Lee 2003) and the rise of digital TV technologies developed first by the Koreans (Lee, Lim, and Song 2005). The rise in mobile phones similarly triggered multiple rounds of technology changes including first the transition from analog to digital, followed by the change from the global system for mobile communications (GSM)/CDMA digital to the emergence of the current generation of smart phones. Another example is the rise and quick adoption of the Japanese (even before the Americans) of radical technological innovations such as the basic oxygen furnace and continuous casting in steel (Lee and Ki 2011). The stories of these industries and their leadership changes suggest the importance of radical innovation. It also presents new generations of technology as windows of opportunity for the late entrant firms of developing countries. Moreover, these stories suggest that the way forward for latecomers is not only in short-cycle time sectors. What matters more is the frequency of the emergence of new opportunities.

If the nature of technical change is competence destroying rather than competence enhancing, the situation will be more advantageous for the late entrants. Such a situation can lead to a shift in the hegemony (Anderson and Tushman 1990). However, even if a sector is prone to competence-destroying discontinuity, that sector is not likely to generate many catch-ups if it also involves a very long cycle time so that discontinuity occurs with very long intervals or very infrequently.[4]

Based on this perspective, the advantage of short-cycle sectors is that the adoption of new technologies, products, and processes is likely to trigger the frequent emergence of newer technologies and products/ processes. Therefore, what matters in the short-cycle sectors is not the

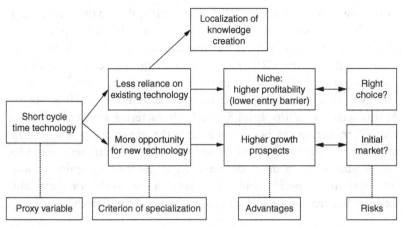

Figure 6.2 Criterion of technological specialization: why the sectors of short cycle matter.

length of the cycle time itself, but the surfacing of more opportunities, with the continuous emergence of new technologies and a reduced reliance on the existing dominant technologies.[5] In short, the criterion for specialization is the entry into a technological sector with less reliance on existing technologies but with greater opportunity for the emergence of new technologies. The variable of a short cycle time is merely a proxy for such criterion. Figure 6.2 explains this idea. The property of new opportunities indicates more and new growth prospects, and the property of less reliance on existing technologies may lead to faster localization of a knowledge-creation mechanism. The figure also illustrates lower entry barriers and the possibility of higher profitability associated with less collision with the technology of advanced countries, fewer royalty payments, and first-/fast-mover advantages or product differentiation.

However, these two properties also involve two kinds of risk, as identified by Lee, Lim, and Song (2005). First, new opportunity is only a potential and does not guarantee the existence of initial markets. Second, less reliance on existing technology indicates greater technical uncertainty, and companies cannot be sure whether their choice will turn out right or wrong *ex post*. Recognition of these risks is also a call for technology policy by the government. However, tools for technology policy are different from traditional industrial policy, which is used in the low-income stage and comprises tariffs, devaluation, and entry controls. As illustrated in Table 6.2 and discussed in detail in the next chapter, technology policy for middle-income countries tends to involve public–private R&D consortia to share the technology choice risk, as well as initial market provision in the form of exclusive technology standards, public procurement, or subsidies for early adopters. In this sense, we differ from Spence's characterization of the middle-income transition, as he observes that the government will assume fewer roles.[6] In general, while the scope for government activities may be narrower in the middle-income stage, it may require a sharp intervention in specific projects to stage a late break or entry into existing but rent-prone technologies or new emerging technologies.

6.6 Detour, emulation, and direct replication

The preceding sections argue that the strategy of technological specialization (in short-cycle technologies) can be regarded as a detour strategy. In this strategy, successful catching-up countries do not attempt to directly imitate the advanced economies, which feature highly original and long-cycle technologies, but move initially in the opposite direction of shorter and less original technologies. This detour concept can be compared with Reinert's (2009: 79) concept of emulation. Defining emulation as an "endeavor to be equal or surpass others in any achievement or quality," Reinert argues that all countries that progressed from poverty to wealth did so by undergoing a period of emulation, that is, of infant industry protection, to work their way into the areas where technological progress is concentrated. He cited the Marshall Plan after the World War II and Airbus as typical examples. Although the present study embraces the need for emulation before following natural comparative advantages later, we have to be cautious, as emulation does not consider the low (emulation and other) capabilities of developing countries, which has been one of the causes of many failures in infant-industry protection.

Developing countries cannot merely emulate all the industries currently dominated by developed countries. For instance, the fact that the USA has a viable aircraft industry does not necessarily mean that Korea should also build one. The target for emulation should be chosen carefully and strategically. Reinert does not deal with this point, and nor does he identify the selection criteria for emulation.

A simple and immature emulation effort may veer toward the path of direct and immediate replication, which this study discourages. In our exposition, the direct replication or high-road strategy is defined by a focus on the same highly original and long-cycle technologies as those in developed countries. However, this strategy may not be viable for developing countries because it goes against their pre-existing comparative advantages. We side with Lin's structural economics, which suggests that latecomers are advised to observe closely the countries slightly ahead of them and then target the mature industries in those countries as their latent comparative advantages.

Moreover, direct emulation may lead to a continued reliance on advanced countries, and prevent the consolidation of indigenous knowledge bases. Therefore, this study suggests a detour into short-cycle technology sectors, which are a niche for latecomers in terms of profitability. In this sense, this detour strategy can be called indirect or selective emulation, and direct replication can be considered direct and unselective emulation. A wrong or even an unwise interpretation of emulation suggests that developing countries should open up their economy for international trade or financial flows immediately, as all rich countries have a fully open economic structure. In what follows, further comparisons and analogies are conducted along this line of thought.

The contrast between a detour and direct replication can be explained through an analogy to the so-called Washington Consensus and an alternative consensus, such as the Beijing–Seoul–Tokyo (BeST) Consensus suggested by Lee and Mathews (2010), or the new structural economics proposed by Lin. The idea of the Washington Consensus is to have developing countries immediately replicate the key features of the current advanced countries by conducting full-scale privatization and liberalization. However, this prescription has led to many failures worldwide or has turned out not to be viable or to be too expensive (Lin 2012a: 38, 2012c: 40-1; Rodrik 1996, 2006). For instance, in some Asian countries, such as Korea and Indonesia in the 1990s, financial liberalization was immediately followed by financial crisis.

In terms of trade liberalization, the experience of Korea and Taiwan, as well as that of Japan, was a detour in the sense that they used to be only half-open or semi-protectionist, and only became more open eventually. In contrast to the Washington Consensus, the BeST consensus suggests that developing countries protect their local industries

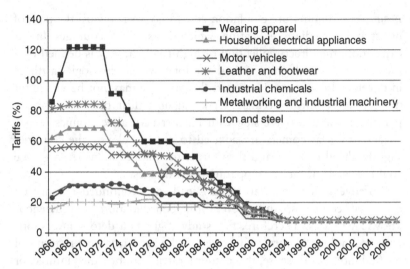

Figure 6.3 Trend of tariffs in Korea and of asymmetric opening.
Source: Drawn using data from Shin and Lee (2012).

initially to enhance their indigenous capabilities and that they are only opened up later. If Korea and Taiwan had been opened up from the beginning, they would not have been as successful in promoting indigenous firms and sustaining their catch-up, and their level would have been similar to that of many other middle-income countries. A hidden assumption of trade liberalization is that local firms are sufficiently competitive to potentially compete against foreign companies or imported goods. This assumption is not true in many cases. In such circumstances, naive trade liberalization may lead to monopoly by foreign goods or the destruction of local industrial bases. A smart or better opening strategy, as discussed in Shin and Lee (2012), is "asymmetric opening" in which latecomer economies liberalize the import of capital goods for the production of final or consumer goods while protecting their consumer goods industries by charging high tariffs on imported goods.

Korea implemented an asymmetric tariff policy for its consumer and capital goods. Figure 6.3 illustrates that Korea charged extremely high tariffs for consumer goods (e.g. around 70 percent for household electrical appliances in the 1970s), which were promoted as export industries, but charged considerably lower tariffs for capital goods, such as machinery. Of course, we can point out that the protection of local firms and entry control will lead to an oligopolistic domestic market. However, a study by Jung and Lee (2010) demonstrates that monopoly rents can be used to fund R&D investment because firms are exposed to the discipline of world export markets while their privileged protection from the government is not free but linked to their export performance.

A similar analogy can be made for the protection of IPR, such as patent rights. A high-standard protection of IPR in developing countries when they are starting to grow may hinder the development of indigenous companies as they cannot obtain the benefits of learning and imitative innovation (Fink and Maskus 2005: 2-3). An econometric study by Kim et al. (2012) demonstrates that a high level of patent rights protection is significantly related to more innovation only in upper-middle- or high-income countries, not in low- and low-middle-income countries. In this case, a reasonable and smart strategy is a detour with loose protection of IPR initially and higher protection later, as in Korea (see WIPO 2012: ch. 2; Kim et al. 2012). Similarly, a key assumption of the desirability of greater protection of IPR that leads to more investment in innovation is that private firms are capable of conducting R&D. However, this is not the case in most developing countries, and in such contexts, higher IPR protection will not generate any tangible change in local R&D activity. Priority should be given to improving local R&D capabilities first, which may require loose IPR protection in the initial stages. Kim et al. (2012) suggest that an effective policy for building R&D capabilities is to recognize and protect minor innovations or adaptive inventions by introducing the system of petit patents (utility models) instead of maintaining a system of regular patents only that protect inventions of high novelty.

A final analogy of detour versus direct replication can be made with regard to the contrast between the "big bang" and gradual policies used when the former socialist planned economies were in a state of transition. Adopting a general equilibrium point of view, the big bang approach involved the immediate transplant of a fully grown free market system into the soil of former Soviet-style economies in Eastern Europe, which led to a prolonged decline in GDP. By contrast, gradualism in China never brought about such negative growth, as it was a detour associated with the preservation of the state sector and the state apparatus (Lin 2012b: 204).

The results of the empirical analysis in this book suggest that late-comers take a detour for sustained catch-up instead of immediately replicating advanced economies in their economic policy making. However, such detour is often a less traveled road and thus may involve more risks and difficulties. The risks of development justify a proactive or facilitating state, as emphasized in the new structural economics of Lin (2012c) as well as recent initiatives by Stiglitz and his group (Cimoli, Dosi, and Stiglitz 2009). The latter justify the proactive role of the government, not only in promoting infant indus-tries, but also in facilitating industrial upgrading and diversification by pointing out issues of information and coordination failure as well as external conditions.

In contrast to the typical arguments for government activism that are based on market failure, the current study emphasizes "capability failure" as a justification for government activism. Typical market-failure-based justification of R&D subsidy notes the positive external-ity of R&D and its resulting undersupply. However, an assumption behind this thinking is that latecomers are already capable of conduct-ing R&D and that they are only conducting less than the optimal amount of R&D. A stark reality in many developing countries is that private firms are not capable of conducting in-house R&D. Thus, they are afraid to pursue R&D, which they consider a very uncertain endeavor. A safer way of doing business for them is merely to buy or to borrow foreign technologies or production facilities and to special-ize in less technical methods or assembly manufacturing. In such states, an effective form of government activism is the provision not only of R&D funding but also various ways of cultivating R&D capability itself, which can begin from an even transfer of R&D outcomes per-formed by public research institutes and a joint public–private R&D consortium, a strategy which was successful in Korea and Taiwan.[7]

The sector-level analysis in Chapter 4 has another justification for technological targeting by the government, as the uncertainty variable negatively affects patenting in advanced countries, in contrast to its insignificant effect on latecomers. This phenomenon is attributed to the fact that latecomers are not on the technology frontier but have more clearly defined (existing) technologies or projects to emulate, whereas advanced countries are at the frontier. Latecomers have a better chance of success if they mobilize all public and private resources to achieve a goal without being bothered by the uncertainty of technological and standard choices involved in new and radical technologies. In other words, another assumption behind the caution on technological targeting is that countries are at the frontier. However, many late-comers are within the frontier and rely on imported technologies, but are often charged monopoly prices for imported goods.

The high prices charged by foreign companies for telephone switches in the 1970s and 1980s were the primary push factor for the Korean government to develop endogenously its telephone switches in the mid 1980s and also for China in the 1990s.[8] When the latecomers attempted to develop their own telephone switches, the required technologies and knowledge were not that difficult to access because they were mature. Thus, several latecomer countries, such as India, Brazil, China, and Korea, succeeded as expected in developing their own switches mostly using public and private R&D collaboration in the 1980s and 1990s. However, initial success was sustained only in Korea and China. Brazil and India traveled a divergent path as a result of different attitudes or industrial policies by the government; without government support for nascent local makers in India and Brazil, firms were incapable of competing against foreign products and faced a gradual slowdown. Conversely, government support in China and in Korea involved initial procurement by the government telephone authorities and even credit allocations for these purchases. Thus, local firms increasingly grew stronger and even made a successful transition toward wireless-based technologies such as CDMA cell phone initia-tives in Korea's Samsung and LG and the emergence of two IT giants ZTE and Huawei in China.[9] These divergent stories of the four coun-tries are elaborated in the next chapter.

Figure 6.4 illustrates a transformation of the industrial structure in Korea from 1960 to 2000. Korea began with long-cycle technology sectors such as apparel as the main export items and gradually shifted to shorter-cycle technology sectors such as automobiles and electron-ics. The share of apparel increased rapidly in the 1960s and the 1970s, with the total export share reaching 10 percent by 1965 and then almost 30 percent by the early 1970s. After this period, the share continued to decline as other higher-value goods took over. The share of apparel declined to approximately 10 percent in 1990 and eventu-ally less than 3 percent by 2000. By contrast, the share of electronics goods and automobiles surpassed that of apparel and footwear. The share of electrical products and electronics increased by approximately

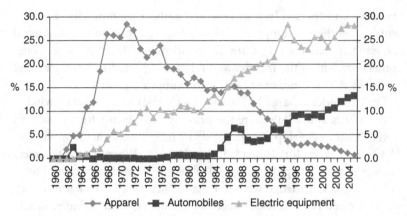

Figure 6.4 Changing trend in the composition of major export items in Korea (% share in total exports), 1960–2005.
Source: drawn by the author using data from the Korea International Trade Association Database (http://www.kita.net) and the United Nations Commodity Trade Statistics Database (http://comtrade.un.org) based on the MTI Code formulated by the Ministry of Knowledge and Economy or by the relevant SITC Rev. 1 Code.

10 percent by the mid 1970s, 20 percent by the early 1990s, and finally close to 30 percent by 2005. The upgrade and diversification would not have occurred so quickly without several five-year economic plans, which assigned different industries for targeted promotion in a particular period, leading to firm-level decision making to move into new industries and to upgrade into a higher-value segment in the same industries.

The next chapter elaborates how such structural changes occurred, focussing on firm-level anecdotes. We will demonstrate that macro-level structural changes have counterparts at the firm-level stories of upgrading and new entries. Examples are numerous, including Hyundai Motors' initial entry as the assembly maker of Ford Motors and a later decision to separate from Ford to create and sell cars with their own brands, as well as Taiwan's decision to enter into the notebook business by relying on the initial R&D of the public research institute.

7 | *How to build up technological capabilities to enter short-cycle technology sectors*

7.1 Introduction

Research interest in the latecomers in economic development can be traced back to Gerschenkron (1962), who emphasizes the advantages of the latecomers, that is, these countries may adopt up-to-date technology after it has fully matured. However, the majority of the early literature has focussed on explaining how developing countries, including the newly industrialized economies, have attempted to catch up with advanced countries by assimilating and adapting the more or less obsolete technology of the advanced countries, as suggested by the so-called product life cycle theory of Vernon (1966).[1] This view is consistent with the low road for development discussed in the preceding chapter, which refers to the situation of typical low- or lower middle-income countries specializing in low-value-added activities or low-end goods in long-technological-cycle fields. This strategy makes sense, and countries tend to achieve a certain degree of economic growth along this road. The next step is to initiate upgrading by switching to a middle road. The experience of successful catching-up economies indicates that switching to a middle road is accompanied by an increase in R&D effort and the arrival of a technological turning point of moving into short-cycle technologies and out of former specialization in long-cycle technologies.

Therefore, an intriguing question is why such a turning point does not occur in other middle-income countries, which continue to traverse the low road. One of the obvious causes of this situation is the weak R&D effort exerted by these middle-income countries. As presented in Figure 1.3, the R&D to GDP ratio of middle-income countries is as low as that of low-income countries, as the ratio does not increase proportionally to per capita income around the range of the middle-income level. An explanation for this weak R&D is market failure arising from the nature of knowledge as a public good. From this perspective, the actual amount of R&D is often less than the optimal amount that will prevail without market failure, such as flaws in capital and risk markets as well as market failure associated with imperfectly competitive industries and a spillover in learning. Therefore, government subsidies to support R&D are suggested, given the externality involved in the production of knowledge.

However, a problem with this market failure view is that it assumes that firms are already capable of conducting R&D, and it is concerned only about the sub-optimality of R&D activities. In other words, the reasons for sub-optimality are found outside the firm, such as in the capital market or risk market. However, the reality in a typical developing country is that private firms do not know how to conduct in-house R&D and thus view it as a very uncertain endeavor with uncertain returns. Therefore, the problem is not less or more R&D but no R&D. In developing countries where firms have low R&D capability, a safer way of doing business is merely to buy or borrow external technologies or production facilities and to specialize in less technical methods or assembly manufacturing. We call this situation a capability failure, different from both market failure (neoclassical view) and system failure (neo-Schumpeterian view).[2]

Therefore, this chapter elaborates the specific ways to cultivate the technological capabilities of firms in developing countries. Effective forms of government activism should include not the simple provision of R&D funds but various ways to cultivate R&D capability itself to correct the situation of capability failure. Chaminade, Intarakumnerd, and Sapprasert (2012) observe that government policy in Thailand is limited only to tax incentives, without implementing explicit measures to encourage Thai firms to assume greater risk in innovation. More effective and alternative forms of intervention may include the transfer of R&D outcomes performed by public research institutes and a public–private R&D consortium in which private firms may participate and learn. Such diverse learning channels are important, as learning failure occurs not only because knowledge is a public good but also because no opportunity is present for effective learning due to historically inherited conditions or policy failure. From this perspective, industrial policy is not about picking winners but about picking good students and matching them with good teachers or bringing them to good schools. Good schools may be in the form of licensing-based learning or public–private joint

R&D projects, in which direct and cooperative learning occur. By contrast, banks that merely supply R&D money may not serve as good schools.

In sum, the capability failure view advocates the importance of increasing the level of capabilities of firms (students) and the various learning methods to be provided over the dynamic course of learning. Therefore, this chapter focusses on how to enhance the capabilities of private firms so that they can escape the middle-income trap by moving away from the long-cycle technology-based to short-cycle technology-based activities and sectors. This journey along the detour requires special driving skills and technological capabilities. By contrast, the journey along the straight road does not require higher skills; therefore, this road is crowded and often sustains heavy traffic. More importantly, the driving skill is not easy to learn; it can be learned only in specialized driving schools. In this sense, this chapter discusses how to learn these specific driving skills in a driving school. This chapter is important because merely recommending short-cycle technology-based sectors is useless or irresponsible unless a discussion on how to enter such sectors is presented.

In what follows, section 7.2 provides an overview of the stages of learning various dimensions of technological capabilities, emphasizing the difficulty of learning how to design products or of acquiring design capability beyond the production technology. Section 7.3 discusses several modes of learning R&D capabilities, namely, co-development with foreign partners, setting up overseas R&D outposts, and involving public–private R&D consortia. Section 7.4 presents the final stage of technological development, which is the case of leapfrogging with the examples of mobile phones and digital TV success in Korea. Section 7.5 provides a summary of how to move into short-cycle technology-based sectors.

7.2 Overview of the learning process and stages

In describing the path of the technological development of latecomer firms, several stages have been identified in the literature. Kim (1997a: 11–14) distinguishes the stages of technological development by categorizing them into the duplicative imitation, the creative imitation, and innovation stages. Another series of stages can be discussed in terms of OEM, own design manufacturing (ODM), and own brand manufacturing (OBM).[3] OEM is a specific form of subcontracting under which a complete, finished product is created according to the exact buyer specifications, with both designs and marketing executed by buyer firms. Some OEM firms evolve into ODM firms, which execute most of the detailed product design, and the customer firms of ODM companies continue to execute the marketing functions. The OBM firms conduct manufacturing, design of new products, R&D for materials, processing of products, and sales and distribution for their own brands. Therefore, the path from OEM to ODM to OBM has become the standard upgrading process for latecomer firms. For example, in their upgrading process, Taiwanese firms followed the steps of OEM, ODM, and OBM, whereas Korean large businesses attempted to switch to OBM at an earlier stage after experiencing a relatively short period of OEM even without fully undergoing the stage of ODM (Lee 2005).

In the early days of Taiwan and Korea, that is, during the 1970s, 1980s, and even 1990s, OEM accounted for a significant share of electronic exports and served as one of the institutional mechanisms that facilitated technological learning.[4] However, the concept of the OEM trap implies that OEM is an easy way of catching up in the early stage of economic growth, but that OEM firms will soon face difficulties when the forerunning buyer firms move their production to other lower-wage production sites (Lee 2005). Therefore, unless these companies eventually produce and sell their own designs and brands, they will remain in the low-value-added segments. These companies and their countries will not assume the status of rich countries. Rasiah (2006) notes the limitations exhibited by Malaysia's rapid export expansion of low-value-added goods. Thus, only a few developing countries made the successful transition from OEM to the next stages of ODM or OBM and the majority of them therefore continued to remain in the OEM form, which implies a small amount of value-added in developing countries.

One related issue is identifying several stages of technological development in terms of objects of learning. The stages can be differentiated in terms of learning of (1) skills; (2) process technology; (3) design technology; and (4) new product development. The basic ideas are presented in Table 7.1. The first and second stages largely correspond to the duplicative imitation and path-following catching up, the third

Table 7.1 *Patterns of catching up and stages of technological development*

| | Stages in catch-up | | | |
	Stage 1	Stage 2	Stage 3	Stage 4
Patterns of catch-up	Duplicative imitation (OEM)	Duplicative imitation (OEM)	Creative imitation (Taiwan: ODM Korea: OBM)	Real innovation (OBM)
Learning object	Path-following Operational skills	Path-following/ stage-skipping Process technology	Stage-skipping Design technology (for existing products)	Path-leading/ path-creating New product development technology
Learning mechanism	Learning by doing (production following manuals and guidance)	Learning by doing (production following product designs)	How to learn? (crisis and switches to in-house R&D, R&D consortia, and overseas R&D outposts)	Co-development Strategic alliances

Source: the author and Lee (2005).

stage corresponds to creative imitation and stage-skipping catching up, and the final stage corresponds to real innovation and path-creating or path-leading catching up. The main idea of identifying the stages of technological development is that the progress up to the first and second stages is relatively easy and occurs in most developing countries, whereas very few firms reach the third stage of learning how to design. Transition into the third stage requires learning and acquisition of design capabilities or R&D capabilities in general. This transition is often perceived as a high entry barrier or crisis stage because latecomer firms experience serious difficulty in learning how to design and produce higher-value-added products.

For instance, South Africa had a very early start, as early as the 1930s, as an assembly site for top Western automobile companies. However, it merely continued as it began, without further growth into an independent automaker with its own designs and brands. By contrast, Hyundai Motors was a late entrant into auto manufacturing when it began its assembly business with Ford in the early 1970s. However, after only a few years, Hyundai separated from Ford and declared its independence in producing and selling cars with its own brand. Now, it is one of the top five global carmakers. One of the first requirements in the journey to independence is the design capability of a company to create its own engines and transmissions. However, a school to learn such skills is not easy to find, as all the major carmakers declined to teach their skills to Hyundai. Thus, Hyundai encountered a moment of learning failure and related capability failure. We will discuss how Hyundai overcame the crisis in the following sections.

However, such a crisis can also be a window of opportunity for the leapfrogging type of catch-up, such as stage-skipping or path-creating, if latecomer firms overcome the crisis by a different means or if they take new opportunities associated with the rise of a new techno-economic paradigm or radical technical change. However, this window of opportunity can be accessed not by all the latecomers but only by those who arrange access to foreign-source technologies, or who are able to create complementary assets for using new technological opportunity. Korean *chaebols* overcame this crisis, and some of them actually succeeded by cross-subsidizing a large amount of R&D funds among affiliates. When even that was not sufficient, they had to form an R&D consortium with the government. For Taiwanese firms of a smaller scale, the solution was the new developmental state; public research units such as the Industrial Technology Research Institute (ITRI) developed the parts and components that were formerly imported and hired private firms to produce them.[5]

Therefore, the following sections discuss how to enhance the technological capability required for shifting from long-cycle to short-cycle technology-based sectors, or from the low-value-added segment to the higher-valued-added segment in the same industries. Such a transition does not occur automatically even if a country is open to trade and FDI. Instead, it always involves deliberate learning and risk-taking by companies and other public actors, combined with exogenously open windows of opportunity. The market mechanism serves not as a triggering factor but as a facilitating factor that stimulates risk-taking action and rewards successful actors.

7.3 Licensing/transfer/FDI-based learning to build absorptive capacity

As Cohen and Levinthal (1990) define absorptive capacity as a firm's ability to identify, value, assimilate, and exploit knowledge from the environment, this capacity has been recognized as one of the major binding constraints for economic development of latecomers. Efforts to develop such capacity should focus not only on enhancing the level of generic human capital but also on providing learning opportunities for workers in private firms. The experience of Korea verifies this point. In the 1960s, when Korea began to modernize with export drives, its human capital base was poor. Thus, the main emphasis was on increasing the general level of human capital, and by the mid 1970s, considerable improvement was evident compared with the previous decade. The other aspect of enhancing absorptive capacity is increasing the imports of technology embodied in equipment combined with training to acquire the know-how and skills needed to operate the imported facilities. Korean firms, especially during the 1960s and 1970s, chose to acquire the know-how (tacit knowledge) that could help them construct and operate manufacturing facilities with which they were initially unfamiliar (Chung and Lee 2011). The typical know-how bundle consisted of not only technological contents in printed form but also related training and services provided on site by expatriate engineers. Korean engineers were occasionally sent to the transferor's firm to learn the implementation process. Chung and Lee (2011) demonstrated through firm-level data on know-how licensing that Korean firms actually experienced a lengthy period of learning, assimilating, and adapting foreign technology in the 1970s before beginning to conduct in-house R&D in the mid 1980s.

Therefore, establishing joint ventures with foreign partners or working in an OEM assembly arrangement with foreign firms is also an effective channel for learning basic operational skills and production technologies (Hobday 2005). Attracting FDI is one of the best strategies to guarantee learning and access to knowledge. However, this strategy may not be reliable for longer-term purposes, and certain conditions must be met, including local controllership and local content requirements. According to Amsden and Chu (2003: 3), technological catch-up requires the use of assets related to project execution, product engineering, and a form of R&D that straddles applied research and exploratory development. If such assets are to be accumulated at all, the responsible party tends to be a nationally owned organization. Thus, ownership matters at least in R&D, and FDI may not be effective as a device through which to learn higher-tier capabilities (e.g. R&D). In their early days, many Korean *chaebols* had FDI or OEM relationships with foreign MNCs, but they took over the management at a later stage. According to Lee and He (2009), during its early days, Samsung Electronics was a joint venture with the Japanese firm Sanyo, in which the Korean company, having no prior experience in the electronics industry, learned know-how and technologies from its partner. However, Samsung eventually bought the equity shares held by Sanyo. Hyundai Motors was an OEM assembler for the US-based Ford, but it eventually separated from the latter. Taiwan's path from OEM to OBM through ODM also involved a great deal of interaction with foreign firms in FDI.

From the production experience in FDI or OEM firms, catching-up firms learn skills or operational know-how while producing the final products according to the foreign-supplied manual on foreign-made plants or production lines.[6] In other words, a manual is followed during operation, and tacit knowledge (know-how and skills) is acquired during the process. Therefore, the process can be called skill formation, which leads to increase in productivity. This productivity increase through learning by doing is the main source for the catching up during this stage. In terms of catching-up patterns, this stage corresponds to path-following catching up. In this stage, as a simple assembly production, the responsibility assumed by local or latecomer firms or entrepreneurs for production tends to be small.

Examples are the cases of Hyundai Motors' assembler agreement with Ford in 1968 for semi-knock-down production as well as Samsung's start-up D-RAM assembly factory in the 1970s in Korea. In the case of Taiwan, examples are the many fully foreign-owned or joint venture firms in the TV industry during the late 1960s and the 1970s that transferred know-how not only to joint venture partners but also to their local part suppliers (Amsden and Chu 2003: 21–4).

After learning the skills, latecomer firms then embark on learning the processing technology or production technology.[7] Latecomer firms acquire processing technology when they produce goods according to designs provided by foreigners. The designs can be those of the products, those of production facility, or both. In any case, acquisition of processing technology means that latecomer firms become capable of setting up their own production facility and assuming responsibility for production. Foreigners provide not only designs but also often dispatch personnel to provide technical guidance in setting up the production facility and/or in producing the goods. In terms of the catching-up pattern, the stage still corresponds to path-following catching up because it attempts to imitate the forerunning firms. Examples of this situation include the path-following catching up by Hyundai in its production of Pony in 1975, with licensed production of the Mitsubishi engine.

Although stage-skipping catching up may be a possibility in this stage, it is still stage-skipping in terms of production but not in terms of R&D or development because latecomer firms are not conducting R&D yet. An example of stage-skipping production includes catching up by Samsung in production (not development) of 64K memory chips (D-RAM). In the 1970s, several Korean firms began wafer-processing memory chips in the form of FDI firms or private OEM with the facility provided by the foreigners. Later, some foreign companies sold their shares to Korean firms, and Korean *chaebols* such as Samsung took over these firms. Samsung first began to produce 64K-bit D-RAM chips in the early 1980s. It bought the 64K D-RAM design from Microelectronics (a US firm) and copied the production facility of Sharp with the help of a small company which also previously built the sharp production facility. However, this instance is a stage-skipping entry because Samsung skipped the 1K to 16K-bit D-RAM to enter directly into the production of 64K-bit D-RAM despite advice from the government to begin with the 1K-bit D-RAM. In the case of Taiwan, many engineers used to working in a foreign-owned TV factory left the firm to start their own firms in related areas.[8] Some targeted local markets and others focussed on OEM for exports, but both assumed responsibility for their own production with technology-licensing agreements with foreign firms.

During the early stages, the forerunning firms provided product or process designs for latecomer firms. However, as the technological capabilities of the latecomer firms grow, buying or obtaining a license for the designs held by the forerunning firms becomes increasingly difficult or expensive because the latter are becoming concerned with the so-called boomerang effects of the transferred technology. In this sense, this stage can also be considered a "crisis" for the catching-up firm.

In the late 1980s many Korean export industries shifted from producing for OEM to marketing internationally under their own brand names (OBM).[9] Most of these goods were still standardized, of low quality, and cheap. Only after the drive to OBM export did Korean firms realize the importance of product differentiation and quality improvement. The lack of design capability caused the early export drives by Korean car producers in the US markets with their own brand to experience serious difficulties after their initial success in the 1980s.[10] However, the dilemma is that merely relying on OEM or licensing is not a long-term solution either. Acquiring design capability for product differentiation and product innovation was difficult, and this was a common dilemma for firms in both Korea and Taiwan.

Korean *chaebols* soon realized that the forerunning firms were no longer willing to provide them with designs, and thus this period constituted the crisis stage in the dynamic path of technological development. For Taiwanese firms, the crisis unfolded as the foreign vendors switched to other lower-wage economies, such as Malaysia, for their OEM orders when the wage rate increased in Taiwan. Taiwanese firms realized that they needed to have the design capability to create their own and more lasting competitive advantages, which would enable them to continue to hold OEM orders from MNCs.

In sum, the nature of the crisis is that products do exist for the latecomers to imitate, but no design of these products is available from the incumbent producers, which are reluctant to transfer the design technology. In the next section, this process of acquiring design or R&D capabilities is discussed comprehensively, as the modes of learning and acquiring design capabilities are diverse.

7.4 Diverse modes of learning design capabilities

Once a latecomer firm builds a certain level of absorptive capacity, it must establish and initiate its own in-house R&D center. Independent R&D efforts are required because foreign firms will become increasingly reluctant to grant technology licenses to the emerging latecomer firms, especially when the latter attempt to enter the skill-intensive markets dominated by advanced countries. With the establishment of in-house R&D laboratories, firms at this stage have to explore more diverse channels of learning and access to foreign knowledge. New alternatives include co-development contracts with foreign R&D specialist firms and/or with public R&D institutes, gaining mastery of the existing literature, setting up overseas R&D outposts, and initiating international mergers and acquisitions (M&As). Arranging access to foreign knowledge and trying new modes of learning is critical because isolated in-house R&D efforts are often insufficient for developing indigenous R&D capabilities. In this regard, these important modes of learning are elaborated as follows.

Co-development with foreign R&D specialist firms[11]

After its break with Ford, Hyundai Motors in Korea ceased the OEM-based production of Ford-branded cars but set up a joint venture with the Japanese carmaker Mitsubishi. The Japanese company provided engines and other key components, and Hyundai assembled them. Hyundai was a licensed producer but not an OEM producer, as it used its own brand in the local market and in exporting. However, when Hyundai wanted to develop its own engines, the 20 percent equity holding Mitsubishi refused to teach Hyundai how to design and produce engines. Most developing country businessmen would have stopped there, but the founding chairman, Mr. Chung, decided to spend an enormous amount of R&D expenditure on engine development (Lee and Lim 2001). Fortunately, Hyundai was able to obtain access to the external knowledge of specialized R&D firms, such as Ricardo Co in the UK. The process was not easy, and Ricardo did not merely provide the design of an engine for Hyundai to develop according to the design. The two entities established a co-development contract to work together, and the final design was a completely new one. They had to test more than a thousand prototypes until they finally succeeded seven years after the first project year of 1984. Hyundai's technological development also involved a process that can be classified as stage-skipping catching up. When Hyundai began to develop engines, the carburetor-based engine was the standard type. However, knowing that the trend of engine technology was moving toward a new electronic-injection-based engine, Hyundai perceived this transition as a window of opportunity and decided to develop this latter type of engine instead of following the old path in developing the standard engine. By succeeding in this project, Hyundai was able to reduce the gap in engine technology in a very short period of time.

Learning by setting up overseas R&D post and access to foreign knowledge

Samsung in Korea entered the production of memory chips in the early 1980s. After several years of foreign-design-based production of memory chips, Samsung decided to localize the process of memory chip design, especially from the generation of 256K D-RAM, as buying the design of memory chips was neither easy nor cheap.[12] Thus, Samsung established an overseas R&D outpost in Silicon Valley and hired many foreign-trained engineers or scientists (which can be called a reverse brain drain). Eventually, Samsung's 256K D-RAM designs turned out better than its Japanese counterparts (Kim 1997b). After Samsung's independent development of the 256K D-RAM, some foreign companies offered to sell Samsung their 1Mb D-RAM designs, but Samsung refused to purchase them because it could develop its own designs. In sum, this case of the development of chip designs can be considered a stage-skipping catching up that relied on access to the external knowledge base in the form of licensing and overseas R&D outposts, taking advantage of the mass production and investment capability of conglomerate firms.

In the case of Taiwan, the era of the electronic calculator, which peaked in the mid-1980s, signified a trend away from OEM toward ODM, which paved the way for notebooks and cell phones later on (Amsden and Chu 2003: 28–32). Young Taiwan-educated engineers contributed to the rise of the industry from the 1970s by copying designs and making them slightly different. Since the early 1980s, Taiwanese manufacturers had mastered the skill of design integration, which enabled them to be the first-to-market (if not lowest in cost) and to win the most profitable original design contract from foreign prime contractors. Despite collaborative relations with foreign vendors, the acquisition of design capability required active learning effort from the Taiwan side.[13] Taiwanese engineers traveled around the world to study large-scale integration applications, and they combined what they saw and learned from Japanese suppliers. In this way, they were able to integrate into a small space a large number of parts and components sourced globally at the lowest prices.

Learning by public–private R&D consortia for entries into new sectors

In Taiwan, the acquisition of more fundamental design capability or the basic design platform was possible with the help of government research institutes such as ITRI. A notable example is the public–private R&D consortium to develop a laptop PC that ran for a year and a half from 1990 to 1991 (Mathews 2002b). This consortium with capital of less than US$2 million developed a common machine architecture for a prototype that could easily translate into a series of standardized components mass produced by manufacturers. The consortium represented a watershed after some previous failures, indicating the potential of an R&D consortium to help establish new "fast follower" industries in Taiwan. A similar watershed is the case of a public–private R&D consortium to develop telephone switches in Korea. Other countries, such as China, India, and Brazil, had a similar experience with telephone switches, although the final outcomes were different because of the different roles played by the government in each country. This case is elaborated as follows.[14]

Most developing countries tended to experience serious telephone service bottlenecks in the 1970s and 1980s. However, most of them had neither their own telecommunications manufacturing equipment industry nor R&D programs. As a result, they imported at high prices most of the equipment and related technologies from abroad, and local technicians merely installed foreign switching systems into the nation's domestic telephone networks. With industrial and commercial bases developing rapidly and populations growing, many countries wanted to develop their own manufacturing capabilities. Thus, they initiated government-led R&D consortia to attempt the local development of telephone switches. This attempt led to the successful localization of telephone switches in the 1980s and 1990s in several latecomer countries, including China, Korea, India, and Brazil (Lee, Mani, and Mu 2012). In these four countries, a common pattern in the indigenous development of digital switches was the tripartite R&D consortium among the government research institutes (GRIs) in charge of R&D functions, state-owned enterprises (SOEs) or the ministry in charge of financing and coordination, and private companies in charge of manufacturing in the initial or later stages.

However, the subsequent waves of industry privatization and market liberalization in Brazil and India as opposed to the consistent infant industry protection in Korea and China distinguish the trajectory of the industries in these four countries (Lee, Mani, and Mu, 2012). On the one hand, the indigenous manufacturers of China and Korea took over from the importers and MNCs. Their enhanced capabilities in wired telecommunication, which had been accumulated over the preceding decades, led to the growth of indigenous capabilities in wireless telecommunication as well. On the other hand, Brazil and India increasingly became net importers of telecom equipment, and their industries are now dominated by affiliates of the MNCs.

In China, the role of the government was decisive when the indigenous Chinese firms began to compete directly with foreign joint ventures in both rural and urban areas. The role of the Chinese government was to provide market protection and incentives for the adoption and use of domestic products.[15] In Korea, the government's support and protection were also important factors for the growth of indigenous developed telephone switches, especially in the form of public procurement in the 1980s. Moreover, in the mid 1980s, the Korean government limited the imports of foreign switches. In Brazil, from 1976 to the 1990s, the Brazilian state attempted to foster the evolution of a domestic local equipment manufacturing industry through a variety of public support measures such as public procurement. However, since the mid 1990s, these policies were abandoned because of political instability and the country later moved to liberalization (e.g. the elimination of market guarantees for local products and local content requirement in the 1990s). The situation is similar in India in that the Indian state discriminated against the wider diffusion of the indigenously designed telephone switches as it freely allowed the imports of foreign telephone switches. Furthermore, with the effective privatization of telecom services, the manufacturing of telecom equipment has become open to imports and indeed FDI.

One of the reasons why all four latecomers were able to develop their own digital switches is that the knowledge system of digital switches was mature and had stable trajectories. Thus, arranging access to knowledge was not difficult whether it was in the form of licensing/joint venture or study of the literature in public domain.

This finding indicates that technology targeting makes more sense when the latecomers are not at the technological frontier and face less uncertainty in terms of selecting the right or wrong objective as the R&D target. Concentrating their human, physical, and financial resources on this target, latecomers will be able to develop products that are similar to the existing products of incumbent companies.

The subsequent variations among the four can be explained in terms of the critical difference in the role of governments in providing coordination and protection with strategic visions, as in the cases of China and Korea, compared with no sustained state activism in the cases of India and Brazil. Furthermore, the initial success led to the developing capabilities of private firms in China and Korea but not in India and Brazil. Based on enhanced capability, Korea and China have taken advantage of the emergence of the new era of wireless telecommunication to manage even a path-creating catch-up, such as the commercialization of the CDMA technology in Korea and the development of the 3G wireless standard (TD-SCDMA) in China. By contrast, if the latecomers fail to improve their own capabilities, then the shift of the technological generation or paradigm can become a further barrier to catching up, as occurred in Brazil and India as their firms failed to make the transition to the mobile era. In sum, paradigm or generation shifts can represent either a window of opportunity (as in China and Korea) or an additional entry barrier (as in India or Brazil). This double-edged nature of technological change is consistent with the empirical findings in Chapter 4 of this book.

7.5 Learning by leapfrogging: mobile phones and digital TV in Korea[16]

Alongside the tradition of neo-Schumpeterian economics, a thesis of leapfrogging has been proposed.[17] This idea of leapfrogging emphasizes the importance of utilizing emerging technological opportunities in the process of catching up. Based on this view, the emergence of digital technology since the 1990s was also an opportunity for latecomers to overtake the forerunners. Especially since the 2000s, Korean companies have emerged as world leaders in digital TV and mobile phones. This section provides a discussion on the emergence and growth of the industry of mobile phones and digital TV in Korea and examines the leapfrogging thesis. The focus is on how the risks of early entry to emerging industries were managed by Korean firms.

Choice over alternative technology standards and public–private consortia

When the Koreans decided to enter the high-definition (HD) TV technology, they faced tough choices regarding technology standards. Initially, they were heavily influenced by the Japanese leaders in analog HD TV. The Japanese group arrived in Korea during the 1988 Seoul Olympic Games and staged a promotional tour of their achievement in the hope that the Koreans would follow them, as they had done in the past. Recognizing that HD TV would be a next-generation hot consumer item with immense technological and market potential, the Korean government established the Committee for Co-development of HD TV in 1989 with the participation of seventeen institutions including private firms, GRIs, and universities.

One year after Korea began the project, GI in the United States, a leading firm in digital TV technology, staged a historic demonstration of the possibility of digital TV in 1990. After this event, the Korean consortium decided to target digital HD TV instead of the Japanese-developed analog HD TV. However, the US standard was not yet determined at that time. In this regard, one interesting strategy by the Korean team was the decision to develop several alternative standards simultaneously, with different private companies in the team assigned to watch and follow different standards. This strategy can be called a "parallel mover" in comparison with the first-mover strategy. Immediately after the so-called "grand coalition" agreed to a common standard for digital TV, the Korean firms became a first mover in terms of launching their first digital TVs compatible with the common standard in the US markets.

In terms of access to foreign knowledge, Korean firms had been closely monitoring the technological activities of GI and other leading firms in the USA. As early as September 1989, Samsung first established an R&D team for digital TV and a US branch (Advanced Media Lab (AML)) in Princeton, New Jersey. In the case of LG, it acquired a minor share of 15 percent of Zenith, a US company with a core technology in digital TV as early as 1990. LG eventually acquired 100 percent of equity of Zenith and was able to use the patented technology without fear of patent violation.

Another entry into short-cycle technologies through the Korean consortium was cell phones, one of the most successful cases of a path-creating or leapfrogging event led by private–public collaboration. When the Korean firms and the government authorities considered entry into this sector, the leader was the US firm Motorola, and the analog system was dominant in the USA, whereas the TDMA-based GSM system was the dominant system in Europe. However, the Korean authorities (i.e. the Ministry of Information and Telecommunication) considered an emerging alternative of CDMA technology with higher efficiency in frequency utilization and higher quality and security in voice transmission. Thus, despite great uncertainty in the development of the world's first CDMA system as well as the strong reservations expressed by the telephone service provider and private manufacturers (e.g. Samsung and LG), the Ministry and the Electronics and Telecommunication Research Institute (ETRI) decided to support CDMA. One of the main reasons for the decision was the consideration that if Korea merely followed the already established standards, the gap between Korea and its forerunners would never be reduced and thus catching up would take even longer. Thus, Korea chose a shorter but riskier path.

The Korean government first designated the CDMA system development a national R&D project as early as 1989. In 1991, the contract to introduce the core technology from and to develop the system together with the US-based Qualcomm was forged. In 1993, the Ministry declared CDMA to be the national standard in telecommunication. Given the high frequency of innovation and the high fluidity of trajectory, the telecommunications industry does not offer latecomers any incentives for R&D effort. Expected profits and other related gains from first-mover advantages served as a strong attraction, and the high risks were shared by the government-led R&D consortium and knowledge alliance with Qualcomm. The ETRI also contributed to reducing technological uncertainty by providing accurate and up-to-date information on technology trends and by identifying the correct R&D targets that were more promising than alternatives.

In the case of both digital TV and mobile phones, the public–private coalition encouraged private firms to maintain this risky R&D activity by channeling R&D funds and forming a network of researchers from firms, universities, and GRIs. In other words, the importance of the government involvement was the fact that this consortium had the effect of providing the private companies with legitimacy for the project, and without this legitimacy their project would have been stopped midstream because private companies could not continue to pour money into a project with an uncertain cash outcome.[18] Moreover, in the consortium, a clear division of labor was stated among the participating units, so that each unit, GRI, or private firm was assigned to different tasks with some intentional overlaps among them, namely, two or more units being assigned the same task to avoid monopoly in the research outcomes.

Implications: technology policy on standards and R&D consortia

The cases of digital TV and mobile phones in Korea demonstrate how the emerging new technological paradigm can serve as a window of opportunity for catching-up firms. This study has also identified the risks facing such a leapfrogging strategy and elaborated how these risks can be overcome by a public–private R&D consortium. This case demonstrates that a path-creating catching-up situation is likely to occur through public–private collaboration when the technological regime of the concerned industry features a fluid trajectory and high risk. This study has the following implications for government policy and firm strategies.[19]

First, a long list of success with public–private R&D consortia, from digital telephone switches to memory chips (D-RAM), wireless phones (CDMA), and finally digital TV in Korea, confirms the positive role of the government and GRIs in technological catch-up by latecomer firms. The private firms that participated in the public–private consortium all acknowledged the important function of the government in providing legitimacy for large projects that are often difficult for private firms to support. The consortium also served as a field to pool domestic resources from various sources, especially resources in the universities. The contribution of public research laboratories is also critical in conducting the role of "technology watch" to interpret and monitor the state-of-the art trend of R&D activities in foreign countries.

Second, in the past or in path-following catch-up, the main channels were license or FDI, whereas the current cases of path-creating or leading catch-up during the paradigm shift period demonstrate the importance of new channels such as co-development with and acquisition of foreign firms as well as collaboration based on complementary assets owned by latecomer firms. Absorption capacity was emphasized in the previous account of technology transfer through license or FDI, whereas now, complementary assets, which have been created with speedy R&D activities and investment in production, seem to be important in these new ways of accessing knowledge.

Third, the critical role of standard setting should be emphasized, especially when the involved technologies are information or other emerging technologies. Isolated development without considering the issue of standards may lead to failure of the entire project. In standard setting, successful collaboration and partnership with rivals or suppliers of complementary products are important. In this competition for standard setting and market creation, the role of the government is to facilitate the adoption of specific standards, and thus it influences the formation of markets at the right time. The role of the government should also be changing, from tariff or R&D subsidy in the old era to standardization policy in the new era.

Finally, the reasons why Japanese digital TV producers lagged Korean digital TV producers can be discussed in terms of the concept of the incumbent's trap or dilemma. Japan had been locked into "analog" HD TV since the 1980s, when it created the first HD TV system. Although the Japanese government attempted to shift to digital TV in 1994, the effort was stifled by the firms that had invested heavily in analog HD TV. This early start and lock-in by the Japanese firms signified the disadvantages and risk of being the technological pioneer, which is close to the so-called innovator's dilemma proposed by Christensen (1997). Japan was the forerunner in taking initiatives toward HD TV, but it was along the trajectory of analog technology. However, Japan's merits turned into debt as the USA and other countries accepted the digital TV as the standard, and the latecomers decided to follow this trajectory. This case eloquently demonstrates that a shift of technological paradigm can penalize the leader while serving as a window of opportunity for latecomers who command complementary assets for using a new technological opportunity.

7.6 How to move to short-cycle technology sectors: a summary

This chapter focusses on how to move from long-cycle technology-based sectors to the short-cycle technology-based sectors and from the low-value-added segment to the higher-valued-added segment in the same industries. The chapter suggests that such a transition does not occur automatically (even if a country is open to trade and FDI), but that it always involves deliberate risk-taking actions by firms and other public actors, which are often combined with exogenously open windows of opportunities. Short-cycle technology-based sectors matter because these sectors are where new opportunities tend to emerge more frequently and are also where more profitable business is available with lower entry barriers. Market mechanism has a role not as a triggering factor but as a facilitating factor that stimulates such risk-taking and provides reward to the successes.

The main business area of the Hyundai business group was construction, one of the long-cycle technology-based sectors. Hyundai entered the shorter- or medium-cycle business of automobiles in the early 1970s as an assembly maker to a foreign company. Such an occurrence is common in many developing countries. However, today's Hyundai Motors and today's Korea, a stronghold in the automobile business, would not have emerged without Hyundai's brave decision to separate from Ford and sell its own brand of cars equipped with their own engines. The role of the government was merely to provide protection for this new firm with high tariff (40 percent to 60 percent) for the first fifteen years until the mid 1980s. The window of opportunity for Hyundai was the transition of engine technology from a carburetor-based engine to a new electronic injection-based engine, which this company chose to develop to save time in catching up.

Taiwan's successful settling down with short-cycle technology-based sectors or higher-value-added segment of the industry would have taken longer if no public-private R&D consortia had been present; the first success was the consortium to develop laptops. Several attempts were made, but all failed prior to this first success. In other words, such a private–private joint effort does not guarantee success, but it is the only way out of the old specialization in long-cycle technology-based sectors (and out of the middle-income trap). In Korean history, the first case of the successful public–private R&D

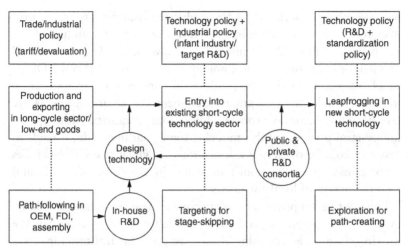

Figure 7.1 Action plan to enter short-cycle technology-based sectors.
Source: the author.

consortium was the one that developed digital telephone switches. This event was also the origin of Korea as a leader in telecommunications and IT devices because that success was the source of the learning and confidence that led to a series of such consortia in memory chips, mobile phones, and finally digital TV. In these cases, the windows of opportunity were the emergence of a new digital technology paradigm and frequent changes in the generation of products. The role of the government ranged from direct participation in R&D and initial public procurement of locally developed products to exclusive standard policy. With this series of public–private R&D consortia to enter new industries, Korea was able to reduce its reliance on the long-cycle technology-based business, namely, textiles and many low-end consumer products such as radios, cookers, ovens, refrigerators, and others.

The discussions in the preceding three sections can be integrated to draw a rough plan to move from long-cycle technology-based sectors to short-cycle technology-based sectors. Figure 7.1 illustrates this discussion (action plans to enter short-cycle technology sectors).

In an initial stage, the latecomer countries tend to specialize in long-cycle technology-based sectors or the low-end segment of the relatively short-cycle technology-based sectors. An example of a long-cycle technology-based sector is textile products, which the latecomers produce for the export market in the OEM arrangement with firms from advanced countries. An example of the low-end or low-value-added segment of the short-cycle technology-based sectors is also the OEM- or FDI-based assembly-type products in consumer electronics, automobiles, or telecommunications equipment. These arrangements are typical of low-income or some middle-income countries. Although the longer-term prospect of this model is somewhat uncertain, it tends to result in some growth in these economies, which is even sometimes accompanied by protectionist measures in the form of tariffs and undervaluation of local currencies.

Now, let us suppose that the latecomers want to break into short-cycle technology-based products or a higher-valued segment of the existing short-cycle technology-based sectors. This transition involves moving from the license-based production of consumer products to their own design-based (IPRs) production of these products. An example of a more discontinuous or stage-skipping entry is the case of the indigenous development of telephone switches discussed in section 7.4. A good target for such entry is products that the latecomers used to be unable to produce but which are based on mature technologies so that access to foreign knowledge may be available. The latecomers had to pay higher prices for their importation into their own countries because they were necessary in their economies. Korea and other economies had to pay very high prices to import telephone switches, and thus the local substituting production of the products meant taking the rents away from the foreign producers and placing them in the hands of indigenous producers. However, such indigenous endeavor tends to involve public and private R&D consortia or private R&D ventures combined with public policy support in the form of R&D subsidies, tariffs, or public procurement. Although this project is still an imitative development of existing products or facilities, it is important because it should be a significant learning experience that is useful for the next stage and that also creates a new engine of growth in more profitable sectors. For Nigeria, which produces oil but exports it as crude oil without refining it for higher value-added, a target should be building an oil refinery in the country. This target is not impossible because the technology to build an oil refinery is old and mature and thus easily available at some cost. Its nature is similar to the Korean decision to build its own steel industry in the early 1970s because Korea did not want to pay higher prices for steel products for the local steel-consuming industries that they wanted to promote, such as automobiles and ships. A recent example is China's move to target and develop a high-speed train as a latecomer. As a large country, China needed such a transportation system, and continuing to rely on foreign technology instead of indigenously producing a train would be expensive.

The final stage is that of true leapfrogging in which latecomers do not imitate existing products or plants but explore the development of new products in short-cycle time-based technologies. For example, a decisive and final watershed in Korean history in which Korea overtook Japan in the IT business involved the indigenous development of mobile phones and digital TVs. China's recent move toward electric engine-based cars and solar and wind power energies is another example. In these areas, advanced and latecomer countries enter at the same time, and thus the latecomer countries are longer latecomers and cannot try to imitate the products of the advanced countries. If the "former" latecomers succeed first, they will become the first movers and their success should be a strong momentum for them to reach beyond the middle-income and join the rich-country club. In this leapfrogging endeavor, the public–private R&D consortium takes on a more vital role, as the risks involved are great and different in nature. Furthermore, coordinated initiatives for exclusive standards and incentives for early adopters are important in reducing the risk of a weak initial market.

Throughout the stages, arranging access to a foreign knowledge base is important for latecomers. Without this access, the latecomers' endeavors are more difficult or likely to fail. Latecomers can utilize diverse access channels, such as tacit knowledge held by specialized R&D firms or individual scientists or engineers in the form of contracts, reverse brain drains, and/or overseas R&D outposts. Latecomer firms sometimes rely on the knowledge and even memory of R&D personnel previously involved in the R&D projects of forerunning companies to imitate, although with some twist, existing product designs or concepts. Latecomers also have to rely on explicit knowledge in the form of licensing, literature, or public information. Generally, the following sequential pattern can be identified.[20]

In the earliest stage, technical guidance from foreign OEM buyers or those working in FDI firms is the primary channel of learning.

Key technology is embodied in imported machinery and equipment. This is learning by doing without the capacity or even intention for a planned technological development.

In the next stage, when the latecomer firms recognize the need for a more systemic learning and structured technological development, such firms tend to resort to technological licensing and actively obtain knowledge from any FDI partners. Licensing was the main method for acquiring foreign technology in Korea during the 1970s and the 1980s. For the Taiwanese monitor industry, which emerged after the TV industry in the 1970s, the main channels were licensing or joint ventures in the 1980s. In this stage, the critical factor for effective learning is the absorption capacity of the latecomer firms, which depends also on the education system and other elements of the NIS of the country. In a number of cases, the distinction between the first two stages may not be that clear.

In the next stage, the latecomer firms establish a certain degree of in-house R&D capacity with a clear idea of the amount and allocation of available resources. With the limitations of licensing or learning from foreign partners increasingly felt, the latecomer firms should rely on public–private R&D consortia, the GRIs, research on existing literature, overseas R&D outposts, co-development contracts with foreign R&D and technology specialist firms, and international M&A. For example, in the early 1990s, a small number of Korean firms established overseas R&D posts mainly to obtain easy and faster access to foreign technologies that were difficult to acquire through imports of license technology. These overseas posts also served as a window on recent trends in technological development.[21]

The final stage is a horizontal collaboration or alliance based on complementary assets. Some Korean firms, like Samsung, have reached this stage, and are now engaged with Intel, Sony, Toshiba, and Microsoft in various modes of alliances. Moreover, in the final catch-up stage, the fact that nationally owned firms have eventually emerged as leaders of the industry even in Taiwan suggests the importance of indigenous ownership of firms in the long-term process of technological catching up.

FDI may not be reliable from a long-term perspective, although it can serve as the initial learning place. This observation on the role of the FDI or international subcontracting does not mean that latecomer countries should not invite foreign firms. Many Korean *chaebols* once had partner or OEM relations with foreign MNCs that served as learning opportunities. Taiwan's path from OEM to OBM through ODM may be a more standard path. Moreover, having arrived at a higher stage of technological development, the catching-up firms may want to form international alliances or even joint ventures to cope with the increasingly fierce global competition and to keep ahead. Several Korean firms have now reached this stage, and the old stand-alone strategy may no longer be effective. However, the alliance strategy is possible and can work only after the latecomer firms have obtained a higher technological capability, which affects their bargaining positions. Thus, the existing technological capability and base of local firms are important because they determine the specific terms of technology-related contracts between local and foreign firms.

We also need to look at the issue beyond the relative roles of private in-house R&D and public–private consortia as well as taking the NIS approach that requires coordination among the firms, government agencies, and academia to begin acquiring design and product development capability. Universities as suppliers of creativity and financial systems as supporters of creativity are important in turning new ideas into actual business. Industries need to collaborate with universities not only because universities are important traditional suppliers of human resources but also because they can conduct R&D for industries as well as directly providing other resources in establishing companies. A new phenomenon called knowledge industrialization has become increasingly important as an increasing number of industries are becoming science based instead of based on on-site experience.

8 | Catching up and leapfrogging in China and India

8.1 Introduction

The preceding chapters focussed on stories of sustained catching-up, mostly from the first-tier East Asian economies of South Korea and Taiwan. Recently, several countries have been observed to follow a similar path of catching-up, with China and India as the leading examples. This chapter discusses these two countries.

Since the early 2010s, China has faced the possibility of falling into the middle-income country trap after three decades of rapid growth, which has been regarded as a success of the Beijing Consensus.[1] After examining China in terms of its innovation capability and the upgrading sequence of the OEM–ODM–OBM, the current chapter presents a positive assessment of China's ability to break free from this trap based on its increasing specialization in short-cycle technology sectors.

India makes an interesting case study because its growth is based on services and not on manufacturing. A critical question is whether it will upgrade to higher-value-added segments, such as has occurred in first-tier Asian economies whose strength lies in their manufacturing sectors. In this chapter, several success stories of leading IT service companies from India are examined. If India succeeds in this respect, then its situation can be regarded as a different type of leapfrogging because India's growth engine will have bypassed manufacturing and jumped directly into services. From a theoretical perspective, India's success with IT service makes sense because the latter can be regarded as another short-cycle technology-based sector as it applies short-cycle technologies, namely IT, to servicing clients. IT service also boasts the frequent emergence of new business opportunities and a lower entry barrier in terms of required capital. The next section compares India and China in terms of the concept of leapfrogging. Section 8.3 examines India's IT service sectors and firms in detail. Section 8.4 first discusses three unique modes of technological learning in China and then explores China's case and its chances of surviving the middle-income country trap by building up technological capabilities or of remaining as a low-end goods producer. Section 8.5 discusses the technological turning points in China and India.

8.2 India's service sector leapfrogging and China's manufacturing sector catching up

Thus far, the accounts of sustained catch-up in the preceding chapter focussed on those that have been driven by the manufacturing sector. An interesting question is whether the service sector can drive economic catch-up. India's case since the 1990s is a possible example of this. A contrast has been drawn between China's manufacturing-led growth and service-led growth.[2] China's impressive catch-up since the 1980s is deemed classical, as its catch-up growth has been accompanied by typical structural changes, with the share of primary sector shrinking over time, whereas that of the secondary and tertiary sectors is increasing. India's case is unusual because the increase in the share of the service sector is matched closely by a decrease in agriculture, whereas the share of the secondary sector remains almost flat.

Figure 8.1 shows the trend in sectoral shares in India and China. In China, the manufacturing sector's contribution to the total GDP has steadily increased, reaching 30 percent by the 2000s and accounting for the sharp decrease in agriculture's contribution to GDP. By contrast, the GDP of India's manufacturing sector has never exceeded 20 percent, remaining constant at around 15 percent for over two decades. However, its service sector has grown steadily since the 1980s, with its GDP share exceeding 50 percent. The growth of India's service sector may be viewed as another story of premature tertiarization typical of developing countries, in which generally low-paying service jobs are generated in the urban informal sector. Although this may be partly true in India, it is not representative of India's whole service sector. In particular, India's IT service industry has generated high-paying jobs and upgraded into higher-value-added segments of the value chain.

Another impressive indicator of India's success is its rising share of service exports in relation to total exports. This share reached 35 percent in the middle of the first decade of the century in India (Figure 8.2), one of the highest in the world, surpassing even that in advanced economies. In contrast, the export share of services in China stayed at

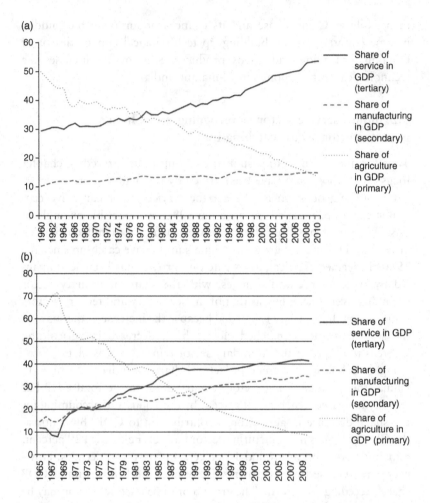

Figure 8.1 GDP shares of the primary, secondary, and tertiary sectors in (a) India; (b) China.
Source: World Bank: world development indicator data and author's own calculations.

around 10 percent in the 2000s. Therefore, if India follows the proven success path of export-led growth, then it is likely to do so through service exports (tertiary) and not through manufacturing (secondary) or agriculture (primary) exports, as in other developing countries.

Growth in most of industrialized countries in the world has been fueled by manufacturing, with the service sector increasing only after this stage of manufacturing-based growth has ended. This pattern has

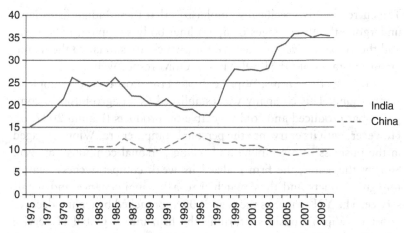

Figure 8.2 Shares of service exports in total exports of China and India (1975-2010).
Source: World Bank: world development indicator data and author's own calculations.

been explained in terms of the income elasticity of services, or services as an intermediate input to manufacturing. However, in India, the service sector has progressed even without going through the usual growth stage in the manufacturing sector. Therefore, the growth of services in India does not fit either the typical demand bias hypothesis of Clark (1940) or the productivity bias hypothesis of Baumol (1967). The former maintains that services tend to grow at a later stage of development because the income elasticity in the demand for services is higher than that for manufacturing, whereas the latter argues that huge increases in manufacturing productivity tend to shed labor from that sector, which is absorbed by the service sector, thus leading to the latter's growth.[3] In reality, service productivity in India is actually higher than that of manufacturing, which is puzzling. Thus, we consider the case of India as leapfrogging in terms of industrial structure because the service sector developed even before the manufacturing sector grew to take some share in the economy.

The next section examines India's IT service sector, focussing on specific cases at the firm level to verify the role of these firms in putting India on the path of impressive catch-up. Based on the cases of the three leading IT service firms, Infosys, Tata Consultancy Services (TCS), and Wipro, we aim to show that these firms have successfully upgraded from their original provision of low-value-added services.

The current study specifically emphasizes that these Indian firms have undergone the three stages of upgrading: body shopping, offshoring, and the global delivery model (GDM), which are similar to the manufacturing stages of OEM, ODM, and OBM respectively.

Among the three firms, Wipro exhibited the most typical example of leapfrogging. This company was established as an agro-business company that produced and sold vegetable oil products (Hamm 2007: 6). However, with its entry into the personal computer era, Wipro engaged in the business of assembling and selling personal computers as well. Shortly thereafter, the firm realized its weak competitiveness against foreign products and thus switched to a PC maintenance and repair service. The Y2K panic as the year 2000 approached brought a decisive boost to Wipro's business, turning the firm into a global IT service company listed on the New York Stock Exchange. Wipro's historical evolution illustrates a company's leapfrogging into IT service, bypassing the stage of IT manufacturing.

8.3 India's IT services industry as another leapfrogging case in short-cycle technology

The IT service industry is a leading growth engine in the Indian economy. This industry is currently led by three giants of TCS, Wipro, and Infosys, which have competed equally with advanced IT service firms in the USA and the European Union. The success of India's IT service industry makes for an interesting case of catching-up growth based on services and not on manufacturing. This section discusses the windows of opportunity that are available to Indian firms, and the types of catching-up or leapfrogging strategies that these firms have adopted to take advantage of these opportunities. It also presents a comparison or analogy of IT service industry with manufacturing industry.

The concept of window of opportunity refers to the idea presented by Perez and Soete (1988), who observed that a new techno-economic paradigm could be a good opportunity for latecomers to stage an entry into new sectors. Windows of opportunity also arise in business cycles, particularly during downturns, because downturn or recession periods cause incumbents to slow down and resources to become cheap, thus reducing costs for late entrants.[4] Other opportunities come with government intervention or changes in industry regulations. Guennif and Ramani (2012) analyze how changes in the regulatory system have given Indian firms the chance to compete in the pharmaceutical industry. Governments have also played prominent roles in several East Asian catch-up cases, such as in the Chinese telecommunications equipment industry and the Korean and Taiwanese high-tech industries.[5]

We argue that the first opportunity for India came with the emergence of a new techno-economic paradigm (or business models), and the second came when the government intervened by changing policies on foreign firms. Given that this techno-economic paradigm shift can happen to other latecomer countries and firms, additional factors that are more specific to Indian firms are identified. We then emphasize that Indian firms have created their own unique path or business model in IT services. In other words, Indian firms were responsible for reinventing the offshoring model and later invented the GDM, which has now become a global industry standard. Focussing on path creation or leapfrogging is aligned with the study conducted by Romijin and Caniëls (2011), in which they question the relevance of incremental capability-building strategies when new knowledge areas emerge.

More importantly, we also identify three stages of upgrading in Indian IT service firms: the body shop model, offshoring, and GDM, which are similar to the three steps of upgrading in manufacturing, OEM, ODM, and OBM respectively.[6] Upgrading enables Indian IT service firms to move into high-value-added segments of the industry instead of staying in the low-value-added segment. IT services contain elements common to an IT service value chain, with consulting and planning at the top of the value chain, followed by system integration, application design, development and maintenance, and programming (coding) at the bottom. Previously, Indian IT service firms provided low-value-added services such as application development, maintenance, and testing. These firms have increasingly turned in strong performances in high-value-added services, such as system analysis and design, system integration, and consulting, and have ventured into business process outsourcing (BPO).

Windows of opportunity for Indian IT service firms

Shift of the techno-economic paradigm and business models
In their struggle against difficulties that emerged during the 1980s, American firms introduced a new production arrangement called offshoring as an alternative to downsizing.[7] According to Grossman

and Rossi-Hansberg (2006), the production chain of the global economy has embraced a new paradigm called "vertical integration of production across borders" or "trade in tasks," in which "tasks," "end-products," and "components" are all subject to international trade through offshoring. India opened its economy after the foreign exchange crisis, providing it with the opportunity to be a new member of the global division of labor. In this case, cost advantage instead of high-quality service was MNCs' main reason for designating India as their offshore center for reaching other countries (e.g. Ireland, Israel, and Singapore). The other reasons are Indian nationals' English-language skills and the zonal time difference of about twelve hours, which provides American firms with a twenty-four-hour work environment.[8]

The shift from hardware technology to client–server in the late 1980s presented another opportunity for India. This shift created a new, huge source of demand for customized software, enabling firms to migrate from the mainframe to client–server systems. In this manner, system integration between the existing mainframe and the new client–server became a significant new market exploited by Indian companies, such as TCS, which had a pool of qualified software manpower.[9] As a result, American firms turned to Indian firms in the areas of low-value-added services and labor-intensive services, such as coding, testing, and software maintenance.

Finally, the Y2K problem and the "dotcom boom" were two important market booms for Indian IT service firms in the late 1990s. Addressing the Y2K problem entailed ensuring that existing programs would not suffer glitches in the new millennium. Around this time, MNCs extensively used Indian companies to solve their Y2K problems. India received considerable business because of its abundant workforce that could capably write many lines of code. The "dotcom boom" also saw Indian technology executives rise to prominence as successful entrepreneurs, chief technical officers, and venture capitalists in Silicon Valley, bringing an overall positive effect on the Indian IT service industry in terms of its reputation and ability to generate more businesses. The presence of qualified Indian "techies" in senior positions in customer firms also helped Indian IT service firms to secure business deals from American firms.

Change in government regulation

India's policy lines have been more inward looking since its independence from the UK in 1947 and particularly along the lines of import substitution industrialization. A stellar example is the Foreign Exchange Regulation Act (FERA) of 1973, one of the policies that helped regulate transactions in foreign exchange and securities with the objective of conserving India's foreign exchange resources. However, in protest against its discriminatory effects on foreign companies, IBM decided to leave India because the FERA required the company to dilute its equity holdings in India to 60 percent.[10]

IBM's exit was an opportunity for other foreign companies, such as Burroughs and International Computers Ltd (ICL) to push the sales of their computers in India. Both companies also depended on Indian programmers to write software conversion programs compatible with their computer systems.[11] This gave Indian programmers the opportunity to acquire technical capability from these two companies and improve their skills in the process. Burroughs also allied itself with TCS, thus enabling TCS to become a world-class IT service firm. Indian firms have also benefitted from the exit of IBM. The Indian government acquired India IBM, nationalized it, and renamed it CMC; it was acquired by TCS in 2002.[12] As a result, various capabilities previously monopolized by India IBM, such as a mainframe support system, infrastructure, skill and human resources, were transferred to many Indian firms and subsequently to TCS during the nationalization period. The acquisition of CMC by TCS was a major milestone in the latter's technical progress.

As India went through the foreign exchange crisis of 1991, it abandoned the Nehru–Mahalanobis model and adopted the Rao–Manmohan model, which veers toward liberalization. With this liberalization came the move to replace FERA's drastic measures with a set of liberal foreign exchange management regulations. This Indian deregulation policy coincided with the accelerated demand for software programming services, as large MNCs moved from mainframe to client–server systems. This move resulted in the large-scale entry of MNCs into India, with the aim of utilizing cheap Indian labor. At the same time, the Indian government reduced import duties on imported software from 1992 to 1995 and provided income tax exemptions from 1993 to 1999. In 1988, the Vajpayee administration also launched a campaign with the slogan "Becoming an IT superpower

by 2008." With this campaign, the administration reformed tax regulations, sold state firms, reduced the financial deficit, expanded the
social infrastructure, promoted foreign investment, increased the software development fund, formed a task force to establish a long-term IT
strategy, and created the Ministry of Information Technology.

Path-creation of Indian firms: the body shop model→offshoring→GDM

The OEM–ODM–OBM path outlines the three observed stages in a
typical catch-up process of latecomers in manufacturing industries.[13]
According to Hobday (2003), firms in East Asian countries, such as
Korea, Taiwan, and Hong Kong, follow a transition path from OEM
to ODM and then to OBM. East Asian manufacturers were OEM firms
which were subcontractors of MNCs from the 1960s to 1970s. In the
1980s, they then moved to ODM, a variation of OEM, before finally
settling for OBM in the 1990s. Thus far, no study has yet presented
a detailed examination of the catch-up process of latecomers in the
service industry, or identified its stages and differences, unlike with the
OEM-ODM-OBM path. Therefore, the current study shows that
Indian IT service firms also followed the processes of catching up and
upgrading through several stages or business models. These firms'
catch-up stage includes three models: body shopping, offshoring, and
GDM. Table 8.1 shows the main features of each model and the three
steps in manufacturing. These three steps can be explained in detail
using TCS as an example, the oldest of three firms involved in the IT
service business included in this study.

The opportunity for body shopping (i.e. dispatching the manpower
of Indian firms to clients) emerged because of a growing shortage of
computer engineers in the USA and Europe since the 1970s, in contrast
to the oversupply of Indian engineers relative to domestic demand.[14]
Moreover, India was a viable manpower resource pool because of the
high international regard for the skills of Indian engineers and the large
Indian diaspora in the USA. IBM's exit from India necessitated the
outsourcing of application development work for Indian companies.[15]
Therefore, in 1971, TCS began sending Indian engineers to Burroughs
for the application development of the police station in Detroit in the
USA. At that time, TCS provided services to American customers in the
form of a body shop (or body staffing), that is, TCS only dispatched

Table 8.1 *Three stages of catch-up in manufacturing vs. IT service*

Manufacturing in East Asia		IT service in India	
Stages	Characteristics	Stages	Characteristics
OEM (own equipment manufacturing)	• Doing assembly-type production using its own equipment but based on designs and orders from MNCs • MNCs in charge of designs, marketing, R&D, and brand management	Body shop	• Manpower of Indian firms sent to clients firms without control over them • As subcontractors, performed simple jobs, such as coding
ODM (own design manufacturing)	• Production with its own designs accepted by vendor MNCs • MNCs in charge of marketing, distribution, and brand management	Offshore	• Now Indian firms managing and controlling their human resources • Prime subcontractors of MNCs • Upgrading to ADM service • Still depend on MNCs for marketing
OBM (own brand manufacturing)	• Producing and selling its own brand products • Now independent and in charge of all value chains	GDM (global delivery model)	• Independence covering all value chains • Combining onsite, offshore, and nearshore services • Upgraded to involve a full range of IT services

Note: stages in manufacturing are based on Hobday (2000, 2003); adaptation using information from Lee, Park, and Krishnan (2011).

Indian manpower to clients, but the latter did not have any responsibility in managing and controlling them.[16] From the late 1960s to the
1970s, TCS served as a subcontractor of multinational IT firms such as
Burroughs, IBM, and ICL. TCS also supplied low-value-added jobs,
such as coding programs of computer hardware produced by multinational IT firms. Thus, the catch-up process of TCS during this period
was similar to OEM because TCS depended largely on MNCs.

Offshoring refers to the production system introduced by American
MNCs to retain their leadership after hurdling the economic difficulties
of the 1980s. These firms enthusiastically introduced this system to
save on costs after experiencing the post-dotcom recession. However,
at that time, offshoring centers served mainly as subsidiaries or captive
development centers that were established overseas by MNCs. An
example of an offshore client is TI, which set up its captive development
center in Bangalore in 1985. The captive development center (subsidiary)
employed cheap Indian manpower and required employees to write
software, which was exclusively supplied to TI in the USA. Although
these subsidiary/offshoring models of MNCs were deemed effective in
terms of cost savings, they posed several disadvantages. Moreover,
MNCs invested a substantial amount of capital and resources as well
as struggling with local regulations and cultural differences to set up and
operate their respective subsidiaries.

Indian IT service firms, specifically Infosys,[17] carefully observed the
captive center of TI and pursued their respective niches. Infosys finally
found that it could deal with all these concerns on behalf of the offshoring subsidiaries of MNCs, so that MNCs would not have to set up
and operate them. In this sense, Infosys and other Indian IT service
firms reinvented the existing offshoring concept as an independent
business model for the IT service industry. The Indian offshore model
spread internationally as a new business model of IT service. Offshoring is a business model that enables the utilization of cheaper labor
offsite, with Indian firms being responsible for managing and controlling manpower. However, the marketing activities of TCS still relied on
multinational IT firms. This dependence is similar to ODM in manufacturing in terms of relying on MNCs for marketing and distribution.
Similar to ODM firms that acquire the capabilities of production and
design, TCS developed its own software and established a new business
model for offshoring that, in turn, performed additional tasks aside
from the usual coding.

The GDM first emerged in the mid 1990s when TCS upgraded its offshore model to a highly advanced business model that effectively combines onsite, offshore, and nearshore businesses. Since the 1990s, the need for further cost reduction has become more pressing among European and US companies. The demand for low-wage service labor has become high, and MNCs see a greater demand for a globally standardized IT service for their offices located around the world. These changes in the client firms motivated IT service firms to maximize the use of standardized jobs utilizing cheap manpower offshore and to minimize interaction with clients on site. Thus emerged so-called nearshore centers, that is, service delivery centers in locations where cultures and languages are similar to those of the clients. In sum, GDM maximizes efficiency and reduces cost by combining onsite, offshore, and nearshore activities at a proper ratio;[18] its essence is that it can deliver a full range of services.

Initially, Indian IT service firms mainly used to provide low-value-added services, such as ADM and testing, in the offshoring model. However, they gradually moved up the value chain through consulting and system integration. The full service range of Indian IT service firms, which spans the opposite ends of the value chain, gives customers various choices. Although some design functions continue to be provided by the client MNCs or their consultants, the high degree of independence and comprehensiveness in business activities is similar to that which characterized OBM firms in manufacturing.

In sum, Indian firms created their own unique paths or business models within the IT service industry, thus leapfrogging to more advanced phases of development. These firms first reinvented the offshoring model and later created the GDM, which became the global industry standard. The companies then underwent three steps of development, gradually progressing from the body shop model to offshoring and finally to GDM.

8.4 Overcoming the middle-income trap: China's strength in short-cycle technologies

China's catch-up and three modes of learning

When China initiated its open door and reform policies in 1978, its per capita income was less than 10 percent of the world average in terms of PPP-adjusted dollars in 2000 prices.[19] According to a calculation derived from the World Bank's world development indicators, as of the time of writing, China's per capita income has reached about half the world average, a truly remarkable achievement. Among transitional economies, China alone has maintained and accelerated its growth during its transition from a socialist planned economy. China's economic success has recently been called the Beijing Consensus.[20] Thus, comparing China with the Washington Consensus and East Asian model is appropriate.

The Washington Consensus can be compared with the East Asian model in terms of policy sequencing and of any element missing from the Washington Consensus. The idea of sequencing originates from Rodrik (1996), who first explored the puzzlingly slow growth of Latin America, the economies of which have more closely followed the Washington Consensus than have those of East Asia. Rodrik's observation, as summarized in Table 8.2, is that although Latin America endorsed and attempted all ten elements of the Consensus more or less simultaneously, East Asian countries (e.g. Korea and Taiwan) adopted only the first half (macroeconomic stabilization, items (1) to (5)) and yet maintained microeconomic intervention by not committing to the second half (i.e. privatization, liberalization, deregulation, etc.) until the later stages.

When we compare the East Asian experience with the elements of the Washington Consensus, we also argue that the mixed results of the latter Consensus are probably related to policy sequencing and missing or neglected policies, such as technology policies and revolutions in higher education.[21] As shown in Part B of Table 8.2, these policy elements are absent from the Washington Consensus, whereas they can be considered the core elements of the East Asian or the BeST Consensus. The difference between successful Asian and less successful Latin American economies is the priority given to policies that enhance long-term growth potential, technology, and specifically higher education.

In these aspects, China seems to have closely followed the East Asian consensus. First, China followed the example of Korea and Taiwan in emphasizing export orientation, following its comparative advantages in labor-intensive products.[22] Second, the similarity is clear not only in terms of the micro-interventions but also in the emphasis on elements missing from the Washington Consensus, such as technology policies and higher education reforms. China has pushed strongly for increased R&D expenditure, reaching the 1 percent ratio in 2000 and currently nearing 2 percent, thus outstripping other middle-income countries by

Table 8.2 *Washington Consensus vs. East Asian Consensus*

A Elements of the Washington Consensus	Korea	Taiwan	China
A1 Macroeconomic stabilization			
1 Fiscal discipline	Yes, generally	Yes	Yes, generally
2 Redirection of public expenditure to health, education, and infrastructure	Yes	Yes	Yes, generally
3 Tax reform, broadening the tax base, and cutting marginal tax rates	Yes, generally	Yes	Yes, since 1994
4 Unified and competitive exchange rates	Yes, except for limited periods	Yes	Yes, since 1994
5 Secure property rights	Yes, except during the early periods	Yes, generally	Mixed
A2 Privatization, deregulation, and liberalization			
6 Deregulation	Limited	Limited	Limited
7 Trade liberalization	Limited until the 1980s	Limited until the 1980s	Limited until 2002
8 Privatization	No: many SOEs in the 1950s and 1960s	No: many SOEs in the 1950s and 1960s	Partly no; SOEs still important
9 Elimination of barriers to foreign direct investment	FDI heavily restricted	FDI subject to state control	FDI regulated in some sectors
10 Financial liberalization	Limited until the 1980s	Limited until the 1980s	Limited until the 1980s
B Elements missing from the Washington Consensus			
11 Export promotion plus import tariffs	Yes, very strong	Yes	Yes, very strong
12 Technology policy for upgrading	Yes, since 1970	Yes, since the 1980s	Given priority since the mid 1990s
13 Higher education revolution	Yes, since the 1980s	Yes, generally	Yes, since the mid 1990s

Sources: Lee, Jee, and Eun (2011) and Lee (2006); originally, part A for Korea and Taiwan are from Rodrik (1996, Table 3), and China and part B are from the current author.

a wide margin. Third, in terms of the tertiary education enrollment ratio, China started in 1990 at a much lower level of 3.4 percent compared with the 20 percent average of nine middle-income countries. However, by 2010, the figure reached 20 percent, a value closer to or higher than those of Brazil, Costa Rica, and Mexico. This rapid progress is related to the higher education revolution and the 20 percent annual increase in the college student population since 1998.

However, it can also be argued that China follows neither the Washington Consensus nor the East Asian model but rather a third model. On the one hand, China boasts a relatively large number of big businesses, such as Lenovo (which acquired the personal computer business of IBM), Haier (the largest refrigerator maker in the world), Changhong, TCL, Konka, Huawei, and other firms. These are brand leaders in Chinese markets that are also successfully competing against MNCs, although they are not yet strong in terms of design capability and mostly undertake final assembly. They may be treading the path of Korean big businesses. Indeed, some firms are similarly leapfrogging straight into OBM without engaging in ODM. On the other hand, Chinese SMEs have developed in close cooperation with MNCs from neighboring economies in Asia and the West. They also seem to be following the Taiwanese or Southeast Asian path of gradual catch-up with the sequential stages of OEM, ODM, and OBM. The size and complexity of China require an economy that exhibits two or more model types, that is, an economy that acts as a combination of large companies, smaller companies, and FDI firms.

Considering the micro- or firm-level dimension of the Chinese economy, a unique strategy for learning technological capabilities and access to foreign knowledge can be observed. As noted by Lee, Jee, and Eun (2011), the unique Chinese features include the following three elements: (1) an emphasis on "forward engineering" (the role of university spin-off firms) in contrast to the reverse engineering of Korea and Taiwan; (2) the acquisition of technology and brands through international M&As; and (3) parallel learning from FDI firms to promote indigenous companies. These three elements comprise the Beijing model, as they have not been explicitly adopted by Korea and Taiwan. These elements actually represent three new modes of learning that are not discussed in the preceding chapter when we discussed learning by co-development, overseas R&D outpost, and public–private consortia. What follows is a brief summary of these three elements.[23]

Parallel learning by trading market for technology

Realizing the attractiveness of China's market size and the bargaining power associated with it, the Chinese government has actively approached multinational suppliers to engage in technology transfer and joint venture negotiations, adopting a purposeful strategy of "trading the (domestic) market for (foreign) technology." Although this strategy has not been entirely successful, there are cases in which it has worked and contributed to technological catch-up, with the tele-communications equipment industry as an excellent example. China took advantage of its large market size to pressure its foreign partner to transfer core technology to the local partner. Shanghai Bell and other joint venture establishments fostered the diffusion of technological know-how on digital telephone switches across the country. Thus, indigenous manufacturers emerged and began to compete directly with joint ventures in the mid 1990s, initially in rural markets and subsequently in urban markets. This process is called "parallel learning" (Eun, Lee and Wu 2006). Although a similar diffusion of knowledge also occurred in Southeast Asian countries, China was more successful in turning diffusion into the promotion of indigenous companies. In this sector, China achieved a stage-skipping catch-up. As China had limited experience in developing and producing electromechanical switches, it skipped the development and production of analog electronic switches and jumped directly to digital automatic switch production. Similar phenomena are taking place in other sectors. The Chinese authorities regard a joint venture as a channel through which learning about technology can take place. Thus, even after its entry into the World Trade Organization, the Chinese government has made no commitment to lifting the cap on foreign shares in joint ventures in key industries, including the automobile, telecommunications, and banking sectors. This continuing restriction on foreign shares is in sharp contrast to the market opening exemplified by the present lowering of tariffs to about 10 percent or less on average, which is lower than the average in most developing countries.

Learning from the academia through forward engineering

China has successfully reared a number of national champion firms in high technology sectors by exploiting their own scientific knowledge base, as exemplified by Lenovo, Founder, Tsinghua Tongfang, and Dongruan. These firms have all been established by and affiliated with academic institutions. These academy-run enterprises are widespread in China. Although their share of the national economy is still minimal, their importance in key high-tech regions, such as Beijing and Shanghai, is substantial. The direct involvement of academic institutions in industrial business is called "forward engineering" (Eun et al. 2006; Lu 2000). In the "reverse engineering" strategy, latecomer firms acquire technological principles by conducting autopsies on final (typically imported) products. Reverse engineering is a *bottom-up* mode, whereas forward engineering is a *top-down* mode of technological development, in which the creators (academic institutions), who already possess scientific knowledge, further process nascent knowledge until it can be applied to commercial uses. Forward engineering is an inherently Chinese characteristic that differentiates China from other East Asian countries. Taiwan and Korea have rarely exploited their academic institutions for technological development, with academia mainly supplying engineers to local firms. By contrast, Chinese universities and research institutes, such as those under the banner of the Chinese Academy of Sciences, have played an active role in commercializing new technologies using the results of their research projects.

Learning by international M&As and going global
Until the 1990s, the Chinese outward FDI was highly regulated compared with the major source countries for FDI. However, a significant shift in policy was made at the Chinese Communist Party's sixteenth Congress in 2002 when the Premier announced a new strategy for encouraging Chinese companies to "Go Global" by investing overseas. The policy change seemed to reflect a desire on the part of the Chinese government to acquire foreign technologies and brands, as can be seen from many M&As targeting foreign companies in the manufacturing sector. This strategy serves the objective of saving time for catch-up, considering that it will take a long time and great effort to build brands and technologies of its own. A well-known case is Lenovo's purchase of the PC division of IBM in 2004 and TCL's acquisition of a German company (Schneide). The move by BOE, a Chinese cathode ray tube (CRT) maker, to acquire the Korean company Hynix's TFT-LCD division (HYDIS) had more to do with the technology than the brand.[24] Similar cases of targeting foreign technologies include Geerly's acquisition of Volvo, D'rong's acquisition of a German

passenger airplane maker (Fairchild-Dornier), and Shanghai Automobile's acquisition of a Korean carmaker SsangYong.

China and the middle-income trap

As China achieves a remarkable catch-up, reaching more than the 20 percent level of the per capita income level of the USA (Figure 1.2), it faces challenges that are shifting over time and becoming increasingly similar to those of other middle-income developing economies.[25] Yao Yang already discussed the end of the Beijing Consensus, noting problems such as corruption, increasing inequality, and policy authoritarianism, and warned about the possibility of China falling into the middle-income country trap. Thus, ascertaining whether China will indeed fall into this trap is an interesting task.

Here, we apply two criteria in assessing China's ability to move beyond the middle-income country trap. Based on the number of studies, the first criterion is whether China is innovative enough to achieve a certain level of technological capability, and the second is whether China has been generating a large number of world-class big businesses comparable with those of other high-income countries.[26]

Recently, there have been several promising signs for China with regard to the first criterion of the technological capability necessary to pass the middle-income trap. First, the increasing number of patent applications abroad (particularly in the USA) seems to reflect the enhanced innovation of Chinese firms. Table 8.3 shows that the number of US patents filed by China reached more than 2,500, much more than that of other middle-income countries, at fewer than 300 patents per year. In terms of growth rates of patents, China is now the first in the world in the first decade of 2000, whereas Korea dominated in the 1990s. Another outlier among the middle-income countries seems to be India, with more than a thousand patents per year.

Another important indicator of China's strength has to do with the fact that Chinese firms filed more patents in short-cycle technologies. As shown in Table 8.4, which classifies US patents by the assignee's nationality, the top thirty technologies in China's US patents are similar to those (shown in Table 3.5) of Korea and Taiwan from 1980 to 1995. The Chinese have more patents in semiconductors, information storage, telecommunications, electrical lighting, electrical heating, X-rays, and computer hardware and software. Table 8.4 also

Table 8.3 *US patents filed by selected countries: 1981 to 2010*

Country	1981	1985	1990	1995	2000	2005	2008	2009	2010
USA	39,218	39,556	47,391	55,739	85,068	74,637	77,502	82,382	107,792
Japan	8,389	12,746	19,525	21,764	31,295	30,341	33,682	35,501	44,814
Germany	6,304	6,718	7,614	6,600	10,235	9,011	8,914	9,000	12,363
United Kingdom	2,471	2,493	2,792	2,481	3,662	3,142	3,087	3,174	4,302
Taiwan	80	174	732	1,620	4,667	5,118	6,339	6,642	8,238
Korea	17	41	225	1,161	3,314	4,352	7,548	8,762	11,671
China	2	1	47	62	119	402	1,225	1,655	2,657
India	6	10	23	37	131	384	634	679	1,098
Mexico	42	32	32	40	76	80	54	60	101
Brazil	23	30	41	63	98	77	101	103	175
Argentina	25	11	17	31	54	24	32	45	45
Malaysia	1	3	3	7	42	88	152	158	202
Philippines	7	5	4	4	2	18	16	23	37
Thailand	2	1	2	8	15	16	22	23	46
Chile	1	2	2	7	15	9	13	21	22
Indonesia	1	1	3	4	6	10	5	3	6

Note: Figures are patent granted.
Source: data from the USPTO.

shows that the weighted average cycle time of China's technology from 2000 to 2005 is 8.07 years, which is closer to the Korean/Taiwanese average of 7.69 from 1980 to 1995 (Table 3.5) than to Brazil/Argentina's average of 9.26 in the same period (Table 3.6).

Another important comparative criterion is whether China measures up to the three important yardsticks of technological catch-up that have been satisfied in Japan, Korea, and Taiwan in the past.[27] These yardsticks are whether (1) resident patenting catches up with non-resident patenting in a host country; (2) regular invention patents catch up with utility model patents (petit patents); and (3) corporate patenting catches up with individual inventor patenting. In Korea, corporate patents caught up with individual patents in 1986, utility models (or petit patents) caught up with invention patents in 1989, and domestic patents outnumbered those of foreigners in 1993. These patterns in Korea indicate a strong R&D capability led by indigenous large corporations. In general, these patterns are important checkpoints because no other latecomer economies aside from Japan, Korea, and Taiwan have achieved such a catch-up. For typical latecomers, the majority of patents are filed by non-resident foreigners.

These three patterns of catch-up all occurred in China in the first decade of 2000. In terms of the number of patent applications, the share of domestic inventors outgrew that of foreigners in 2003, with domestic inventors filing more than 50,000 applications.[28] In 2004, the number of regular invention patents overtook the number of utility model patents. Then, in 2007, the number of patent applications by corporations overtook that of individual inventors, signifying the growing importance of corporate innovation.

Now we turn to the second criterion of the number of world-class big businesses. Evidence is accumulating at the micro-level, supporting the rapid rise of big businesses and their capabilities in China.[29] A study confirms the significant and robust relationship between the number of big businesses, such as the Fortune 500 firms, and national economic growth even after controlling for the size factor.[30] This study shows that among the latecomer countries, a few successful ones like China and Korea have more big businesses than predicted by country size, which can be a basis for arguing that going beyond the status of middle-income countries requires generating a certain number of such big businesses.

According to Table 8.5, as of 2010, China had twenty-three companies in the *Financial Times* (FT) top 500 and an impressive

Table 8.4 *Top thirty technologies in China's US patents and their cycle times, 2000 to 2005*

Class	Counts	Cycle time	Class name	Subcategory	Sub-cat name
502	51	8.97	Catalyst, solid sorbent	19	Miscellaneous chemical
514	50	8.20	Drug, bio-affecting and body treating	31	Drugs
435	36	8.22	Molecular biology and microbiology	33	Biotechnology
438	32	6.07	Semiconductor device	46	Semiconductor devices
361	30	8.04	Electrical systems and devices	45	Power systems
360	29	6.47	Dynamic magnetic information storage	24	Information storage
257	28	7.02	Transistors, solid-state diodes	46	Semiconductor devices
424	27	8.52	Drug, bio-affecting and body treating	31	Drugs
455	27	6.17	Telecommunications	21	Communications
208	22	9.28	Mineral oils: processes and products	19	Miscellaneous chemical
29	18	9.43	Metal working	52	Metal working
585	18	9.53	Chemistry of hydrocarbon compounds	19	Miscellaneous chemical
362	16	7.76	Illumination	42	Electrical lighting
423	16	9.74	Chemistry of inorganic compounds	19	Miscellaneous chemical
526	13	9.45	Synthetic resins or natural rubbers	15	Resins
280	12	8.21	Land vehicles	55	Transportation
324	12	8.28	Electricity: measuring and testing	43	Measuring and testing
385	12	6.12	Optical waveguides	21	Communications
219	11	8.96	Electric heating	49	Miscellaneous electrical

359	11	7.53	Optics: systems and elements	54	Optics
363	11	6.99	Electric power conversion systems	45	Power systems
378	11	7.63	X-ray or gamma ray systems or devices	44	Nuclear and X-rays
530	11	7.25	Chemistry: natural resins or derivatives	15	Resins
62	10	9.66	Refrigeration	69	Miscellaneous others
451	10	9.93	Abrading	51	Materials-processing and handling
428	9	8.36	Stock material or miscellaneous articles	69	Miscellaneous others
439	9	7.98	Electrical connectors	41	Electrical devices
446	9	10.84	Amusement devices: toys	62	Amusement devices
525	9	9.18	Synthetic resins or natural rubbers	15	Resins
206	8	10.21	Special receptacle or package	68	Receptacles
252	8	7.06	Compositions	19	Miscellaneous chemical
370	8	5.38	Multiplex communications	21	Communications
375	8	7.06	Pulse or digital communications	21	Communications
556	8	8.91	Organic compounds	14	Organic compounds
702	8	6.65	Data processing: measuring, testing	22	Computer hardware and software
Sum	608	8.07	% of the period total (1107) = 54.9%		

Note: the value 8.07 at the bottom of the table is the average time weighted by counts.

Source: author's own calculation using the NBER data file (https://sites.google.com/site/patentdataproject/Home).

Table 8.5 *Number of global companies by country, 2000 to 2010*

		2000	2004	2007	2008	2009	2010
FT 500 (rank by market capitalization)	USA	218	231	184	169	181	163
	Japan	77	55	49	39	49	42
	China	–	–	8	25	27	23
	India	3	2	8	13	10	16
	Korea	5	3	6	5	5	6
	Germany	20	19	20	22	20	19
	France	26	28	32	31	23	27
	UK	46	42	41	35	32	32
Fortune Global 500	USA	179	189	162	153	140	139
	Japan	107	82	67	64	68	71
	China	10	15	24	29	37	46
	India	1	4	6	7	7	8
	Korea	12	11	14	15	14	10
	Germany	37	34	37	37	39	37
	France	37	37	38	39	40	39
	UK	38	35	33	34	26	29

Source: adapted from Table 5 in Lee, Jee, and Eun (2011) which uses figures from: http://money.cnn.com/magazines/fortune/global500/; http://specials.ft.com/ln/specials/global_ft500004.htm http://specials.ft.com/ln/specials/global_ft500004.htm.

forty-six in the Fortune 500 list in 2010 and more recently sixty-three in 2011. In terms of the number of Fortune Global 500 companies, as of 2012, China now far surpasses all major European countries, such as France (thirty-nine), Germany (thirty-seven), and the United Kingdom (twenty-nine), and commands the second largest number after only the USA. However, the fact that China boasts only a limited number of big companies from the manufacturing sector, such as Bao Steel, Shanghai Auto, and First Automotive, are a part of China's weakness, although this share of manufacturing is fast increasing over time. These observations of emerging Chinese companies are in sharp contrast to the gloomy description of Chinese companies during the 1990s given in a number of studies.[31] At that period, China did not have any companies in the UK R&D scoreboard and FT 500; China only had ten listed companies in the Fortune Global 500.

Furthermore, we see many cases of Chinese indigenous firms upgrading to the status of OBM and globally competitive companies. China now boasts a relatively large number of big firms, such as Lenovo, Haier, Changhong, TCL, and Huawei, among others, which are considered brand leaders in their respective sectors. Some of these Chinese companies are not just leaders in the domestic market but global players across a wide spectrum of industries as well. One fascinating case is that of the China International Marine Container Group (CIMC), which has dominated the world of global shipping containers in recent years, boasting a market share of over 55 percent.[32] A significant characteristic of this company is that it has gradually penetrated every segment of the container market, including high-end segment products with refrigeration, electronic tracking, internal tanks, and folding mechanisms, all of which are niches that specialized European container-makers believed they could defend. In learning to innovate, this firm uses various channels, such as licensing and many M&As of existing companies in Korea and Europe.

An increasing number of success stories and the previously stated figures serve as powerful counter-arguments against the belittling of Chinese companies. They also serve as evidence that Chinese companies are no longer simply low-end or OEM producers. They are now in the process of upgrading into higher-end-brand producers and leapfrogging into emerging technologies such as renewable energies.

8.5 Technological turning points in China and India

To verify whether China has reached the "turning point" in technological specialization, Figure 8.3 draws a trend of the average cycle times of technologies from the US patents held by China and India. The average cycle time of China reached its peak around the mid 1990s, ten years later than Korea or Taiwan, and has turned to a clear downward trend toward the eight-year line from its peak of ten years. Although the time series is a little short, we can conclude that China has already passed the turning point. However, as shown in comparison, the case of India is not yet certain. India's cycle time seems to have reached its peak of about eleven years around the late 1990s, but its downward trend is not yet certain, as it is hovering around the ten-year line, even

Table 8.6 *Top thirty technologies in India's US patents and their cycle times, 2000 to 2005*

Class	Count	Cycle time	Class name	Sub-category	Sub-cat name
424	142	8.52	Drug, bio-affecting and body treating compositions	31	Drugs
514	132	8.20	Drug, bio-affecting and body treating compositions	31	Drugs
435	104	8.22	Chemistry: molecular biology and microbiology	33	Biotechnology
568	50	9.81	Organic compounds – part of class 532–570 series	14	Organic compounds
549	49	9.50	Organic compounds – part of class 532–570 series	14	Organic compounds
546	41	8.36	Organic compounds – part of class 532–570 series	14	Organic compounds
423	38	9.74	Chemistry of inorganic compounds	19	Miscellaneous chemical
564	32	10.64	Organic compounds – part of class 532–570 series	14	Organic compounds
540	25	8.15	Organic compounds – part of class 532–570 series	14	Organic compounds
548	25	8.83	Organic compounds – part of class 532–570 series	14	Organic compounds
502	24	8.97	Catalyst, solid sorbent, or support	19	Miscellaneous chemical
562	21	10.32	Organic compounds – part of class 532–570 series	14	Organic compounds
560	20	10.01	Organic compounds – part of class 532–570 series	14	Organic compounds
544	19	8.38	Organic compounds – part of class 532–570 series	14	Organic compounds
536	18	8.38	Organic compounds – part of class 532–570 series	14	Organic compounds
326	15	5.66	Electronic digital logic circuitry	46	Semiconductor devices
426	15	10.28	Food or edible material: compositions and products	61	Agriculture, husbandry, food
702	15	6.65	Data processing: measuring, calibrating, or testing	22	Computer hardware and software

252	14	7.06	Compositions	19	Miscellaneous chemical
526	13	9.45	Synthetic resins or natural rubbers	15	Resins
210	12	9.90	Liquid purification or separation	19	Miscellaneous chemical
800	12	6.16	Multicellular living organisms and unmodified parts		
327	11	7.54	Miscellaneous electrical nonlinear devices, circuits, and systems	41	Electrical devices
528	11	9.12	Synthetic resins or natural rubbers	15	Resins
73	8	9.13	Measuring and testing	43	Measuring and testing
504	8	7.98	Plant protecting and regulating compositions	11	Agriculture, food, textiles
264	7	10.11	Plastic and nonmetallic article shaping or treating	51	Materials-processing and handling
324	7	8.28	Electricity: measuring and testing	43	Measuring and testing
525	7	9.18	Synthetic resins or natural rubbers	15	Resins
75	6	9.29	Specialized metallurgical processes, compositions	52	Metal-working
208	6	9.28	Mineral oils: processes and products	19	Miscellaneous chemical
365	6	5.74	Static information storage and retrieval	24	Information storage
554	6	10.32	Organic compounds – part of class 532–570 series	14	Organic compounds
585	6	9.53	Chemistry of hydrocarbon compounds	19	Miscellaneous chemical
Total	925	8.71	% of the period total (1111) = 83%		

Note: the value 8.71 at the bottom of cycle time is the average time weighted by counts.
Source: author's own calculation using the NBER data file.

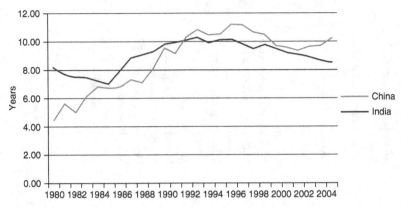

Figure 8.3 Technological turning points in China and India: average cycle time in patents.
Note: for smoothing, five-year moving averages are shown.
Source: author's own calculation using the NBER data file, (https://sites.google. com/site/patentdataproject/Home).

showing recent signs of getting longer again. As shown in Table 8.6, the average cycle time of technologies in India's US patents was 8.7 years in the first half of the 2000s, which can be regarded as somewhat longer than that of China (8.07) but shorter than the Brazil/Argentina's average of 9.26 in the same period.

Based on this discussion, we conclude with caution that Chinese industry will rise to become an industry populated by high-end or brand producers and will not simply remain as a low-end-good or OEM-based industry. In general, China is achieving a "compressed catch-up" with the developed world, avoiding some of the risks involved in the process. By following the East Asian sequencing instead of the Washington Consensus, China has avoided the risk of the "liberalization trap," in which premature financial liberalization leads to a crisis-reform cycle or macroeconomic instability. In this sense, the current Beijing model seems a natural extension of the earlier gradual, pragmatic approach to economic reform, which has been largely responsible for China's early success. If we broaden our perspective beyond the area of technology, China is facing more challenges, such as issues of rising inequality, environmental degradation, and corruption. Although these topics are serious problems, they fall outside the scope of this book.

PART IV

Technological turning points and conclusion

9 | Hypothesizing a theory of technological turning points

9.1 Introduction

This chapter addresses a number of issues that remain to be discussed on the topic of specialization in short-cycle technologies. The first has to do with whether a single variable of cycle times of technologies can sufficiently explain the complex process of technological development. The second is the generalizability of the technological turning point phenomenon, specifically whether this turning point can and should occur in every successful catching-up economy. Given that the curve of cycle time always exhibits short-term vertical fluctuations, a third question that remains to be answered is how to ascertain whether an economy is in fact experiencing such a turning point. Finally, specialization in short-cycle technologies may not be the only path toward successful technological development for latecomers and a closer consideration of alternatives is in order.

9.2 A single-variable theory?

Given this book's heavy emphasis on the cycle time of technologies, one may wonder whether, as a single variable, cycle time can sufficiently explain the complex process of technological development. However, cycle times reflect changes in many other aspects of technological development, and as an explanatory variable, it performs much better than alternatives in the literature such as technological opportunity. In the remainder of this section, we discuss the relationship of cycle time to other variables including technological diversification, localization of knowledge creation, and technological opportunity.

The first variable we examine is that of technological diversification. We find that the process of technological diversification has actually been accompanied by the process of increasing specialization in short-cycle time technologies. Korea and Taiwan's cycle-time curves have shown a gradual shortening since the mid 1980s. This gradual shortening does not mean that these economies have increasingly specialized in only a small number of sectors, but rather that they kept entering into progressively newer sectors with shorter cycle times. This is essentially a process of industrial diversification.

Figure 9.1(a) shows the number of technological fields in which Korea and Germany have registered patents out of 417 three-digit fields in the US patent classification system. It is clear from the figure that Korea has engaged keenly in technological diversification since the mid 1980s. It has registered patents in a growing number of fields, starting with just 50 fields in the 1980s to achieve more than 250 fields by the year 2000. Although its number of patents is still fewer than that of Germany, with patents in more than 350 fields, Korea has made an impressive catch-up. The graph indicates that the process of entering into shorter-cycle technologies since the mid 1980s (Figure 1.4) also involves a process of technological diversification. Figure 9.1(b) shows the same technological diversification, but with figures normalized by dividing the number of patent classes registered by each country by the total number of patent classes (417). High-income countries have generally registered patents in about 40 percent of the 417 classes in the US patent system. The gains made by Korea and Taiwan are impressive, especially when compared to other middle-income countries which started at the same level. By the early 1990s, Korea and Taiwan had effectively surpassed the level of average high-income countries and had reached the 60 percent level that is more akin to that of the top G5 countries.

These findings are related to Imbs and Wacziarg's (2003) U-shaped curve showing the evolution of sectoral concentration in relation to per capita income. They show that countries tend initially to diversify their economic activity so that it becomes more equally spread across various sectors, and that there comes a point relatively late in the development process at which they begin to specialize again. Supporting the trend to first diversify, scholars have identified the diversification of export structure as a necessary condition for sustained export performance and economic growth, and as a key challenge faced by developing countries.[1]

The gradual nature of diversification begs the question of which sectors diversification should encompass. Although Hidalgo et al. (2007) consider proximity between product spaces to be an important

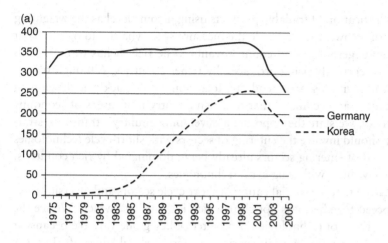

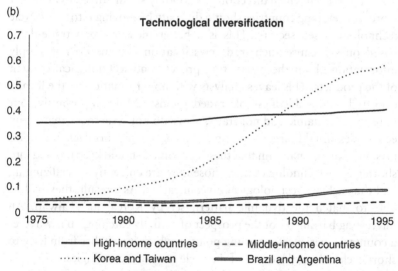

Figure 9.1 Technological diversification in selected countries: (a) the number of fields with patents registered by Korea and Germany; (b) the number of filed patents divided by 417, total number of classes.

Note: five-year moving averages are shown for smoothing the curves.

Source: drawn by the author using the NBER patent data.

variable in determining the feasibility of diversification, they consider the matter to be more about distance and less about specific directions of specialization based on the nature of the products in question. To this end, Hausman et al. (2007) developed a measure of the sophistication of tradable products using income level as the weighting factor. However, this made the measure somewhat tautological. That is, it suggests that if a country wants to be rich, it has to move into goods currently being produced by richer countries. Although typical research in this area tends to focus on how quickly a developing country can become similar to a rich country in its areas of economic activity, we state the opposite: a developing country's transition strategy should involve the entering of sectors with short-cycle technologies instead of entering sectors already being dominated by rich countries, namely those with long-cycle technologies.

Given that the specialization in short-cycle sectors and diversification proceed together, it is not clear which is "causing" which. We see the cycle times of technologies as a better policy-guide variable because it indicates to us in which direction an economy should diversify. In other words, developing countries should diversify by moving into short-cycle technology-based sectors. This is a better measure than trade-data-based ones because such trade classification systems do not supply information about the production process and technological content of the products. This leaves analysts with no information on the locally captured value-addedness of traded goods.[2] More importantly, our criterion is dynamic and not static, as we do not state that catching-up economies should target a specific or fixed list of short-cycle technologies. Instead, we maintain that these economies should keep moving into shorter-cycle technologies than those they are currently specializing in, and thus achieve technological diversification. As a result, they will be able to match the dynamic pattern set by Korea and Taiwan. An interesting barometer of the prospect of actually catching up is whether a country experiences a turning point at which it switches from long to short cycles along the curve of the cycle time of technologies.

Both Korea and Taiwan exhibit dual diversification, in that their diversification is both inter-sectoral and intra-sectoral. Inter-sectoral diversification involves the entering of new industries with higher added value, whereas intra-sectoral diversification involves the entering of higher-value-added segments within the same industry. One example of intra-sectoral upgrading or diversification is in the Korean and Taiwanese semiconductor firms that move up the value chain. Many examples of successive entries into higher-value-added industries also exist, such as that of the Tatung group in Taiwan and the Samsung Group in Korea.[3]

In this process of dual diversification and upgrading, the old sectors do not simply give up, but instead upgrade into higher-value-added segments within the same industry. These new, higher-value-added segments are usually based on short-cycle technologies. This process is also a type of diversification, specifically an intra-sector diversification into higher ends. In sum, cycle times are gradually shortened when an economy engages in both intra- and inter-sector diversification. A middle-income economy that fails to realize this dual diversification may become a victim of the "adding-up" problem and the middle-income trap. To avoid this trap, an economy should find new industries or activities that are beyond the capabilities of its next-tier neighbors. Because older industries tend to degrade into lower-value-added activities as they mature, it is important for successful catch-up for an economy to enter into such new industries at progressively earlier stages over time.[4] Without such progressively earlier entry, an economy is doomed to lower-wage activities or industries, with little chance of long-term success.

The second variable we consider is the localization of knowledge creation and diffusion within a national economy, which is an important aspect of structural transformation. This study has found that the localization of knowledge creation occurs increasingly once a country has moved into short-cycle technology-based sectors. As mentioned earlier, this phenomenon occurs because short cycle times quickly obviate existing technologies, and the reliance on existing or older technologies that are already dominated by incumbent countries is reduced. Increasing the localization of knowledge creation takes longer if latecomers try to move into long-cycle technologies. In such cases, the latecomers increase their technological dependence on advanced economies by citing more patents held by them, thus slowing the process of local knowledge creation and diffusion.

As shown in Figure 3.1, the average degree of localization (measured in terms of country-level self-citation) ranged between 8 percent and 10 percent in high income countries. By the year 2000, after about fifteen years of rapid catch-up, Korea and Taiwan's average localization equaled this level. Other middle-income countries did not catch up to a similar level.

Other factors that may affect the speed of the localization of knowledge creation have to be taken into account, one of which is the type and ownership of firms and specifically whether a company is locally owned or foreign. If technological catch-up is led more by foreign firms through measures such as FDI or the creation of subsidiaries of MNCs, a greater reliance is placed on the knowledge base of the parent firm and of the global network. In such a situation, the process of knowledge localization and diffusion may take longer. Although Taiwan relied initially on foreign firms for its economic growth, it has been able to increase its knowledge localization over time because of the gradual generation of locally owned firms (Amsden and Chu 2003: 12–13). Many IT firms in Taiwan are also spin-offs of the same governmental institute, namely ITRI, and thus tend to be naturally networked. Their tendency to share knowledge among themselves has led to a much higher degree of knowledge localization in Taiwan than in Korea (Lee and Yoon 2010).

The above discussion suggests that the variable of localization of knowledge creation and diffusion is more about the question of who is in charge of the catching-up process. In comparison, the variable of cycle time of technologies relates more to how to achieve the catch-up. Both aspects are complementary.

Finally, we argue that cycle time is a better variable for "good" technological specialization than other alternatives such as technological opportunity as measured by the growth rate of patents per field. This opportunity variable has been used in the literature as an indicator of "good" technological specialization, but a robust relationship has yet to be found.[5] Our own analysis in Chapter 4 also confirms the absence of a significant relationship between the variable of technological opportunity and technological catch-up in the cases of Korea and Taiwan. From a latecomer's point of view, specialization in high-opportunity sectors is desirable, but involves a greater risk because such sectors are more crowded with already established companies. Short-cycle technologies are thus a better choice for latecomers because they pose a smaller disadvantage to those who need to rely less on existing technology. Short-cycle technologies are also promising sectors which hold a greater possibility for the emergence of new technologies to replace the old. In other words, short cycle times incur a higher probability, but high opportunity cannot guarantee latecomers this badly needed aspect. Latecomers are thus no longer latecomers in short-cycle sectors as everybody is a newcomer.

In the meantime, we do not posit that there is no strong incumbent company in the short-cycle technology sectors. As a matter of fact, cumulativeness as indicated by the share of patents held by persistent inventors is not necessarily low in these sectors (as shown in Chapter 4). Giants exist in every sector, but the short-cycle technology sector is where some old giants tend to weaken suddenly or face a sudden downfall. The sudden decline of Nokia and Sony are cases in point. By contrast, the old giants tend to persist more successfully in long-cycle sectors such as medicine.

This study has considered many variables representing innovation systems of various dimensions. These include the cycle time of technologies, originality, localization of knowledge creation, innovator concentration, and technological diversification. The study has tried also to identify key variables responsible for growth and catch-up in a number of latecomer economies. We first introduced in Chapter 4 the criterion of whether a particular variable could show clear-cut change in the successful catching-up economies over the catching-up period (or since the mid 1980s). We considered also whether the change indicated by the variable was significantly different from that of other less successful economies. In subsequent chapters, we tested the relationship by econometric analysis.

Two variables, that of originality and innovator concentration, did not pass the test. Economies that were successful in catching up and other developing countries did not differ in their accounts. In contrast, we find that the degree of knowledge localization and technological diversification in economies that have successfully caught up has rapidly increased over time. At the same time, such countries have specialized increasingly in short-cycle technologies. Thus, these three variables seem to hold the key to the question of the mechanism of economic catch-up. As discussed above, they appear also to occur together and to complement each other. Statistically, there is very high degree (as high as 0.7) of correlation between knowledge localization and technological diversification. In contrast, the variable of cycle time does not show such a high correlation with either of the two variables. Also, while advanced countries all tend to show high degrees of knowledge localization and technological diversification, they all seem to have more patents in the long-cycle technologies, which is exactly the opposite of the case with successful catching-up economies. Also, as verified in Chapters 3 and 5, although the variable of knowledge localization shows rapid increases over time in catching-up economies, the variable is significant in the performance equation only in advanced economies and their firms.

The nature of technological diversification appears similar to that of knowledge localization, as has been confirmed in the firm-level analysis conducted in Chapter 5 and by other efforts.[6]

Based on this information, we take both diversification and localization as the end-state variables, and cycle time as an effective transition variable that guides us to the end-state. As explained above, the variable of cycle times of technologies indicates in which direction an economy should diversify. It also promotes faster localization of knowledge creation because a short cycle time means less reliance on existing or old technologies dominated by the incumbent countries. Another way of positioning the three variables is to say that each of them represents one of the major questions of who, how, and what related to technological catch-up. In other words, we can ask "what" catch-up is and define technological catch-up as becoming more like the advanced economies in terms of diversification. The answer then to the questions of "who" will do it and "how" will be that it is more likely to be led by locally owned companies that gradually specialize in short-cycle technologies.

Although typical studies in this area tend to advise latecomer economies to try to become similar to the rich countries in terms of trade and industrial structure, these studies do not mention how latecomers can maintain competitiveness and succeed against the incumbents in the same industries. For instance, they point out that the industrial structure of advanced economies is highly diversified and thus recommend that developing countries should also try to diversify. But they do not tell us how to diversify and what direction to take first. In comparison, the current study suggests that latecomers should avoid both the immediate emulation of rich countries and direct market competition with them. Instead, they should look for their own niches in short-cycle sectors, where they can enjoy a certain level of profitability, as demonstrated by the positive correlation between profitability and specialization in short-cycle technologies discussed in Chapter 5.

A better chance for profitability in short-cycle technologies may be related to the factor of imitation possibility. A recent book by Raustiala and Sprigman (2012: 43–4) observes that imitation tends to reduce the life cycle of products, which is a phenomenon called induced obsolescence. We can thus deduce that the industries with shorter life cycles should be those where the possibility of imitation is the highest. These tend to be the industries where the latecomers perceive greater opportunity for doing business while requiring less rigorous or advanced R&D.

9.3 Turning points in other economies

In acknowledging the important role played by the phenomenon of the technological turning point, it becomes important for us to ascertain whether an economy is indeed experiencing such a turning point. This consideration is important, given that the cycle-time curve will always show short-term vertical fluctuations. One technical solution to this problem is to use the five-year (or higher) moving average instead of annual cycle time data to capture trends and in this way, to minimize the impact of short-term oscillations. Beyond this technical answer, let us discuss how to properly use the curve to analyze the technological development of an economy. This discussion relates particularly to the generalizability of turning points in the context of a wide range of countries.

The issue of the generalizability of the turning point is primarily about whether such a point can be reached by economies other than Korea and Taiwan. Section 8.5 states that China seems to have passed such a turning point in the late 1990s. However, given that the time series is short, we cannot be completely sure that this will actually become a longer trend. One way to decide is to measure the cycle times of China's technologies. If we draw graphs of several groups of economies, the cycle times typically range from five years at the bottom to eleven years at the top, with eight years as the middle point. Therefore, if a country's cycle-time curve shows a clear downward slope and passes the eight-year benchmark, we can be sure that it has passed the turning point and is driving smoothly toward a specialization in short-cycle technologies. As shown in Figure 8.3, China seems to satisfy this condition. Its curve shows a clear, smooth downward slope since the late 1990s, and it approached the eight-year mark in 2005. Additional data points are necessary to more conclusively see if China reaches the range of seven years, which is the case for Korea and Taiwan.

As discussed in section 8.5, India has yet to satisfy this condition. Although it exhibited a peak at eleven years around the late 1990s, its downward journey after peaking has not been straightforward. Instead of passing the nine-year range, it went back up to the ten-year line in 2005. However, India presents a more promising case than Brazil or Argentina, as the curves of these two countries increased again in the 2000s after a short period of declining in the late 1990s, reaching above the ten-year line in 2005 (Figure 9.2(a)). Therefore, we can state

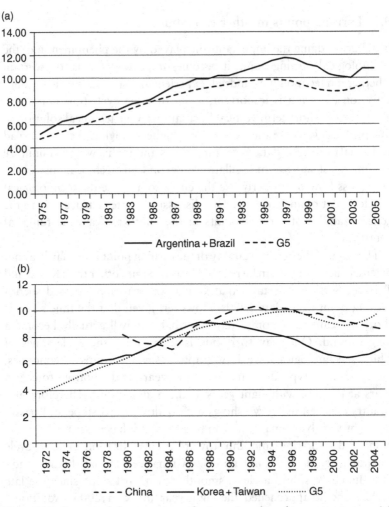

Figure 9.2 Curves of the average cycle times in selected country groups: (a) Brazil and Argentina combined and G5 countries; (b) Korea and Taiwan, China, and the G5 countries.
Note: the G5 countries consist of Canada, Italy, France, Germany, and the United Kingdom. Five-year moving averages are shown in order to smoothen the curves.
Source: drawn by the author using the NBER patent data.

with certainty that these Latin American countries have not yet passed the turning point. If a country pursues a primary commodity- or resource-based development strategy, an upward trend may still emerge, as has been the case since the early 2000s for Brazil and Argentina.

Can an advanced economy show a similar pattern of passing through the turning point? Our answer is no, unless it experiences a major collapse in its industrial structure or it radically restructures its industry toward short-cycle technologies. However, given that cycle times cannot increase infinitely, we may expect some oscillation around high values. Figure 9–2(a) shows the combined curve of the G5 countries, which has oscillated between nine and ten years since the 1990s but has never dropped below nine years.

Figure 9–2(b) compares the curves produced by plotting figures from China, from all the G5 countries, and from Korea and Taiwan combined. First, the figure shows how short the combined cycle times of Korea and Taiwan are compared to those of the G5. The average cycle times in Korea and Taiwan were around six years in 2000, and a gap of about three years has existed between these two countries and the G5 in every corresponding year since the mid 1990s. Second, China seems to be paralleling Korea and Taiwan even though it is about ten or fifteen years behind. Third, as noted in Chapter 6, Korea and Taiwan, both together and individually, have exhibited an upward trend since the early 2000s. We tentatively interpret this as a sign that the technological bases of these economies are maturing as they enter the post-catch-up period.

This last observation is more controversial because we do not know whether the phenomenon in question is a new trend or merely a short-term oscillation. The former case can be called a second turning point, as it signals that the former catching-up economies have ceased further specialization in short cycles. However, regardless of whether this phenomenon is a major turning point or an oscillation, it is in a sense natural and expected because the curve cannot keep moving into infinitely shorter cycle times. Therefore, it is safe to say that the phenomenon in question is a turning point in the sense that the movement toward shorter and shorter cycle times has ceased, although it may not necessarily indicate a decisive move toward technologies with longer cycle times. The question that then arises is when this second turning point should arrive? How long does it take between the first and second turning points? Judging from the curve, it appears that a gap of about fifteen years exists between the two turning points. However, how can we be certain that the curve will turn again and decrease back toward short cycle times?

To answer this question, we first need to gather some additional information on the degree to which knowledge creation and diffusion is localized. This is measured by intranational self-citation. In Chapter 3 (Figure 3.1), we point out that the degree of localization in Korea and Taiwan increased steadily starting in the mid 1980s, and caught up with the level of the G5 by the late 1990s. Given that this ratio is a benchmark for the technological development of latecomers, it reiterates the fact that Korea and Taiwan achieved this catch-up by not moving into the same long-cycle technological fields as the advanced economies and G5 countries, but by moving in the opposite direction toward short-cycle technology fields. That Korea and Taiwan reached a comparable level of localization of knowledge creation by the late 1990s indicates that the industries of these economies were ready to enter a new era. Therefore, we can infer that the second turning point will arrive at approximately the same time at which the localization of knowledge creation reaches the level of advanced economies. Otherwise, any upturn of the curve will only be temporary, and it may turn back again and reach a lower point than before.

More importantly, the actual shape of the curve is affected by other factors such as the country's size, historical legacy, its geography and its climate. For example, the lowest degree of specialization into short-cycle technologies may not be as low for a giant economy like China as it would be for a smaller economy such as Korea. Furthermore, larger economies may be able to increase the localization of knowledge creation more quickly than smaller ones, and as a result, the second turning point may come within a shorter period of time. India's pharmaceutical industry had a very early head start in the 1950s, thanks mainly to strong government initiatives to control local diseases. Given that the pharmaceutical sector is traditionally dominated by long-cycle technologies, the average cycle time of Indian technology remained longer than that of other countries even after it moved significantly toward IT services.

9.4 Resource-based development and other alternatives

Often, prospective newcomers find that it is in fact too late for them to enter certain high-tech industries. In such a case, they may be better off pursing alternative means of economic advancement, such as the pursuit of natural-resource-based industrialization. Indeed, the strong growth of the Brazilian economy in the decade between 2000 and 2010 has been attributed to the export of several key natural resources, and

Chile's salmon industry is another example of natural-resource-based industrialization.[7] Thus, we cannot rule out alternative specializations as key proponents of economic betterment.

According to Table 6.2, a natural-resource-based industry can be viewed as a type of specialization following factor endowments in a way that is similar to the specialization that occurs in labor-intensive industries. It is also intrinsically subject to the medium- or long-term risks of exhausting the very resources with which it was initially endowed, and to the risk that competing production sites emerge in other countries. The challenge is then how to add value to this industry. A combination of new technological imports and R&D efforts is required so that resource-based businesses can be transformed into a segment in the manufacturing category. Otherwise, the natural-resource-based industry cannot serve as a stepping stone toward the development of a high-income economy. Figures 1.1 and 1.2 show that although Brazil grew at a higher rate in the 2000s than in previous decades, this cannot be considered a period of catching-up because the gap with the USA in terms of per capita income was not narrowed. Experts on Latin America, such as Perez (2008), have also described resource-based development as offering only a short window of opportunity. However, such development can also serve as the basis for a self-funded developmental leap, possibly into new emerging industries.

Perez (2008) makes the following analogy between East Asia and Latin America: East Asian tigers acquired their initial capability in the fabrication industries of the 1960s and 1970s, and they used this capability to place themselves in an advantageous position within the emerging ICT paradigm-based industries of the 1990s. Latin American economies can similarly use their current resource exports as a platform and a source of funding with which to begin to enhance their capabilities in preparation for entering the next technological revolution. Perez considers resource-based development as a seed for the future that can help Latin America leapfrog into emerging technologies that combine biotechnology, nanotechnology, bioelectronics, new materials, and new energies.

Historically, important initiatives have generally taken place in the larger, latecomer economies such as those of China, Brazil, and India. As Mathews (2008a) describes, these countries are forging ahead in their search for new development paths that are powered not by traditional fossil fuels, but by alternative energy sources, such as biofuel and other renewable energies. Mathews notes the criticism emerging against these new energy sources, such as that they are not environmentally sustainable (taking land from crops) and that they are low in their input–output energy efficiency (energy-intensive cultivation). However, this criticism has less relevance in the context of such large developing countries where sunshine and desolate landscapes are not in short supply. There is vast scope for producing biofuel using degraded land. Such countries are moving decisively in the direction of new low-carbon economies by developing a range of alternatives, such as wind, solar, and thermal energy, as well as photovoltaic and biogas digesters. In fact, China is leading the game in the area of photovoltaic panel capacity development, leaving even Korea behind in its progress. Brazil has already had some success in producing ethanol-based automobile engines. These new initiatives call for new industrial policy that takes the "latecomer effect" into account and sustains the initiatives through new mandates and incentives.

With nationwide efforts to mobilize physical, financial, and human resources, some latecomers should be able to attain leadership in new technological areas. This exactly describes the concept of leapfrogging as discussed in section 1.3. Leapfrogging into new areas is an effective means of avoiding direct collision with incumbent countries and their technologies. It can result in the development of a profitable niche based on fast or first-mover advantages. Of course, there are risks involved with this strategy, as discussed in section 7.5. The fact that new technologies tend to emerge suddenly and exogenously implies that new windows of opportunity always open up for new entrants. An important advantage of latecomers is also that they are not restricted to the use of technologies that are pre-existing or dominant. The incumbents, in contrast, are faced with the opposite dilemma of whether to keep using existing technologies and paradigms or abandon their investments in favor of new advancements.

Is it reasonable to assume that every middle-income country should specialize in the same short-cycle technologies? This question is analogous to the risk involved when all low-income countries adopt a labor-intensive specialization strategy. In other words, this is the adding-up problem because countries all have to compete against each other in the same areas of specialization. However, whereas specialization based on factor endowments is relatively fixed with few opportunities for change, specialization in short-cycle technologies does not entail having a fixed list of technologies; instead, it suggests specializing in a field or sector where new technologies always emerge to replace obsolete ones. For instance, the Tatung Company in Taiwan has made successive entries into different segments in the broadly defined IT industry since the 1960s.[8] This pattern applies particularly in the IT industry because it allows a continuous movement into new technologies. The nature of the IT industry enables the frequent creation of new generations of products, and this leads to prevalence of short cycle times. In contrast, specializing in a labor-intensive industry, such as clothing industry, does not provide many new opportunities or possibilities for product diversification.

Specializing in short-cycle sectors implies that the economy does not remain long within its existing lines of business, but is always moving into new lines. This is consistent with the concept of leapfrogging. The main criterion by which to assess the potential for technological specialization should be whether the *technological sector has a lesser reliance on existing technologies, and it presents greater opportunity for the emergence of new technologies* (Figure 6.2). Certainly, industries based on digital technologies meet this criterion, along with others based on technologies such as those used in finding new and renewable sources of energy.

9.5 Remaining issues

This book often uses Korean and Taiwanese firms and industries as examples of successful catch-up, leaving us with an intriguing question: did the policy makers in these countries have the criterion of short cycle time in mind as they planned their economic development? While the answer to this question is no, they were in fact always asking themselves, "What's next?" They looked keenly at which industries and businesses were likely to emerge in the immediate future and thought carefully about how to enter the emerging ones. New or emerging industries or businesses are often those with short-cycle technologies because they rely less on existing technology. Therefore, without specifically planning to do so, in effect the policy makers were always pursuing short-cycle industries.

According to Lin's framework, if policy makers choose to target an industry that is new to a latecomer country but mature in the forerunning countries, the industry must offer a latent comparative advantage (Lin 2012c: 154-5). After a certain amount of technological capability has been built up in the latecomer economy, it can then target another industry that is new to both the latecomer and forerunning economies. This is an effort at leapfrogging, and China is already doing this in various industries. Its efforts to this end are exemplified in particular by its solar power and wind power initiatives. Korea also succeeded in leapfrogging in the 1990s through mobile phones and digital TV, as discussed in Chapter 7.

A less explored issue is how latecomer firms in the short-cycle sector can compete against the incumbents from advanced economies. In general terms, this is a question of competiveness among the many firms operating in the same short-cycle-time sector. We have discussed the necessity of initial government support and the sharing of risks and funds, but other dimensions exist, such as corporate strategy, culture, and decision making, which fall outside the realm of industrial policy. Nonetheless the question of how the Korean firms were able to compete against Japanese firms remains, especially since the Korean firms entered business lines in which Japanese firms were well established.

One possible reason for Korea's success is that prompt decision making and timely investment are of critical importance in short-cycle sectors. Therefore, the direct ownership-based management prevalent amongst the Korean *chaebols* presented them with a number of advantages over Japanese firms that were more typically managed by salaried professional managers. Although family ownership is not necessarily required, we can say in principle that short-cycle sectors demand quick decision-making processes and that the corporate management has to be set up to allow for this. Incumbent firms with long histories tend to be more cautious in their decision making and they tend also to be more complacent in their perception and judgment of market conditions, making them less likely to win in the short-cycle technology sectors compared to latecomer firms. While timely decision making is important, quick execution and implementation often matter more in the short-cycle sectors. Latecomer firms from developing countries can be said to have certain advantages in this regard, with longer or more flexible work hours motivated by their strong commitment to catching up with the incumbents.[9] This hypothetical idea should be further explored in future studies.

10 | *Summary and concluding remarks*

10.1 Summary

A number of studies have focussed on the poverty trap, which is a highly relevant topic for low-income countries. By contrast, relatively few studies have investigated the sustaining of growth beyond the middle-income level. Although several studies have proposed that developing countries can take off by targeting industries in which they have comparative advantage, few have discussed the issue of sustaining growth after the initial short-lived spurt of development. Therefore, the questions that motivate this study are as follows. Which factors lead to growth that can be sustained for an extended period? Which factors bring about a short-lived process of catch-up, particularly for middle-income developing countries?

The current study proposes that technological capability is a key factor for sustainable progress. A detailed analysis of the innovation system at three levels (i.e. firm, sector, and country) is conducted using a neo-Schumpeterian perspective. Within each of these three levels, we examine different aspects of innovation systems, including the cycle times of technologies, the localization of knowledge creation and diffusion, the concentration of knowledge creation among innovators, and the originality of technologies.

Empirical analysis shows that successful catching-up economies and their firms gradually specialize in shorter-cycle technologies, thus promoting the localization of knowledge diffusion and creation, as well as enabling further development based on indigenous capabilities. This strategy is a rational one, because sectors with short technological cycle times see the frequent emergence of new technologies and the rapid obsolescence of existing ones. Therefore, latecomer economies need not master the existing technologies dominated by advanced economies, which tend to command more patents in sectors with long cycle times. Furthermore, a complementary relationship exists between

223

specialization in short-cycle technologies and the localization of knowledge creation, because using short-cycle technologies means relying less on existing ones dominated by advanced countries. More importantly, the criterion used in this book is not static but dynamic, as we do not argue that catching-up economies should target a certain or fixed list of short-cycle technologies. Instead, we encourage a dynamic movement into shorter- and shorter-cycle technologies, thereby achieving technological diversification. As demonstrated by Korea and Taiwan, the process of moving into shorter-cycle sectors since the mid 1980s is actually a process of technological diversification.

Technological diversification accompanied by a specialization in short-cycle technologies can be considered a "detour" strategy because the latecomer economies do not attempt to replicate the highly original, long-cycle technologies common in advanced economies. Latecomer countries that have successfully caught up with developed ones were found to have moved initially in the opposite direction toward short-cycle or low-originality technologies. However, as they advanced in their technological development, their own success enabled them to move toward more diverse fields that included technologies with greater originality and long cycle times. This maturing phenomenon has taken place in East Asian countries since the turn of the century. In contrast, however, the less successful middle-income countries, such as Brazil and Argentina, adopted a direct replication strategy focussing on more original and long-cycle technologies. This strategy may have led to a continuous reliance on advanced foreign countries which held the required knowledge, which in turn created few opportunities to localize knowledge creation.

Part II of this book demonstrated the double-edged nature of short-cycle technologies: they can serve either as windows of opportunity or as additional barriers to entry. Although Korea and Taiwan were successful in playing catch-up in the short-cycle sectors, other lower-tier countries encountered difficulties. This disparity can be attributed to the notion of truncated learning, according to which frequent technological changes interfere with the effectiveness of learning, and acquired knowledge becomes obsolete or useless with the advent of new technologies. As shown in Chapters 3 and 4, Latin American countries tend to register more patents in long-cycle sectors, and their economic growth tends to be positively associated with specialization in long-cycle technologies.

The current study proposes a broad roadmap that recommends technological specialization for middle-income developing countries and trade-based specialization for low-income developing countries. The existing literature encourages low-income countries to follow trade-based specialization to exploit comparative advantages associated with their natural resource endowments. In this manner, as predicted by the product life cycle theory, such countries can command international competitiveness in certain industries typically inherited from higher-income countries. Following this line of action, low-income countries may reach middle-income status. However, in countries that employ initial comparative advantages, labor-intensive industries depend on low wages and thus face medium-term risks associated with wage rate increases. Worse, new and lower-cost labor sites in next-tier countries always emerge to take these countries' positions in the global value chain. Therefore, developing countries may be caught in the middle-income country trap associated with the so-called adding-up problem. Moving upward for higher-value-added activities in the same industries and/or gaining entry into newly emerging ones presents a longer-term challenge for developing countries.

A developing country intending to move beyond the middle-income stage can implement technological specialization in short-cycle or emerging technologies, or establish upgraded niches in new segments of current industries. However, these transitions require technological capabilities based on learning and local R&D effort. One effective catch-up strategy is for latecomers to first attempt to enter mature segments in medium- to short-cycle technology sectors, as seen in the indigenous development of telephone switches in Korea, China, India, and Brazil. Upon successful entry, a more ambitious strategy of leapfrogging into emerging technologies may be attempted. An example of this is the development of cell phones and digital TV in Korea or 3G wireless standards in China. Technological specialization involving leapfrogging may, however, present a number of risks, such as the incorrect selection of technologies or standards, and the uncertain availability of an initial market for these technologies. Therefore, gaining entry into new, emerging industries requires government assistance in the form of technological policies that promote public–private R&D consortia, exclusive standard policies, and procurement and user subsidies for initial market provision. These strategies entail much risk but present the only available path toward achieving higher profitability, faster growth, and eventually, high-income status. As such, the above method can be described as a "detour via niche" strategy, which in hindsight may be viewed as a shortcut. Toward the end of this path, a latecomer economy can eventually achieve similar status to the high-income countries that focus on developing long-cycle, short-cycle, and more original technologies.

The rationality of all middle-income countries specializing in the same short-cycle technologies can be questioned. Such an inquiry is analogous to the adding-up problem, which refers to the risks involved in the labor-intensive specialization practiced by all low-income countries. In other words, developing countries that compete against each other in the same area of specialization risk eliminating their initiatives and disrupting the very industries in which they have advantages. Thus, a specialization based on factor endowments is relatively fixed, with few opportunities for change. However, specializing in short-cycle technologies does not entail a fixed list of technologies. Instead, the implication in sectors with short-cycle technologies is that new technologies always emerge to replace existing ones. In other words, the criterion for technological specialization is less about the cycle length itself, but more about the technological sectors that rely less on existing technologies and offer greater opportunities with newly emerging technologies. The short-cycle time variable is merely a proxy for such a criterion. Continuous technological emergence suggests the availability to new entrants of fresh windows of opportunity that are not confined to the old, dominant technologies. This concept is the exact opposite of the product life cycle concept in which latecomers merely inherit old or mature industries (or segments thereof) from the incumbent economies.

10.2 Contributions and limitations

This study conducts a multinational, quantitative analysis of economic catch-up across three dimensions (i.e. firms, sectors, and countries) based on a single consistent framework focussed on the innovation system. This multi-level analysis identifies a consistent set of catch-up determinants: technological cycle time (short cycles) as the transition variable, and the related localization of knowledge creation and technological diversification as the end-point variables Thus, the current study provides rigorous and generalizable findings at both the macro- and micro-levels, and justifies the findings of earlier case studies and qualitative analyses on the importance of knowledge and innovation systems in economic catch-up beyond the middle-income stages of development.

With these results, the current study proposes a comprehensive policy framework for development, as well as a clear-cut criterion for the technological specialization of middle-income countries. The literature on technological specialization has so far failed to provide this. The concepts offered by the current study also differ from the traditional recommendation to focus on trade-based specialization, which is more suitable for low-income countries. Middle-income countries need to specialize in technological sectors that rely less on existing technologies, and that afford the greater opportunities associated with new technologies.

This study also provides a yardstick with which one can assess whether a middle-income country is stuck in the middle-income trap, or if it is in fact moving beyond that to reach the high-income stage. We label this phenomenon the technological turning point, or the point at which cycle time, as measured by the patent portfolio of a country, reaches a peak and the country turns to technologies with short cycle times. Korea and Taiwan passed this turning point in the mid 1980s, and China seems to have reached this point in the mid 1990s, as shown by the graph of cycle times in Chapter 8. The Indian graph also shows a peak in its cycle time in the late 1990s, but a downward trend is not yet clear enough for us to declare that the technological turning point has been passed.

This study contributes significantly to the existing body of knowledge, as no literature has explicitly and theoretically addressed specialization conditions for middle-income countries. The growth identification and facilitation framework of Lin (2012c: 155–6) advises latecomers to closely observe the countries slightly ahead of them, and then to target the mature industries in those countries as their latent comparative advantages. Although such recommendations are a very effective and practical guide for targeting profitable industries, the current study complements that of Lin by providing a theoretical criterion for specialization, namely in sectors based on short-cycle technology. Of course, the whole process should be a gradual movement into shorter-cycle sectors involving multiple stages. At a certain point, however, it becomes prudent to take the risk of leapfrogging into even shorter-cycle sectors and thus reducing catch-up time. In other words, one of the distinctive policy arguments of this book is that sustained catch-up requires not only an entrance into mature industries (which are still new to the latecomers), but also leapfrogging into emerging industries that are new to both the advanced and developing countries.

This book also provides a detailed elaboration of how to build the technological capability required for the journey toward short-cycle technology-based sectors (Chapter 7), focussing on the role of the government or public research institutes and public–private partnerships. We consider capability building to be one of the most binding elements in catching-up growth.

One of the limitations of this multi-dimensional study is the exclusion of the direct interaction of variables representing different dimensions. For example, firm-, sector-, and country-level variables can be grouped together in a single equation, and various interaction terms among them can be created and examined. This aspect is important and interesting, and has already attracted the attention of researchers.[1] This multi-level interaction analysis requires the merging of multinational data at the firm or sector level, which is a greater challenge.

Although we have been able to define and measure several variables in the same manner at all three levels (e.g. cycle time of technologies), certain variables defy our attempts. For instance, the degree of innovation concentration can be measured at the country level but not at the firm level. Furthermore, similar variables tend to assume different names. One example is the variable of localization of knowledge creation, which, when measured at the country level, is essentially equivalent to the appropriability variable at the sector level (which in turn is measured as the percentage of self-citations in the patents in that sector) and to the self-citation ratio measured at the firm level.

Similar analysis can be extended to more countries in more recent times and to include recent cases of economic progress. This will allow us to determine whether the same findings hold in different settings, and to clarify which areas require qualification or modification. Future studies can also focus on the same successful developing economies, such as Korea and Taiwan, in more recent periods. Such research could determine whether these countries behave differently during their post-catch-up periods and whether they are currently converging smoothly with traditional advanced economies.

Appendix tables

Table A1.1 *Economic growth and (a) high-income countries; (b) upper- and low-middle-income countries*

	GDP per capita (in constant 2000 US$)		Annual growth rate of GDP per capita, 1980–95 (%)
	1980	1995	
(a) High-income countries			
Korea, Republic of	3,223	9,164	7.21
Taiwan	4,672	11,287	6.06
Singapore	8,926	19,152	5.22
Hong Kong, China	11,344	22,637	4.71
Luxembourg	19,406	34,032	3.82
Ireland	9,720	16,463	3.58
Japan	23,897	35,304	2.64
Norway	23,148	33,939	2.58
Portugal	6,022	8,789	2.55
Israel	12,270	16,850	2.14
Spain	8,646	11,863	2.13
United Kingdom	15,541	21,176	2.08
Germany	15,727	20,952	1.93
Austria	15,744	20,953	1.92
United States	22,568	29,942	1.90
Italy	12,998	17,085	1.84
Australia	13,860	17,827	1.69
Belgium	15,344	19,680	1.67
Netherlands	15,761	19,956	1.59
Denmark	20,999	26,510	1.57
France	15,810	19,820	1.52
Sweden	19,064	23,121	1.29
Finland	15,431	18,637	1.27
Canada	16,578	19,837	1.20
New Zealand	13,928	16,556	1.16
Iceland	21,685	24,555	0.83
Switzerland	28,646	31,623	0.66
Greece	8,615	8,900	0.22
Average	14,985	20,593	2.14

Table A1.1 (*cont.*)

	GDP per capita (in constant 2000 US$)		Annual growth rate of GDP per capita, 1980–95 (%)
	1980	1995	
(b) Upper-middle- income countries			
Malaysia	1,848	3,468	4.28
Chile	2,494	4,295	3.69
Turkey	1,897	2,660	2.28
Costa Rica	3,314	3,655	0.65
Hungary	3,604	3,748	0.26
Brazil	3,255	3,376	0.24
Argentina	7,551	7,335	−0.19
Mexico	5,121	4,899	−0.30
Venezuela	6,066	5,336	−0.85
South Africa	3,436	2,872	−1.19
Saudi Arabia	16,424	9,131	−3.84
Poland	N/A	3,362	N/A
Average	5,001	4,616	−0.53
Lower-middle-income countries			
China	173	603	8.68
Thailand	798	2,048	6.48
Indonesia	361	753	5.02
India	222	371	3.47
Egypt	934	1,321	2.34
Colombia	1,616	2,077	1.69
Bulgaria	1,335	1,567	1.08
Iran	1,278	1,373	0.48
Romania	1,872	1,768	−0.38
Philippines	990	916	−0.52
Russian Federation	N/A	1,618	N/A
Average	958	1,280	1.95

Note: high-income countries are defined as those where GDP per capita in 2000 constant prices exceeds $10,000 and those that have more than ten US patents in every period. A tax haven (Bahamas) and countries that have dissolved such as Yugoslavia and Czechoslovakia are excluded.

Upper-middle-income countries are defined as those with GDP per capita in 2000 constant prices between $3,000 and $10,000, whereas lower middle-income countries are those with less than $3,000. In both groups, only those countries with more than ten US patents in every period are included. Those that already dissolved are excluded, such as Yugoslavia and Czechoslovakia. N/A means no data available for a certain year.

Source: Drawn up using the data from world development indicators by the World Bank.

Table A3.1 *NIS index by country*

Country	No. of patents	No. of assignees	HHI	CR5	Intra-national	Cycle time	Quality	Originality
(a) Values with patent data with application year of 1990								
United States	53,302	9,954	0.00	0.07	0.27	10.20	339,092	0.39
Japan	22,113	2,005	0.01	0.21	0.35	7.70	118,396	0.32
Germany	7,508	1,543	0.02	0.24	0.19	9.80	26,248	0.32
France	3,053	856	0.01	0.13	0.11	9.97	11,401	0.33
United Kingdom	2,596	845	0.01	0.12	0.10	10.21	10,870	0.34
Canada	1,940	656	0.01	0.09	0.07	10.86	9,190	0.34
Italy	1,284	542	0.01	0.12	0.10	10.13	4,142	0.32
Switzerland	1,199	362	0.04	0.29	0.15	9.99	4,262	0.34
Taiwan	932	106	0.08	0.09	0.08	9.68	3,857	0.25
Netherlands	919	233	0.13	0.45	0.10	9.59	3,825	0.32
Sweden	659	276	0.02	0.18	0.11	9.85	3,141	0.33
South Korea	510	53	0.29	0.68	0.03	7.46	2,341	0.30
Australia	449	215	0.01	0.08	0.04	11.75	1,797	0.32
Austria	396	133	0.02	0.17	0.15	10.48	1,119	0.31
Finland	350	107	0.04	0.34	0.10	10.50	1,398	0.34
Belgium	336	121	0.04	0.31	0.09	9.64	1,262	0.30
Israel	326	135	0.02	0.15	0.07	10.28	1,914	0.32
Denmark	232	103	0.04	0.30	0.08	10.23	1,073	0.29
Spain	146	67	0.02	0.13	0.02	11.00	407	0.28
Norway	119	60	0.03	0.23	0.05	10.62	564	0.31
South Africa	98	45	0.03	0.16	0.06	11.19	312	0.35
Hungary	86	27	0.15	0.55	0.10	10.28	189	0.26
Ireland	54	31	0.06	0.26	0.10	9.63	290	0.41
China, Hong Kong	50	23	0.05	0.12	0.02	9.88	214	0.30
New Zealand	44	23	0.06	0.25	0.02	12.30	175	0.35
China, People's Republic	43	24	0.05	0.19	0.02	9.60	133	0.25
Brazil	41	18	0.13	0.49	0.08	11.75	130	0.32
Mexico	34	13	0.12	0.35	0.06	12.33	88	0.35
Venezuela	28	10	0.27	0.64	0.03	12.53	53	0.37
Argentina	27	4	0.25	0.15	0.04	10.54	181	0.29
India	25	11	0.17	0.56	0.02	10.70	67	0.29

Table A3.1 (*cont.*)

Country	No. of patents	No. of assignees	HHI	CR5	Intra-national	Cycle time	Quality	Originality
Luxembourg	25	10	0.14	0.72	0.06	10.92	76	0.32
Singapore	19	10	0.15	0.68	0.01	8.67	97	0.34
Greece	10	3	0.33	0.30	0.02	12.88	30	0.32
Bulgaria	9	8	0.13	0.56	0.07	11.49	13	0.46
Poland	8	5	0.20	0.63	0.00	11.40	23	0.29
Chile	7	4	0.28	0.71	0.00	11.18	13	0.24
Colombia	7	3	0.33	0.43	0.00	8.59	24	0.30
Philippines	7	3	0.33	0.43	0.10	9.62	29	0.14
Malaysia	5	2	0.63	0.80	0.00	8.77	21	0.50
Thailand	5	1	1.00	0.20	0.00	13.76	18	0.32
Portugal	4	3	0.38	1.00	0.32	12.05	6	0.35
Turkey	4	2	0.50	0.50	0.14	10.57	4	0.22
Indonesia	3	2	0.50	0.67	0.00	12.27	8	0.39
Saudi Arabia	3	0	0.00	0.00	0.03	18.51	5	0.80
Costa Rica	2	0	0.00	0.00	0.00	9.77	5	0.28
Iran	2	1	1.00	0.50	0.21	9.00	5	0.25
Egypt	1	1	1.00	1.00	0.00	7.14	13	0.74
Iceland	1	0	0.00	0.00	0.00	10.00	0	0.00
Average	2,021	381	0.19	0.35	0.08	10.56	11,194	0.33
Median	44	23	0.06	0.29	0.06	10.28	181	0.32
(b) Values with patent data with application year of 1995								
United States	77,699	13,197	0.00	0.07	0.34	10.72	110,181	0.44
Japan	27,761	2,153	0.02	0.23	0.36	8.30	35,058	0.35
Germany	8,329	1,667	0.02	0.24	0.19	10.41	6,638	0.35
France	3,568	838	0.01	0.17	0.14	10.44	2,800	0.35
United Kingdom	3,286	1,030	0.01	0.10	0.07	10.25	3,181	0.38
Canada	2,917	996	0.00	0.08	0.08	11.51	3,195	0.39
Taiwan	2,235	242	0.09	0.26	0.13	8.75	3,936	0.28
South Korea	2,092	146	0.13	0.62	0.07	7.34	2,944	0.30
Italy	1,453	545	0.02	0.18	0.12	11.48	1,151	0.34
Switzerland	1,306	408	0.02	0.22	0.16	11.10	948	0.38
Sweden	1,066	326	0.03	0.29	0.08	10.57	998	0.38
Netherlands	1,008	265	0.13	0.46	0.09	10.38	850	0.37
Belgium	667	162	0.06	0.39	0.10	10.43	683	0.32
Israel	655	261	0.02	0.18	0.06	10.47	758	0.38
Australia	600	293	0.01	0.11	0.05	12.12	448	0.35
Finland	522	149	0.04	0.34	0.10	10.32	501	0.35

Table A3.1 (*cont.*)

Country	No. of patents	No. of assignees	HHI	CR5	Intra-national	Cycle time	Quality	Originality
Denmark	434	153	0.11	0.40	0.08	12.24	273	0.33
Austria	433	141	0.02	0.18	0.09	11.83	266	0.35
Spain	203	101	0.02	0.12	0.02	11.53	80	0.33
Norway	180	70	0.05	0.33	0.05	12.20	181	0.33
Russian Federation	143	79	0.02	0.15	0.01	12.35	93	0.38
China, Hong Kong	100	57	0.02	0.11	0.02	11.61	89	0.32
South Africa	98	47	0.03	0.10	0.05	12.22	66	0.00
Singapore	96	43	0.05	0.39	0.02	9.53	144	0.35
New Zealand	88	36	0.04	0.19	0.02	13.53	69	0.31
Ireland	76	41	0.08	0.36	0.03	10.62	64	0.35
China People's Republic	63	33	0.05	0.22	0.01	10.67	34	0.35
Brazil	60	31	0.05	0.25	0.01	11.66	28	0.39
India	51	23	0.13	0.55	0.03	11.72	30	0.33
Hungary	50	23	0.06	0.34	0.06	9.61	40	0.35
Mexico	50	20	0.07	0.30	0.04	12.74	30	0.27
Argentina	35	11	0.10	0.17	0.07	10.26	40	0.41
Venezuela	22	4	0.67	0.73	0.08	12.31	24	0.44
Luxembourg	20	10	0.14	0.70	0.03	12.96	42	0.39
Malaysia	19	7	0.16	0.42	0.01	10.70	19	0.32
Saudi Arabia	19	1	1.00	0.05	0.05	15.60	6	0.59
Greece	15	9	0.11	0.33	0.02	11.09	7	0.35
Thailand	12	5	0.22	0.58	0.00	10.00	15	0.33
Colombia	10	3	0.38	0.40	0.00	11.23	8	0.31
Chile	9	5	0.20	0.56	0.02	14.05	2	0.48
Poland	9	6	0.18	0.67	0.02	11.67	7	0.48
Portugal	7	5	0.20	0.71	0.00	11.29	14	0.41
Iceland	6	4	0.25	0.67	0.00	9.35	11	0.38
Indonesia	5	4	0.25	0.80	0.02	13.49	2	0.65
Philippines	5	2	0.50	0.40	0.04	14.36	3	0.54
Bulgaria	4	1	1.00	0.25	0.00	11.57	2	0.32
Costa Rica	4	3	0.33	0.75	0.04	13.11	0	0.49
Turkey	3	2	0.50	0.67	0.00	11.41	1	0.55
Iran	1	1	1.00	1.00	0.00	11.33	0	0.00
Average	2,806	483	0.18	0.36	0.06	11.31	3,591	0.37
Median	88	41	0.07	0.33	0.04	11.33	66	0.35

Table A4.1 *Correlations among the eight regime variables*

	Opportun	Cumul	Cumul2	Appro	Originality	Fluidity	Initial stock	Cycle time	Access
Opportun	1								
Cumul	−0.09333	1							
	0.0707								
Cumul2	0.04369	0.71209	1						
	0.3983	<.0001							
Appro	0.09325	−0.14629	0.28208	1					
	0.0709	0.0045	<.0001						
Originality	0.15006	−0.13502	−0.30683	−0.32446	1				
	0.0035	0.0088	<.0001	<.0001					
Fluidity	0.61824	0.02842	0.10406	−0.06787	0.2709	1			
	<.0001	0.5828	0.0437	0.1891	<.0001				
Initial stock	−0.26434	0.4555	0.30702	−0.12642	−0.1208	−0.33559	1		
	<.0001	<.0001	<.0001	0.0142	0.0191	<.0001			
Cycle time	−0.07908	−0.54383	−0.45836	0.37458	−0.05774	−0.34144	−0.1574	1	
	0.1259	<.0001	<.0001	<.0001	0.264	<.0001	0.0022		
Access	0.00007	−0.15607	−0.15111	0.04104	−0.1305	−0.1143	−0.08341	0.25974	1
	0.9989	0.0024	0.0033	0.4275	0.0113	0.0267	0.1063	<.0001	

Note: the correlation coefficients are located at the top, and the levels of significance are located at the bottom.

Table A5.1 *Descriptive statistics for the variables used in regressions*

Variables	Mean	Std Dev.	Min	Max
US firms				
Growth (%)	8.78	25.82	−100.00	335.59
ROA (%)	9.31	10.37	−55.03	52.21
ROS (%)	4.67	56.18	−2479.19	51.04
Sales/workers (US$ million)	0.19	0.11	0	0.81
Tobin's Q	1.75	1.14	0.46	11.93
Patent count	21.47	52.09	1.00	509.00
HHI	0.51	0.35	0.02	1.00
Originality	0.42	0.18	0.00	0.89
Cycle time (years)	14.01	7.44	1	46.68
Self-citation ratio	0.12	0.13	0.00	1.00
No. of employees	16,282.52	50,616.23	23.00	775,100.0
Investment propensity (%)	0.99	5.72	−60.29	74.23
Debt-to-equity ratio (%)	267.97	6,609.26	−63,150.0	387,388.1
Capital–labor ratio (US$ million)	0.06	0.09	0.00007	1.37
Korean firms				
Growth (%)	11.94	17.08	−12.69	103.97
ROA (%)	8.19	4.91	−4.98	31.74
ROS	9.92%	7.03%	−24.69%	44.22%
Sales/workers (KRW thousand)	231,740.00	175,300.90	5,408.26	1,277,812.00
Sales/workers (US$ million)	0.29	0.22	0.01	1.66
Tobin's Q	1.01	0.13	0.71	1.43
Patent count	9.98	30.39	1.00	219.00
HHI	0.71	0.35	0.05	1.00
Originality	0.30	0.24	0.00	0.83
Cycle time (years)	11.76	7.09	0	40.50
Self-citation	0.04	0.11	0.00	1.00
No. of employees	6,836.07	11,005.36	25.00	60,898.00
Investment propensity (%)	2.57	7.12	−11.73	31.41
Debt to equity ratio (%)	301.71	366.58	−3,620.92	2,671.22
Capital–labor ratio (KRW thousand)	120,041.30	154,853.20	1,954.74	1,170,768.00
Capital–labor ratio (US$ million)	0.15	0.19	0.002	1.46

Table A5.2 Correlation coefficient matrix

	Patent count	HHI	Originality	Technology cycle	Self-citation	No. of workers	Investment propensity	Debt-to-equity ratio	Capital-labor ratio
US firms									
Patent count	1								
HHI index	-0.403	1							
Originality	0.005	-0.123	1						
Tech. cycle	-0.149	0.106	0.022	1					
Self-citation	0.205	-0.135	-0.028	-0.110	1				
No. of workers	0.533	-0.212	-0.001	0.015	0.023	1			
Investment propensity	0.046	-0.044	0.033	-0.042	0.015	0.010	1		
Debt-to-equity ratio	-0.005	0.034	0.043	-0.008	-0.018	0.005	0.022	1	
Capital labor ratio	0.123	-0.102	0.024	-0.022	0.043	0.037	0.052	0.067	1
Korean firms									
Patent count	1								
HHI index	-0.480	1							
Originality	-0.046	-0.014	1						
Tech. cycle	-0.108	0.082	0.088	1					
Self-citation	0.050	-0.150	-0.037	-0.126	1				
No. of workers	0.396	-0.475	-0.074	-0.068	0.021	1			
Investment propensity	0.101	-0.010	-0.078	-0.096	-0.065	0.024	1		
Debt-to-equity ratio	0.018	0.066	-0.021	0.042	0.019	-0.038	0.028	1	
Capital-labor ratio	-0.050	-0.115	0.083	-0.069	-0.097	0.102	-0.038	-0.291	1

Table A5.3 *Sectoral distribution of Korean firms used in regressions (unit: no. of firms, %)*

Industry name (8th KSIC code – 2-digit)	1992	1993	1994	1995	1991–95
Furniture; not elsewhere classified	0(0)	0(0)	2(2.90)	0(0)	2(1.65)
Other machinery and equipment	1(2.38)	1(1.96)	3(4.35)	3(3.90)	7(5.79)
Other transport equipment	2(4.76)	2(3.92)	2(2.90)	2(2.60)	2(1.65)
Electrical machinery and parts not elsewhere counted	2(4.76)	2(3.92)	3(4.35)	2(2.60)	4(3.31)
Wholesale and commission trade	3(7.14)	1(1.96)	0(0)	1(1.30)	5(4.13)
Apparel and fur articles	0(0)	0(0)	1(1.45)	0(0)	1(0.83)
Real estate activities	0(0)	0(0)	1(1.45)	0(0)	1(0.83)
Other non-metallic mineral products	1(2.38)	3(5.88)	1(1.45)	3(3.90)	4(3.31)
Food products and beverages	3(7.14)	7(13.73)	5(7.25)	3(3.90)	10(8.26)
Medical, precision, and optical instruments	2(4.76)	1(1.96)	1(1.45)	5(6.49)	5(4.13)
Motor vehicles, trailers and semitrailers	4(9.52)	3(5.88)	7(10.14)	9(11.69)	11(9.09)
Electricity and gas supply	0(0)	1(1.96)	1(1.45)	1(1.30)	1(0.83)
Professional and scientific services	5(11.90)	4(7.84)	5(7.25)	6(7.79)	7(5.79)
Specialized construction	0(0)	0(0)	0(0)	1(1.30)	1(0.83)
Electronic components	6(14.29)	9(17.65)	12(17.39)	9(11.69)	17(14.05)
Basic metals	1(2.38)	2(3.92)	2(2.90)	4(5.19)	6(4.96)
Fabricated metal products	2(4.76)	0(0)	1(1.45)	2(2.60)	3(2.48)

Table A5.3 (*cont.*)

Industry name (8th KSIC code – 2-digit)	1992	1993	1994	1995	1991–95
General construction	2(4.76)	0(0)	2(2.90)	1(1.30)	2(1.65)
Computers and office machinery	0(0)	0(0)	1(1.45)	2(2.60)	2(1.65)
Refined petroleum products	0(0)	1(1.96)	1(1.45)	1(1.30)	1(0.83)
Telecommunication services	1(2.38)	1(1.96)	1(1.45)	1(1.30)	1(0.83)
Pulp, paper and paper products	0(0)	0(0)	1(1.45)	0(0)	1(0.83)
Chemicals and chemical products	7(16.67)	13(25.49)	16(23.19)	21(27.27)	27(22.31)
Total	42(100)	51(100)	69(100)	77(100)	121(100)

Notes

1 Introduction

1 Although Amsden (1989), Chang (1994), and the World Bank (1993) appreciate the early achievements in Asia, a concern for limited catch-up in other parts of the world is expressed by Rodrik (2003, 1999) and the World Bank (2005). For similar concerns, see also Easterly (2001) and Loayza, Fajnzylber, and Calcleron (2005).

2 Williamson (1990) first used the term Washington Consensus.

3 Notable examples include Knack and Keefer (1995) and Rodrik (1996).

4 The so-called institution supremacy view has been verified in such works as Acemoglu, Johnson, and Robinson (2001; 2002), Rodrik, Subramian, and Trebbi (2004), and most recently in Acemoglu and Robinson (2012). However, these works do not deal with the question of the middle-income trap.

5 See Commission on Growth and Development report (2008).

6 This argument is made by Hausman, Pritchelt, and Rodrik (2005) and Jones and Olken (2005).

7 See Lee and Kim (2009, Table 1) and Paus (2009).

8 For similar definitions and more discussions, see Lin (2012c: 216), Williamson (2012), Yusuf and Nabeshima (2009), and World Bank (2010: 27; 2012: 12).

9 Examples include Eichengreen, Park, and Shin (2011), Griffith (2011), Ohno (2010), and Pause (2009).

10 This observation is made by Mazzoleni and Nelson (2007).

11 Although not shown here, a similar figure was drawn with Japan as the benchmark. It again showed that Korea was unable to reduce the gap with Japan in the 1960s and 1970s, and reduced the gap with Japan only after the mid 1980s.

12 From Lee and Kim (2009; Table 1.E).

13 For details, see Lee and Kim (2010), which is a chapter in Odagiri et al. (2010).

14 See OECD (1996: 27).

15 Cited from Lee (2006).

16 The study on productivity was by Jung and Lee (2010).

17 Information provided in Lee and Kim (2009).
18 See World Bank (2005: 11).
19 This case of digital TV is thoroughly explained by Lee, Lim, and Song (2005). For a direct comparison between Samsung and Sony, see Joo and Lee (2010).
20 This concept was first discussed by Tushman and Anderson (1986).
21 Definition of the mean backward citation is from Jaffe and Trajtenberg (2002: 421). But their book did not call it the cycle time of technologies. Park and Lee (2006) is one of the first researches to call this a measure of the cycle times of technology.
22 Table 4.1 presents actual data on the cycle time of these technologies.
23 Tatung's story is taken from Khan (2002), which is also discussed by Lee and Mathews (2012).
24 For dramatically changing composition of Samsung's sales by industries, refer to Figure 3.3 of Chang (2003).
25 The adding-up problem may provoke a protectionist response in the form of tariffs, quotas, or other barriers in the markets, including those of advanced countries (Spence 2011: 122–5).
26 On this point, see Amsden and Chu (2003: 167).

2 Knowledge as a key factor for economic catch-up

1 This view is expressed by Mazzoleni and Nelson (2007).
2 Such studies include the following: Verspagen (1991), Nelson (1995), Nelson and Pack (1999), Fagerberg and Godinho (2005), Lee (2005), Mazzoleni and Nelson (2007), and Nelson (2008a, 2008b).
3 This observation is expressed by Fagerberg and Godinho (2005) and Mazzoleni and Nelson (2007).
4 Dosi (1982) used the term "technological paradigm" when he attempted to account for both continuous changes and discontinuities in techno-logical innovation. Continuous changes are usually related to progress along a technological trajectory defined by a technological paradigm, whereas discontinuities are associated with the emergence of a new paradigm.
5 The notion of the technological regime defines the nature of technology according to a knowledge-based theory of production and defines the particular knowledge environment where problem-solving activities occur (Winter 1984). Other studies on this concept include the following: Breschi et al. (2000), Malerba (2002), Malerba and Orsenigo (1996), and Malerba, Orsenigo, and Peretto (1997).
6 Examples are Edquist (1997), Freeman (1987), Lundvall (1993), and Nelson (1993).

7 For a Schumpeterian theory of the firm, see Nelson (1991, 2008c) and Winter (2006).
8 For a discussion on the distinctive nature of neo-Schumpeterian economics, see Dosi et al. (1988: Chs. 1, 2, and 3).
9 Lee and Yoon (2010) refer to this aspect as international knowledge diffusion.
10 Sectoral concentration or technological diversification is further discussed in Chapter 9.
11 See Archibugi and Pianta (1996) for a full discussion on the costs and benefits of the patent data. For similar points, see Griliches (1990), Hall, Jaffe, and Trajtenberg (2001), OECD (1994) and Pavitt (1985).
12 On the usefulness of patents' citation data and their characteristics, refer to Jaffe et al. (1993) and Hall et al. (2001).
13 Mahmood and Singh (2003) made this observation.

3 Knowledge and country-level catch-up

1 Studies on the binding constraints include Hausmann et al. (2008) and Rodrik (2006).
2 See Appendix Table A3.1 for a list of countries and values of each NIS variable for each country.
3 This way of measuring the localization of knowledge creation is intended to control the size effects, so that a country cites more of its own nationality patents simply because of the size of the country and thus the size of patent pools. Technically, this formula may generate negative values, but it does not in the cases included in this study. An alternative is to use the ratios, not the difference.
4 Acemoglu et al. (2001, 2002), Glaeser et al. (2004), and Rodrik et al. (2004) all use cross-sectional estimation, which has the advantage of using time-invariant variables such as geography as a regressor. However, problems associated with cross-section estimations are often serious, and most of the results are fragile and subject to an omitted variable bias. Moreover, finding a good instrumental variable to mitigate the potential endogeneity is difficult. Therefore, a fixed-effect panel estimation (Islam 1995), which reduces omitted variable bias and time-invariant heterogeneity, is first provided in this study. However, as time-varying country effects and endogeneity are not controlled in this method, we also use the system-GMM method developed by Arellano and Bover (1995) and Blundell and Bond (1998), and applied by Bond, Hoeffler and Temple (2001). This method is known to reduce a small sample bias that characterizes first-differenced GMM used by Caselli, Esquivel, and Lefort (1996).

242   *Notes to pages 63–80*

5 Additional regressions covering the four Asian countries as the basis and with the dummy variables for the high-income countries are run. In this switched regression, the coefficient of the cycle variable is negative and significant. The results are available upon request.
6 Schott (2004) shows that when exporting the same products, rich nations export the varieties of higher unit value, whereas poorer nations export those of lower unit value.

4 Knowledge and sector-level catch-up

1 In a similar context, Dosi (1982) uses the term "technological paradigm."
2 Technological regimes are not the only factors that affect technological performance. See Laursen and Meliciani (2002) for the relationship between domestic and international linkages and technological competitiveness, and Dosi, Pavitt, and Soete (1990) for a diverse work on trade and technological specializations.
3 For details, see Lee, Mani, and Mu (2012).
4 The concept of uncertainty of technological trajectory concerns the degree that the future trajectory of an industry can be predicted. When predicting how industries will evolve in the future is difficult, the level of uncertainty is greater.
5 Malerba and Orsenigo (1996) determine whether a relationship exists between sectoral patterns of innovative activities and international technological specialization. They posit the international specialization of a country, in terms of revealed technological advantages, as the dependent variable. The independent variables are the measures used to identify the Schumpeterian patterns of innovation and technological regimes. Breschi et al. (2000) take four measures of Schumpeterian patterns of innovation, such as entry and exit, and stability or concentration of inventors, as the dependent variables and estimate the effects of the technological regime variables on the pattern of innovation. However, this chapter measures the regime variables not by any objective variable, such as patent, but by the responses to survey questions.
6 This section heavily relies on Park and Lee (2006).
7 Dosi (1988) also analyzes the processes leading from technological opportunities to actual innovative efforts and changes in the structures and performance of industries.
8 Park and Lee (2006) use both measures to obtain consistent results.
9 Distinguishing the cumulativeness of technological advancement from the technological cycle time is possible. Although both comprise cumulativeness in a broad sense, the first represents the cumulativeness

of technology in the organization dimension, whereas the latter represents the inverse of cumulativeness of technology itself.

10 Park and Lee (2006) find that this reasoning is true in the cases of Korean large businesses and Taiwanese SMEs.

11 In the second data set, the nationalities of patents are identified as those of assignees.

12 Archibugi and Pianta (1992) argue that the total amount of resources devoted by each country to science and technology is inversely related to the degree of specialization across technological fields. Only large countries can afford to distribute their innovations more uniformly across technologies.

13 The structure of the regression model here follows that of Park and Lee (2006).

14 In Korea, 292 sectors show technological catch-up and 84 sectors do not. In Taiwan, 320 sectors show technological catch-up and 56 sectors do not (Park and Lee 2006).

15 If the numerical value produced by that option is less than 10, the multicollinearity problem is considered not serious. Multicollinearity is also checked by the EVIEW program (singular matrix check). In testing significance of the estimated coefficients, we have used the White heteroskeclasticity-consistent standard errors.

16 As in Park and Lee (2006), we conduct this study because we want to determine the common feature of catch-up economies despite the many differences between Korea and Taiwan.

17 As previously asserted by Malerba and Orsenigo (1996), we cannot say much about the direction of causation between the sectoral level of catch-up and the factor of technological regimes. Rather, we interpret the result of the regression simply in evidence of the existence or absence of correlation between the variables that represent them.

18 The two interpretations below are from Park and Lee (2006).

19 Albert (1998) also notes the short technological cycle time of Japan, Korea, and Taiwan, and observes that there is a marked shortening of the cycle times for Taiwan in the automotive and IT sectors and for Korea in the IT sector.

20 For more details on the cases of CDMA phones and digital TV, see Lee and Lim (2001) and Lee, Lim, and Song (2005).

21 I owe this point to Richard Nelson.

5 Knowledge and firm-level catch-up: Korean versus US firms

1 Lee and Shim (1995) examine the determinants of sales growth of US and Japanese firms. They investigate the effects of strategic variables

(e.g. R&D intensity, advertisement intensity, capital intensity, capital utilization, debt leverage, size, labor productivity, and export activity). Gedajlovic and Shapiro (1998) study the effects of ownership concentration and diversification on the profitability of firms in the USA, the UK, Germany, France, and Canada, and find that the effects are different across firms because of the heterogeneous governance structures of Anglo-Saxon and European styles. D'Souza, Megginson and Nash (2005) analyze 130 firms from twenty-three advanced OECD countries to examine their post-privatization performance, with a focus on trade openness and the overall improvement of macroeconomic conditions.

2 For a review, see Hoopes, Madsen, and Walker (2003).
3 Other studies include Granovetter (1994), Guillen (2000), Khanna (2000), and Khanna and Palepu (1997, 1999a, 2000a).
4 For instance, India (Ghemawat and Khanna 1998), Chile (Khanna and Palepu 2000b; Khanna and Palepu 1999b), Hong Kong (Au, Peng, and Wang 2000), and China (Keister 1998; Lee and Kang 2010).
5 See Joo and Lee (2010) for detailed comparison of Samsungand Sony.
6 Test results are available upon request. In the random effect models, sectoral dummies are used but not shown.

6 Toward a knowledge-based theory of economic catch-up

1 For example, Wang, Wei, and Wong (2010), who define leapfrogging as the share of sophisticated products, observed no relationship of this variable with economic growth. However, leapfrogging occurred in only a few successful catching-up economies. Thus, cross-country regressions cannot capture it unless a separate dummy is used for such countries, as we have done in Chapter 3.
2 The acquisition process is explained in section 7.2 of the next chapter and in many previous studies (Lee and Lim 2001; Mathews 2002b; Lee, Lim, and Song 2005) and is summarized in a survey article of Lee (2005).
3 For the theory of catch-up cycle and its application to steel industry, see Lee and Ki (2011).
4 Of course, if we are concerned not about the sectoral level but at the technological level, every competence-destroying technical change is an opportunity for latecomers or entrants, regardless of the sector to which it belongs.
5 Table A4.1 illustrates a highly positive correlation between short cycle time and cumulativeness of technologies, where cumulativeness is measured by the degree to which persistent inventors tend to dominate the invention in specific classes of technologies. This concept is similar to that of entry barriers to invention in specific fields.

6 Spence (2011: 102) also recognizes many problems in the middle-income stage but states that transition in the middle-income stage in general requires the government to play fewer roles.

7 For details, see Mathews (2002b), Lee and Lim (2001), Lee, Lim, and Song (2005), and OECD (1996).

8 For details, see Lee, Mani, and Mu (2012). For China in the 1990s, see Mu and Lee (2005).

9 For details, see Lee, Cho, and Jin (2009).

7 How to build up technological capabilities to enter short-cycle technology sectors

1 For a similar view, see Dahlman, Westphal, and Kim (1985), Kim (1980, 1997a), OECD (1992), and Utterback and Abernathy (1975).

2 Lee (2013) provides further discussion of three kinds of failure, namely, market, system, and capability failure. On system failure, Metcalfe (2005) argued that the process of innovation depends on the emergence and success of innovation systems connecting the various actors (components) engaged in the process. Then the need for government activism arises, because effective interaction among the actors in the innovation systems does not exist naturally but has to be constructed and instituted for a purpose. In particular, some scholars (i.e. Bergek et al. 2008, Dodgson et al. 2011) observed that system failure often exists where missing or weak connections (and synergies) among actors tend to lead to lower performance. However, the problem in developing countries is more urgently about extremely weak levels of capability of firms rather than interaction among actors.

3 The explanations of these three terms are obtained from Hobday (1995: 37–8, 192–3).

4 This figure is taken from Hobday (2000: 133).

5 This observation is from Amsden and Chu (2003: 77).

6 What follows is a summary of the explanation provided in Lee (2005).

7 Again the part on learning process technology is based on Lee (2005).

8 Amsden and Chu (2003: 23–4).

9 See OECD (1996: 27).

10 See Guillen (2001: 164–5).

11 This part relies on information from Lee and Lim (2001).

12 For more on the story on Samsung, see Kim (1997b) and Lee (2005).

13 For details, see Amsden and Chu (2003), specifically 28–32.

14 This sub-section is a summary of Lee, Mani, and Mu (2012) and Mu and Lee (2005).

15 This observation is based on Mu and Lee (2005).

16 This section is a compact summary of the main argument of Lee and Lim (2001) and Lee, Lim, and Song (2005).
17 The neo-Schumpeterians include Freeman (1987, 1995), Freeman and Soete (1997), and Perez and Soete (1988).
18 The interviewed R&D staff of both Samsung and LG acknowledged this as one important benefit of the consortium.
19 These implications are also explained in Lee, Lim, and Song (2005).
20 The sequential modes of knowledge accesses are first discussed in Lee (2005).
21 This point is made in OECD (1996: 97)

8 Catching up and leapfrogging in China and India

1 For a recent treatment of the Beijing Consensus, see Yao (2010).
2 For instance, see Winters and Yusuf (2007).
3 This uniqueness of the Indian service sector in view of these two views is first explained by Ok (2010) in a book edited by the author.
4 The role of downturns in semiconductor and LCD industries is analyzed by Mathews (2005).
5 See Chapter 7 of this book, Lee and Lim (2001), Mathews (2002a, 2002b), and Mu and Lee (2005).
6 For an early treatment of these three forms, see Hobday (1995: 37–8, 2003).
7 This part is a summary of a section in Lee, Park, and Krishnan (2011), which is co-authored by the current author.
8 This point is based on Madhani (2008).
9 For details, see Athreye (2005) and Krishnan and Vallabhaneni (2010).
10 Information in this regard is based on Mizuho Corporate Bank (2008: 10).
11 This information is from Athreye (2005).
12 This information is from Mizuho Corporate Bank (2008: 34).
13 This part is a summary of a section in Lee, Park, and Krishnan (2011), which is co-authored by the current author.
14 This observation is based on Bhatnagar (2006).
15 This observation is based on Bhatnagar (2006).
16 Refer to the article "Tata Group: On a Giant Shoulder" published on July 25, 2003 (http://dquindia.ciol.com).
17 According to our interview with a staff member of Infosys in August 2010, Infosys considers itself the founder of the offshore business model.
18 A nearshore company is physically located closer to customers, making it more responsive to customer needs than offshore companies.
19 See Lee (2010).
20 One of the earliest uses of the term Beijing Consensus is Ramo (2004), who defines it as a combination of emphases on innovation, sustainability and equality, and self-determination.

21 This argument was first made in Lee (2006) and Lee and Mathews (2010) when they discussed the BeST Consensus.

22 See Lee, Lin, and Chang (2005) and Lin (2012b).

23 This summary is based on the three elements of the Beijing model elaborated in Lee, Jee, and Eun (2011). For forward engineering and the university-run enterprises, see Eun et al. (2006). For parallel learning, see Mu and Lee (2005).

24 As a CRT maker, BOE had been attempting for a long time to acquire TFT-LCD technology by inviting foreign partners to enter into ventures with the company. However, after unsuccessful deals with a Japanese company, BOE turned to M&A and finally bought HYDIS in 2003. After the acquisition of HYDIS, BOE built a fifth-generation TFT-LCD panel line in Beijing. HYDIS's technology and know-how played a significant role in the development process. For instance, in 2006, more than 120 former HYDIS Korean engineers worked at BOE sites in Beijing (Jee et al. 2005: 221–2). Re-cited from Lee et al. (2011).

25 As observed by Naughton (2007: 5) and Yao (2010).

26 The first criterion is based on the study of Lee and Kim (2009), which verifies that for upper-middle- and high-income countries, economic growth depends on innovation. The second criterion is based on Lee, Kim, Park, and Sanidas (2013), who found that one source of the difference between high- versus middle-income countries is whether a country has world-class (e.g. Fortune 500) large businesses.

27 These criteria are proposed in Lee and Kim (2010).

28 For details, see Lee (2010), particularly Figure 2.

29 The discussion on big business and their capability in China is based heavily on the work of this author, that is, Lee, Jee, and Eun (2011).

30 For details, see Lee et al. (2013).

31 An example is that by Nolan (2002).

32 This observation and the case of the CIMC are based on Zeng and Williamson (2007: 3–14).

9 Hypothesizing a theory of technological turning points

1 For instance, Hausman, Hwang, and Rodrik (2007) argue the importance of diversification of export products into more sophisticated products.

2 Trade data contain no actual information about the process by which products are made, and thus technological content cannot be assessed based on trade data (Sturgeon and Gereffi 2012). More importantly, although a developing country is observed by trade data to export high-tech goods, the most valuable value-added components of these

goods are often produced in a third country. For example, only $4 out of the $299 retail price of an Apple iPod goes to China (Linden, Kraemer, and Dedrick 2007).

3 For the semi-conductor case, see Mathews (2005). Tatung's story is taken from Khan (2002), which is also discussed in Lee and Mathews (2012). For the dramatically changing composition of Samsung's sales by industry, refer to Figure 3.3 of Chang (2003).

4 On this point, see Amsden and Chu (2003: 167).

5 Certain studies have dealt with the issue of selecting criteria for technological specialization. Most of these studies focus on specialization into sectors with higher opportunities as measured by the higher growth rates of patents in the sector. However, Meliciani (2002) failed to confirm any significant relationship between such specialization and economic growth.

6 Although not shown here, we have tried additional regression with the variable of technological diversification measured as the number of classes with patents registered by each country divided by the total number of patent classes (417) in the similar country-panel models as in Chapter 3. We find that the impact of this variable is marginally significant in the economic growth of advanced economies, but insignificant in successful catching-up economies. This is exactly what we have obtained with regard to the localization variable (see Table 3.4).

7 See Chandra (2006) on the salmon industry in Chile.

8 This item on Tatung is from Khan (2002).

9 Amsden and Hikino (1994) observe that the latecomer firms tend to command "project execution capabilities," including the skills required to establish or expand operating and other corporate facilities.

10 Summary and concluding remarks

1 Jung and Lee (2010), for example, used firm-level regressions with both firm- and sector-level variables that affected the productivity catch-up of Korean firms compared with that of Japanese firms. The study by Srholic and Fagerberg (2010) also represents an effort toward this direction.

Bibliography

Abramovitz, Moses 1986. "Catching up, Forging Ahead, and Falling Behind," *Journal of Economic History* 46(2): 385–406.

Acemoglu, Daron, and James A. Robinson 2012. *Why Nations Fail.* New York: Crown Business.

Acemoglu, Daron, Simon Johnson, and James A. Robinson 2001. "The Colonial Origins of Comparative Development: An Empirical Investigation," *American Economic Review* 91(5): 1369–1401.

2002. "Reversal of Fortune: Geography and Institutions in the Making of the Modern World Income Distribution," *Quarterly Journal of Economics* 117(4): 1231–94.

Albert, Michael B. 1998. *The New Innovators: Global Patenting Trends in Five Sectors.* New York: US Department of Commerce, Office of Technology Policy.

Amann, Edmund, and John Cantwell (eds.) *Innovative Firms in Emerging Market Countries.* (Oxford University Press, 2012).

Amsden, Alice 1989. *Asia's Next Giant: South Korea and Late Industrialization.* Oxford University Press.

2001. *The Rise of the Rest.* New York: Oxford University Press.

Amsden, Alice, and Wan-Wen Chu 2003. *Beyond Late Development: Taiwan's Upgrading Policies.* Cambridge, MA: MIT Press.

Amsden, Alice, and Takashi Hikino 1994. "Project Execution Capability, Organizational Know-how and Conglomerate Growth in Late Industrialization," *Industrial and Corporate Change* 3(1): 111–47.

Anderson, Philip, and Michael Tushman 1990. "Technological Discontinuity and Dominant Designs: A Cyclical Model of Technological Change," *Administrative Science Quarterly* 35(4): 604–33.

Archibugi, D., and M. Pianta 1992. "Specialization and Size of Technological Activities in Industrial Countries: The Analysis of Patent Data," *Research Policy* 21(1): 79–93.

1996. "Measuring Technological Change through Patents and Innovation Surveys," *Technovation* 16(9): 451–68.

Arellano, M., and O. Bover 1995. "Another Look at Instrumental Variable Estimation of Error-Component Models," *Journal of Econometrics* 68(1): 29–51.

Athreye, S. S. 2005. "Indian Software Industry and its Evolving Service Capability," *Industrial and Corporate Change* 14(3): 393–418.

Au, K., M. W. Peng, and D. Wang 2000. "Interlocking Directorates, Firm Strategies, and Performance in Hong Kong: Towards a Research Agenda," *Asia Pacific Journal of Management* 17(1): 29–47.

Baumol, W. J. 1967. "Macro-economics of Unbalanced Growth: The Anatomy of Urban Crisis," *American Economic Review* 57(3): 415–26.

Bell, R. M., and Pavitt, K. 1993. "Technological Accumulation and Industrial Growth: Contrasts between Developed and Developing Countries," *Industrial and Corporate Change* 2(1): 157–210.

Bergek, Anna, Staffan Jacobsson, Bo Carlsson, Sven Lindmark, and Annika Rickne 2008. "Analyzing the Functional Dynamics of Technological Innovation Systems: A Scheme of Analysis," *Research Policy* 37(3): 407–29.

Bhatnagar, Subhash 2006. "India's Software Industry," in Vandana Chandra (ed.), *Technology, Adaptation, and Exports: How Some Developing Countries Got it Right*, pp. 95–124. Washington, DC: The World Bank.

Blundell, R., and S. Bond 1998. "Initial Conditions and Moment Conditions in Dynamic Panel Data Models," *Journal of Econometrics* 87(1): 115–43.

Bond, S., A. Hoeffler, and J. Temple 2001. "GMM Estimation of Empirical Growth Models," Center for Economic Policy Research Discussion Paper 3048.

Breschi, Stefano, Franco Malerba, and Luigi Orsenigo 2000. "Technological Regimes and Schumpeterian Patterns of Innovation," *Economic Journal* 110(463): 388–410.

Caselli, F., G. Esquivel, and F. Lefort 1996. "Reopening the Convergence Debate: A New Look at Cross-country Growth Empirics," *Journal of Economic Growth* 1(3): 363–89.

Chaminade, Cristina, Patarapong Intarakumnerd, and Koson Sapprasert 2012. "Measuring Systemic Problems in National Innovation Systems: An Application to Thailand," *Research Policy* 41(8): 1476–88.

Chandra, Vandana, 2006. *Technology, Adaptation, and Exports: How Some Developing Countries Got it Right*. Washington, DC: The World Bank.

Chang, Ha-Joon 1994. *The Political Economy of Industrial Policy*. New York: St. Martin's Press.

Chang, S. J. 2003. *Financial Crisis and Transformation of Korean Business Groups*. Cambridge University Press.

Chang, S., and J. Hong 2000. "Economic Performance of Group-Affiliated Companies in Korea: Intergroup Resource Sharing and Internal Business Transitions," *Academy of Management Journal* 43(3): 429–48.

Cheong, Kwang Soo, Kineung Choo, and Keun Lee 2010. "Understanding the Behavior of Business Groups: A Dynamic Model and Empirical Analysis," *Journal of Economic Behavior and Organization* 76(2): 141–52.

Choo, K., K. Lee, K. Ryu, and J. Yoon 2009. "Changing Performance of Business Groups over Two Decades: Technological Capabilities and Investment Inefficiency in Korean Chaebols," *Economic Development and Cultural Change* 57(2): 359–86.

Christensen, C. M. 1997. *The Innovator's Dilemma: When New Technologies Cause Great Firms to Fail.* Boston: Harvard Business School Press.

Chung, Moon Young, and Keun Lee 2011. "How Absorptive Capacity is Formed? Technology Licensing to Indigenous R&D and Innovation in Korea," Paper at the Asia-Pacific Economic and Business History Conference 2011, held in Berkeley, California, USA.

Cimoli, Mario, Giovanni Dosi, and Joseph E. Stiglitz 2009. *Industrial Policy and Development: The Political Economy of Capabilities Accumulation.* New York: Oxford University Press.

Clark, Colin 1940. *The Conditions of Economic Progress.* London: Macmillan.

Cohen, Wesley M., and Daniel A. Levinthal 1990. "Absorptive Capacity: A New Perspective on Learning and Innovation," *Administrative Science Quarterly* 35(1): 128–52.

Commission on Growth and Development 2008. *The Growth Report: Strategies for Sustained Growth and Inclusive Development.* Washington DC: The World Bank.

Dahlman, C., L. E. Westphal, and L. Kim 1985. "Reflections on Acquisition of Technological Capability," in N. Rosenberg and C. Frischtak (eds.), *International Technology Transfer: Concepts, Measures and Comparisons*, pp. 167–221. New York: Praeger.

Dodgson, Mark, Alan Hughes, John Foster, and J. S. Metcalfe 2011. "Systems Thinking, Market Failure, and the Development of Innovation Policy: The Case of Australia," *Research Policy* 40(9): 1145–56.

Dosi, G. 1982. "Technological Paradigms and Technological Trajectories: A Suggested Interpretation of the Determinants and Directions of Technical Change," *Research Policy* 11(3): 147–62.

1988. "Sources, Procedures, and Microeconomic Effects of Innovation," *Journal of Economic Literature* 26(3): 1120–71.

Dosi, G., K. Pavitt, and L. Soete 1990. *The Economics of Technical Change and International Trade.* New York University Press.

Dosi, G., C. Freeman, R. Nelson, G. Silverberg, and L. Soete 1988. *Technical Change and Economic Theory*. London: Pinter Publishers.

D'Souza, J., W. Megginson, and R. Nash 2005. "Effect of Institutional and Firm-specific Characteristics on Post-privatization Performance: Evidence from Developed Countries," *Journal of Corporate Finance* 11(5): 747–66.

Easterly, William 2001. "The Lost Decade: Developing Countries' Stagnation in Spite of Policy Reform 1980–1990," *Journal of Economic Growth* 6(2): 135–57.

Edquist, C. 1997. "Systems of Innovation Approaches: Their Emergence and Characteristics," in C. Edquist, (ed.), *Systems of Innovation: Technologies, Institutions and Organizations*, pp. 1–35. London: Pinter Publishers/ Cassell.

Eichengreen, B., D. Park, and K. Shin 2011. "When Fast Growing Economies Slow Down," NBER Working Paper No. 16919.

Eun, Jong-Hak, K. Lee, and G. Wu 2006. "Explaining the 'University-run Enterprises' in China: A Theoretical Framework for University–Industry Relationship in Developing Countries and its Application to China," *Research Policy* 35(9): 1329–46.

Fagerberg, Jan, and Manuel Godinho 2005. "Innovation and Catching-up," in David C. Mowery, Jan Fagerberg, and Richard R. Nelson (eds.), *The Oxford Handbook of Innovation*, pp. 514–43. New York: Oxford University Press.

Ferris, S. P., K. A. Kim, and P. Kitsabunnarat 2003. "The Costs (and Benefits?) of Diversified Business Groups: The Case of Korean Chaebols," *Journal of Banking & Finance* 27(2): 251–73.

Fink, Carsten, and Keith Maskus 2005. *Intellectual Property and Development*. New York: The World Bank and Oxford University Press.

Freeman, Cris 1987. *Technology Policy and Economic Performance: Lessons from Japan*. London: Pinter Publishers.

1995. "The 'National System of Innovation' in Historical Perspective," *Cambridge Journal of Economics* 19(1): 5–24.

Freeman, C. and L. Soete 1997. "Development and the Diffusion of Technology," in C. Freeman and L. Soete (eds.), *The Economics of Industrial Innovation*, pp. 351–65. London: Pinter Publishers.

Gedajlovic, E. and D. M. Shapiro 1998. "Management and Ownership Effects: Evidence from Five Countries," *Strategic Management Journal* 19(6): 533–53.

Gerschenkron, Alexander 1962. *Economic Backwardness in Historical Perspective*. Cambridge, MA: Harvard University Press.

Ghemawat, P., and T. Khanna 1998. "The Nature of Diversified Business Groups: A Research Design and Two Case Studies," *Journal of Industrial Economics* 46(1): 35–61.

Glaeser, Edward, Rafael La Porta, Florencio Lopez-de-Silanes, and Andrei Shleifer 2004. "Do Institutions Cause Growth?," *Journal of Economic Growth* 9(3): 271–303.

Goto, Akira 1982. "Business Groups in a Market Economy," *European Economic Review* 19(1): 53–70.

Granstrand, O., P. Patel, and K. Pavitt 1997. "Multi-technology Corporations: Why they have 'Distributed' rather than 'Distinctive Core' Competencies," *California Management Review*, 39(4): 8–25.

Granovetter, M. S. 1994. "Business Groups," in N. J. Smelser and R. Swedberg (eds.), *Handbook of Economic Sociology*, pp. 453–75. Princeton University Press.

Griffith, B. 2011. "Middle Income Trap," in R. Nallari et al. (eds.), *Frontiers in Development Policy*, pp. 39–44. Washington, DC: The World Bank.

Griffith, R., S. Redding and J. Van Reenen 2004. "Mapping the Two Faces of R&D: Productivity Growth in a Panel of OECD Industries," *Review of Economics and Statistics* 86(4): 883–95.

Griliches, Z. 1990. "Patent Statistics as Economic Indicators: A Survey," *Journal of Economic Literature* 28(4): 1661–1707.

Grossman, G. M. and E. Rossi-Hansberg 2006. "The rise of offshoring: It's not wine for cloth anymore," Presented at a symposium on The New Economic Geography: Effects and Policy Implications, 59–102.

Guennif, S., and S. V. Ramani 2012. "Explaining Divergence in Catching-up in Pharma between India and Brazil Using the NSI Framework," *Research Policy* 41(2): 430–41.

Guillen, M. 2000. "Business Groups in Emerging Economies: A Resource-based View," *Academy of Management Journal* 43(3): 362–80.

2001. *The Limits of Convergence: Globalization and Organizational Change in Argentina, South Korea, and Spain.* Princeton University Press.

Hall, Bronwyn H., A. B. Jaffe, and M. Trajtenberg 2001. "The NBER Patent Citations Data File: Lesson, Insights and Methodological Tools," NBER Working Papers 8498.

Hamm, Steve 2007. *Bangalore Tiger: How Indian Tech Upstart Wipro is Rewriting the Rules of Global Competition.* New Delhi: Tata McGraw-Hill.

Hasan, Iftekhar, and Christopher L. Tucci 2010. "The Innovation–Economic Growth Nexus: Global Evidence," *Research Policy* 39(10): 1264–76.

Hausman, R., D. Hwang, and D. Rodrik 2007. "What You Export Matters," *Journal of Economic Growth* 12(1): 1–25.

Hausmann, R., L. Pritchett, and D. Rodrik 2005. "Growth Accelerations," *Journal of Economic Growth* 10(4): 303–29.

Hausmann, R., D. Rodrik, and A. Velasco 2008. "Growth Diagnostics," in N. Serra and J. E. Stiglitz (eds.), *The Washington Consensus Reconsidered*

Towards a New Global Governance, pp. 324–55. New York: Oxford University Press.

Hidalgo, C. A., B. Klinge, A. L. Barabási, and R. Hausmann 2007. "The Product Space Conditions the Development of Nations," *Science* 317(5837): 482–7.

Hobday, Michael 1995. *Innovation in East Asia: The Challenge to Japan*. London: Edward Elgar.

    2000. "East versus Southeast Asian Innovation Systems: Comparing OEM- and TNC-led Growth in Electronics," in L. Kim and R. Nelson (eds.), *Technology, Learning and Innovation: Experiences of Newly Industrializing Economies*, pp. 129–69. Cambridge University Press.

    2003. "Innovation in Asian Industrialization: A Gerschenkronian Perspective," *Oxford Development Studies* 31(3): 293–314.

    2005. "Firm-level Innovation Models: Perspectives on Research in Developed and Developing Countries," *Technology Analysis & Strategic Management* 17(2): 121–46.

Hoopes, D. G., T. L. Madsen, and G. Walker 2003. "Why is There a Resource-based View? Toward a Theory of Competitive Heterogeneity," *Strategic Management Journal* 24(10): 889–902.

Hu, A. G. Z., and A. Jaffe 2003. "Patent Citations and International Knowledge Flow: The Cases of Korea and Taiwan," *International Journal of Industrial Organization* 21(6): 849–80.

Imbs, Jean, and Romain Wacziarg 2003. "Stages of Diversification," *American Economic Review* 93(1): 63–86.

Islam, N. 1995. "Growth Empirics: A Panel Data Approach", *Quarterly Journal of Economics* 110(4): 1127–70.

Jaffe, Adam B., and M. Trajtenberg 2002. *Patents, Citations, and Innovations: A Window on the Knowledge Economy*. Cambridge, MA: MIT Press.

Jaffe, Adam B., M. Trajtenberg, and M. S. Forgaty 2000. "Knowledge Spillovers and Patent Citations: Evidence from A Survey of Inventors," *American Economic Review* 90(2): 215–18.

Jaffe, Adam B., M. Trajtenberg, and R. Henderson 1993. "Geographic Localization of Knowledge Spillovers as Evidenced by Patent Citations," *Quarterly Journal of Economics* 108(3): 577–98.

Jee, M., E.-H. Choi, N. Lee, S.-J. Kim, and G. H. Paik 2005. *Development of China's Firms and Industries: The Impacts on Korea (in Korean)*. Seoul: Korea Institute for International Economic Policy.

Jensen, J. B., and R. H. McGuckin 1997. "Firm Performance and Evolution: Empirical Regularities in the US Microdata," *Industrial and Corporative Changes* 6(1): 25–47.

Jensen, M., B. Johnson, E. Lorenz and B.-A. Lundvall 2007. "Forms of Knowledge, Modes of Innovation and Innovation Systems," *Research Policy* 36(5): 680–93.

Jones, Benjamin F., and Benjamin A. Olken 2005. "The Anatomy of Start-Stop Growth," NBER Working Papers 11528.

Jones, Benjamin F. and Bruce A. Weinberg 2001. "Age Dynamics in Scientific Creativity." *PNAS (Proceedings of the National Academy of the Sciences)* 108 (November 22): 18,910–14.

Joo, S. H., and K. Lee 2010. "Samsung's Catch-up with Sony: An Analysis Using US Patent Data," *Journal of the Asia Pacific Economy* 15(3): 271–87.

Jung, Moosup, and Keun Lee 2010. "Sectoral Systems of Innovation and Productivity Catch-up: Determinants of the Productivity Gap Between Korean and Japanese Firms," *Industrial and Corporate Change* 19(4): 1037–69.

Keister, Lisa A. 1998. "Engineering Growth: Business Group Structure and Firm Performance in China's Transition Economy," *American Journal of Sociology* 104(2): 404–40.

Khan, Haider 2002. "Innovation and Growth: A Schumpeterian Model of Innovation applied to Taiwan," *Oxford Development Studies* 30(3): 289–306.

Khanna, T. 2000. "Business Groups and Social Welfare: Existing Evidence and Unanswered Questions," *European Economic Review* 44(4): 748–61.

Khanna, T., and K. Palepu 1997. "Why Focused Strategies may be Wrong for Emerging Markets," *Harvard Business Review* 75(4): 41–8.

1999a. "The Right Way to Restructure Conglomerates in Emerging Markets," *Harvard Business Review* 77(4): 125–35.

1999b. "Policy Shocks, Market Intermediaries, and Corporate Strategy: Evidence from Chile and India," *Journal of Economics and Management Strategy* 8(2): 271–310.

2000a. "Is Group Affiliation Profitable in Emerging Markets: An Analysis of Indian Diversified Business Groups," *Journal of Finance* 55(2): 867–91.

2000b. "The Future of Business Groups: Long Run Evidence from Chile," *Academy of Management Journal* 43(3): 268–85.

Khanna, T., and Y. Yafeh 2007. "Business Groups in Emerging Markets: Paragons or Parasites?," *Journal of Economic Literature* 45(2): 331–72.

Kim, Linsu 1997a. *Imitation to Innovation: The Dynamics of Korea's Technological Learning.* Boston: Harvard Business School Press.

1997b. "The Dynamics of Samsung's Technological Learning in Semi-Conductors," *California Management Review* 39(3): 86–100.

1980. "Stages of Development of Industrial Technology in a Developing Country: A Model," *Research Policy* 9(3): 254–77.

Kim, C. W., and K. Lee 2003. "Innovation, Technological Regimes, and Organizational Selection in Industry Evolution: A 'history friendly model' of DRAM industry", *Industrial and Corporate Change* 12(5): 1195–1221.

Kim, S. J., and Y. Kim 2000. "Growth Gains from Trade and Education," *Journal of International Economics* 50(2): 519–45.

Kim, Yee Kyoung, Keun Lee, Walter G. Park, and Kineung Choo 2012. "Appropriate Intellectual Property Protection and Economic Growth in Countries at Different Levels of Development," *Research Policy* 41(2): 358–75.

Knack, Stephen and Philip Keefer 1995. "Institutions and Economic Performance: Cross-Country Tests Using Alternative Institutional Measures," *Economics and Politics* 7(3): 207–27.

Kodama, Fumio 1992. "Technology Fusion and the New R&D," *Harvard Business Review* 70(4): 70–8.

Krishnan, T. R., and S. K. Vallabhaneni 2010. "Catch-up in Technology-driven Services: The Case of the Indian Software Services Industry," *Seoul Journal of Economics* 23(2): 263–81.

Lall, Sanjaya 1992. "Technological Capabilities and Industrialization," *World Development* 20(2): 165–86.

2000. "The Technological Structure and Performance of Developing Country Manufactured Exports, 1985–1998," *Oxford Development Studies* 28(3): 337–69.

Laursen, K., and V. Meliciani 2002. "The Relative Importance of International vis-à-vis National Technological Spillovers for Market Share Dynamics," *Industrial and Corporate Change* 11(4): 875–94.

Lee, J., and E. Shim 1995. "Moderating Effects of R&D on Corporate Growth in US and Japanese Hitech Industries: An Empirical Study," *The Journal of High Technology Management Research* 6(2): 179–91.

Lee, K. 2005. "Making a Technological Catch-up: Barriers and Opportunities," *Asian Journal of Technology Innovation* 13(2): 97–131.

2006. "The Washington Consensus and East Asian Sequencing: Understanding Reform in East and South Asia," in J. Fanelli and G. McMahon (eds.), *Understanding Market Reforms*. Volume II: *Motivation, Implementation and Sustainability*, pp. 99–140. Gordonsville, US: Palgrave MacMillan.

2010. "Thirty Years of Catch-up in China, compared with Korea," in Ho-Mao Wu and Yang Yao (eds.), *Reform and Development in New Thinking in Industrial Policy China*, pp. 224–42. New York: Routledge.

2013 (forthcoming). "Capability Failure and Industrial Policy to Move beyond the Middle-Income Trap: From Trade-based to Technology-based Specialization," in J. Lin and J. Stiglitz (eds.), *New Thinking in Industrial Policy*. Palgrave.

Lee, K., and X. He 2009. "Capability of the Samsung Group in Project Execution and Vertical Integration: Created in Korea and Replicated in China," *Asian Business & Management* 8(3): 277–99.

Lee, K., and Young-Sam Kang 2010. "Business Groups in China," in Asli Colpan, Takashi Hikino, and James Lincoln (eds.), *Oxford Handbook of Business Groups*, pp. 210–36. Oxford University Press.

Lee, K., and Jeehoon Ki 2011. "Changes in Industrial Leadership and Catch-Up by Latecomers: Toward a Theory of Catch-up Cycle from the Case in the World Steel Industry," Presented at a seminar held in the UNU-MERIT, Netherlands, and also at the Asia-Pacific Economic Association in Busan.

Lee, K., and B.-Y. Kim 2009. "Both Institutions and Policies Matter but Differently at Different Income Groups of Countries: Determinants of Long Run Economic Growth Revisited," *World Development* 37(3): 533–49.

Lee, K., and Y. K. Kim 2010. "IPR and Technological Catch-Up in Korea," in Hiroyuki Odagiri, Akira Goto, Atsushi Sunami, Richard R. Nelson (eds.), *Intellectual Property Rights, Development, and Catch Up: An International Comparative Study*, pp. 133–62. Oxford University Press.

Lee, K., and C. Lim 2001. "Technological Regimes, Catching-up and Leap-frogging: Findings from the Korean Industries," *Research Policy* 30(3): 459–83.

Lee, K., and J. Mathews 2010. "From the Washington Consensus to the BeST Consensus for World Development," *Asian-Pacific Economic Literature* 24(1): 86–103.

2012. "Ch 6. Firms in Korea and Taiwan: Upgrading in the Same Industry and Entries into New Industries for Sustained Catch-up," in John Cantwell and Ed Amann (eds.), *The Innovative firms in the Emerging Market Economies*, pp. 223–48. Oxford University Press.

Lee, K., and T. Temesgen 2009. "What Makes Firms Grow in Developing Countries? An Extension of the Resource-based Theory of Firm Growth and Empirical Analysis," *International Journal of Technological Learning, Innovation and Development* 2(3): 139–72.

Lee, K., and M. Yoon 2010. "International, Intra-national, and Inter-firm Knowledge Diffusion and Technological Catch-up: The US, Japan, Korea, and Taiwan in the Memory Chip Industry," *Technology Analysis and Strategic Management* 22(5): 553–70.

Lee, K., S.-J. Cho, and J. Jin 2009. "Dynamics of Catch-up in Mobile Phones and Automobiles in China: Sectoral Systems of Innovation Perspective," *China Economic Journal* 2(1): 25–53.

Lee, K., M. Jee, and J. H. Eun 2011. "Assessing China's Economic Catch-Up at the Firm Level and Beyond: Washington Consensus, East Asian Consensus and the Beijing Model," *Industry and Innovation* 18(5): 487–507.

Lee, K., J. Y. Kim, and O. Lee 2010. "Long-term Evolution of the Firm Value and Behavior of Business Groups: Korean Chaebols between Weak Premium, Strong Discount, and Strong Premium," *Journal of the Japanese and International Economies* 24(3): 412–40.

Lee, K., C. Lim, and D. Park 2003. *The Role of Industrial Property Rights in Technological Development in the Republic of Korean*. Geneva: WIPO.

Lee, K., C. Lim, and W. Song 2005. "Emerging Digital Technology as a Window of Opportunity and Technological Leapfrogging: Catch-up in Digital TV by the Korean Firms," *International Journal of Technology Management* 29(1–2): 40–63.

Lee, K., J. Lin, and H. Chang 2005. "Late Marketization vs. Late Industrialization: Convergence or Divergence in East Asia," *Asian-Pacific Economic Literature* 19(1): 42–59.

Lee, K., S. Mani, and Q. Mu 2012. "Divergent Stories of Catch-up in Telecom: China, India, Brazil, and Korea," in F. Malerba and R. Nelson (eds.), *Economic Development as a Learning Process*, pp. 21–71. Cheltenham, UK: Edward Elgar.

Lee, K., T. Y. Park and Rishikesha Krishnan 2011. "Catching-up or Leapfrogging in the Indian IT Service Sector: Windows of Opportunity, Path-creating, and Moving up the Value Chain," Revised version of the paper presented at the Asialics Conference held in Taipei.

Lee, K., B.-Y. Kim, Y.-Y. Park, and E. Sanidas 2013. "Big Business and National Economic Growth," *Journal of Comparative Economics* 41:2, 561–82.

Leff, Nathaniel H. 1978. "Industrial Organization and Entrepreneurship in the Developing Countries: The Economic Groups," *Economic Development and Cultural Change* 26(4): 661–75.

Levin, R., A. Klevorik, R. Nelson, and S. Winter 1987. "Appropriating Returns from Industrial Research and Development," *Brookings Papers on Economic Activity* 1987(3): 783–831.

Lin, Justin Y. 2012a. *New Structural Economics: A Framework for Rethinking Development and Policy*. Washington, DC: The World Bank.

2012b. *Demystifying the Chinese Economy*. Cambridge University Press.

2012c. *The Quest for Prosperity: How Developing Economies Can Take Off*. Princeton University Press.

Linden, G., K. Kraemer, and J. Dedrick 2007. "Who Captures Value in a Global Innovation System? The Case of Apple's iPod," Personal Computing Industry Center (PCIC) Working Paper.

Loayza, Norman, Pablo Fajnzylber, and Cesar Calderon 2005. *Economic Growth in Latin America and the Caribbean*, Washington, DC: The World Bank.

Lu, Qiwen 2000. *China's Leap into the Information Age: Innovation and Organization in the Computer Industry*. Oxford University Press.

Lucas, Robert 1988. "On the Mechanics of Economic Development," *Journal of Monetary Economics* 22(1): 3–42.

Lundvall, Bengt-Ake 1992. *National Systems of Innovation: Towards a Theory of Innovation and Interative Learning*. London: Pinter Publishers.

1993. "User-Producer Relationships, National Systems of Innovation and Internationalization," Ch. 12 in D. Foray and C. Freeman (eds.), *Technology and the Wealth of Nations: The Dynamics of Constructed Advantage*, pp. 277–300. London, New York: Pinter Publishers.

Lundvall, Bengt-Ake, Jan Vang, K. J. Joseph, and Cristina Chaminade 2009. "Innovation System Research and Developing Countries," in Bengt-Ake Lundvall, K. J. Joseph, Cristina Chaminade and Jan Vang (eds.), *Handbook of Innovation Systems and Developing Countries*, pp. 1–32. Cheltenham, UK/Northampton, US: Edward Elgar.

Madhani, P. M. 2008. "Indian Software Success Story: A Resource-based View of Competitive Advantage," *The Icfaian Journal of Management Research* 7(8): 61–83.

Mahmood, Ishtiaq P., and Jasjit Singh 2003. "Technological Dynamism in Asia," *Research Policy* 32(6): 1031–54.

Malerba, Franco 2002. "Sectoral Systems of Innovation and Production," *Research Policy* 31(2): 247–64.

2004. *Sectoral Systems of Innovation: Concepts, Issues and Analyses of Six Major Sectors in Europe*. Cambridge University Press.

Malerba, F., and R. Nelson 2012. *Economic Development as a Learning Process*. Cheltenham: Edward Elgar.

Malerba, F., and L. Orsenigo 1996. "Schumpeterian Patterns of Innovation are Technology-specific," *Research Policy* 25(3): 451–78.

Malerba, F., L. Orsenigo, and P. Peretto 1997. "Persistence of Innovative Activities, Sectoral Patterns of Innovation and International Technological Specialization," *International Journal of Industrial Organization* 15(6): 801–26.

Mathews, John A. 2002a. "Competitive Advantages of the Latecomer Firm: A Resource-based Account of Industrial Catch-up Strategies," *Asia Pacific Journal of Management* 19(4): 467–88.

2002b. "The Origins and Dynamics of Taiwan's R&D Consortia," *Research Policy* 31(4): 633–51.

2005. "Strategy and the Crystal Cycle," *California Management Review* 47(2): 6–32.

2008a. "Energizing Industrial Development," *Transnational Corporations* 17(3): 59–83.

2008b. "China, India and Brazil: Tiger Technologies, Dragon Multinationals and the Building of National Systems of Economic Learning," *Asian Business & Management* 8(1): 5–32.

Mazzoleni, R., and R. Nelson 2007. "The Roles of Research at Universities and Public Labs in Economic Catch-up," *Research Policy* 36(10): 1512–28.

Meliciani, V. 2002. "The Impact of Technological Specialisation on National Performance in a Balance-of-Payments-Constrained Growth Model," *Structural Change and Economic Dynamics* 13(1): 101–18.

Metcalfe, J. S. 2005. "Systems Failure and the Case for Innovation Policy," in Patrick Llerena, Mireille Matt, Arman Avadikyan (eds.), *Innovation Policy in a Knowledge-based Economy: Theory and Practice*, pp. 47–74. Germany: Springer.

Mizuho Corporate Bank 2008. *Mizuho Industry Research: India-based Globalization in the IT Services Industry* 28(2). Tokyo: Industry Research Division of Mizuho Corporate Bank.

Morel, C. M., T. Acharya, D. Broun, A. Dangi, C. Elias, N. K. Ganguly, C. A. Gardner, R. K. Gupta, J. Haycock and A. D. Heher 2005. "Health Innovation Networks to Help Developing Countries Address Neglected Diseases," *Science* 309 (5733): 401–4.

Mu, Qing, and Keun Lee 2005. "Knowledge Diffusion, Market Segmentation and Technological Catch-up: The Case of the Telecommunication Industry in China," *Research Policy* 34(6): 759–83.

Naughton, Barry 2007. *The Chinese Economy: Transitions and Growth.* Cambridge, MA: The MIT Press.

Nelson, R. 1991. "Why Do Firms Differ and How Does it Matter?," *Strategic Management Journal* 12(S2): 61–74.

1993. *National Innovation Systems: A Comparative Analysis.* New York: Oxford University Press.

1995. "Recent Evolutionary Theorizing about Economic Change," *Journal of Economic Literature* 33(1): 48–90.

2008a. "Economic Development from the Perspective of Evolutionary Economic Theory," *Oxford Development Studies* 36(1): 9–21.

2008b. "What Enables Rapid Economic Progress: What are the Needed Institutions?," *Research Policy* 37(1): 1–11.

2008c. "Why Do Firms Differ and How Does it Matter? A Revisitation," *Seoul Journal of Economics* 21(4): 607–19.

Nelson, R., and H. Pack 1999. "The Asian Miracle and Modern Growth Theory," *Economic Journal* 109(457): 416–36.

Nelson, R., and S. Winter 1982. *An Evolutionary Theory of Economic Change*. Cambridge, MA: Harvard University Press.

Nolan, Peter 2002. "China and the Global Business Revolution," *Cambridge Journal of Economics* 26(1): 119–37.

Nonaka, Ikujiro, and Hirotaka Takeuchi 1995. *The Knowledge-Creating Company: How Japanese Companies Create the Dynamics of Innovation*. New York: Oxford University Press.

Odagiri, Hiroyuki, Akira Goto, Atsushi Sunami and Richard R. Nelson 2010. *Intellectual Property Rights, Development, and Catch-up: An International Comparative Study*. Oxford University Press.

OECD 1992. *Technology and Economy: The Key Relationships*. Paris: OECD.

1994. *The Measurement of Scientific and Technological Activities Using Patent Data as Science and Technology Indicators (Patent Manual)*.

1996. *Reviews of National Science and Technology Policy: Republic of Korea*. Paris: OECD.

Ohno, K. 2010. "Overcoming the Middle Income Trap," in L. Yueh (ed.), *Future of Asian Trade and Growth*, pp. 199–221. London: Routledge.

Ok, Woosuk 2010. "Growth of the Indian Economy and Service Industry," ch. 3 in Keun Lee (ed.), *Comparison of IT Service Industry of India and Korea* (in Korean), pp. 18–61. Seoul: STEPI.

Park, K., and K. Lee 2006. "Linking Technological Regimes and Technological Catch-up: Analysis of Korea and Taiwan using the US Patent Data," *Industrial and Corporate Change* 15(4): 715–53.

Patel, P., and K. Pavitt 1997. "The Technological Competencies of World's Largest Firms: Complex and Path-dependent, but not Much Variety," *Research Policy* 26(2): 141–56.

Paus, E. 2009. "Latin America's Middle Income Trap," *Americas Quarterly*, http://www.americasquarterly.org/node/2142.

Pavitt, K. 1985. "Patent Statistics as Indicators of Innovative Activities: Possibilities and Problems," *Scientometrics* 7(1–2): 77–99.

Penrose, E. T. 1995[1959]. *The Theory of the Growth of the Firm*. New York: Oxford University Press.

Perez, Carlota 2008. "A Vision for Latin America: A Resource-based Strategy for Technological Dynamism and Social Inclusion," Globelics Working Paper No. WPG0804.

Perez, C., and L. Soete 1988. "Catching-up in Technology: Entry Barriers and Windows of Opportunity," in Dosi et al. (eds.), *Technical Change and Economic Theory*, pp. 458–79. London: Pinter Publishers.

Posner, M. V. 1961. "International Trade and Technical Change," *Oxford Economic Papers* 13(3): 323–41.

Rabellotti, Roberta 2006. *Upgrading to Compete: Global Value Chains, Clusters and SMEs in Latin America*. Washington, DC: IDB.

Ramo, Joshua C. 2004. *Beijing Consensus*. London: Foreign Policy Center.

Rasiah, Rajah 2006. "Electronics in Malaysia: Export Expansion but Slow Technical Change," in Vandana Chandra (ed.), *Technology, Adaptation, and Exports: How Some Developing Countries Got it Right*, pp. 127–62. Washington, DC: The World Bank.

Raustiala, Kal, and Christopher Sprigman 2012. *The Knockoff Economy: How Imitation Sparks Innovation*. New York: Oxford University Press.

Reinert, Erik 2009. "Emulation versus Comparative Advantages: Competing and Complementary Principles in the History of Economic Policy," in M. Cimoli, G. Dosi, and J. Stiglitz (eds.), *Industrial Policy and Development: The Political Economy of Capabilities Accumulation*, pp. 79–106. Oxford and New York: Oxford University Press.

Rodrik, Dani 1996. "Understanding Economic Policy Reforms," *Journal of Economic Literature* 34(1): 9–41.

1999. "Where Did All the Growth Go? External Shocks, Social Conflict, and Growth Collapses," *Journal of Economic Growth* 4(4): 385–412.

2003. *In Search of Prosperity: Analytic Narratives on Economic Growth*. Princeton University Press.

2006. "Goodbye Washington Consensus Hello Washington Confusion? A Review of the World Bank's Economic Growth in the 1990s: Learning from a Decade of Reform," *Journal of Economic Literature* 44(4): 973–87.

2008. "Understanding South Africa's Economic Puzzles," *The Economics of Transition, The European Bank for Reconstruction and Development*, 16(4): 769–97.

Rodrik, Dani, Arvind Subramanian, and Francesco Trebbi 2004. "Institutions Rule: The Primacy of Institutions Over Geography and Integration in Economic Development," *Journal of Economic Growth* 9(2): 131–65.

Romijin, H., and Caniëls, M. 2011. "Pathways of Technological Change in Developing Countries: Review and New Agenda," *Development Policy Review* 29(3): 359–80.

Schott, P. 2004. "Across-Product versus Within-Product Specialization in International Trade," *Quarterly Journal of Economics* 119(2): 647–78.

Senge, P. 1992. *The Fifth Discipline: The Art and Practice of the Learning Organization*. New York: Doubleday.

Shin, Hochul, and Keun Lee 2012. "Asymmetric Protection Leading not to Productivity but Export Share Changes: The Case of Korean Industries, 1967–1993," *Economics of Transition* 20(4): 745–85.

Spence, Michael 2011. *The Next Convergence: The Future of Economic Growth in a Multispeed World.* New York: FSG Books.

Srholic, M., and Fagerberg, J. 2010. "What Capabilities Does it Take to Escape the Low-growth Trap," Paper presented at the 2010 International Schumpeterian Society Conference, held in Aalborg, June 21–4.

Stolpe, Michael 2002. "Determinants of Knowledge Diffusion as Evidenced in Patent Data: The Case of Liquid Crystal Display Technology," *Research Policy* 31(7): 1181–98.

Sturgeon, Timothy, and Gary Gereffi 2012. "Measuring Success in the Global Economy: International Trade, Industrial Upgrading, and Business Function Outsourcing in Global Value Chains," in C. Pietro-belli and Rasiah (eds.), *Evidence-Based Development Economics*, pp. 249–80. Kuala Lumpur: University of Malaya Press.

Teece, David 1986. "Profiting from Technological Innovation: Implications for Integration, Collaboration, Licensing and Public Policy," *Research Policy* 15(6): 285–305.

2000. "Firm Capabilities and Economic Development," in L. Kim and R. Nelson (eds.), *Technology, Learning and Innovation*, pp. 105–128. Cambridge University Press.

Trajtenberg, Manuel 2001. "Innovation in Israel 1968–97: A Comparative Analysis Using Patent Data," *Research Policy* 30(3): 363–89.

Trajtenberg, Manuel, Rebecca Henderson, and Adam B. Jaffe 1997. "University vs. Corporate Patents: A Window on the Basicness of Innovations," *Economics of Innovation and New Technology* 5(1): 19–50.

Tushman, Michael, and Philip Anderson 1986. "Technological Discontinuity and Organizational Environments," *Administrative Science Quarterly* 31(3): 439–65.

Tybout, J. 2000. "Manufacturing Firms in Developing Countries: How Well do They do, and Why?," *Journal of Economic Literature* 38(1): 11–44.

Utterback, J. M., and W. J. Abernathy 1975. "A Dynamic Model of Process and Product Innovation," *Omega* 3(6): 640–56.

Vernon, Raymond 1966. "International Investment and International Trade in the Product Cycle," *The Quarterly Journal of Economics* 80(2): 190–207.

Verspagen, Bart 1991. "A New Statistical Approach to Catching Up or Falling Behind," *Structural Change and Economic Dynamics* 2(1991): 359–80.

Wang, Zhi, Shang-Jin Wei, Anna Wong 2010. "Does a Leapfrogging Growth Strategy Raise Growth Rate? Some International Evidence," NBER Working Paper No. 16390.

Williamson, John 1990. "What Washington means by policy reform", in J. Williamson (ed.), *Latin American Adjustment: How Much Has Happened?*, Washington, DC: Institute for International Economics.

Williamson, John 2012. "Some Basic Disagreements on Development," Presentation at High-Level Knowledge Forum on Expanding the Frontiers in Development Policy, hosted by the KDI, held in Seoul.

Winter, S. 1984. "Schumpeterian Competition in Alternative Technological Regimes," *Journal of Economic Behavior and Organization* 5(3–4): 287–320.

  2006. "Toward a neo-Schumpeterian Theory of the Firm," *Industrial and Corporate Change* 15(1): 125–41.

Winters, A., and S. Yusuf 2007. *Dancing with Giants: China, India and the Global Economy*. Washington, DC: The World Bank.

WIPO 2012. *Economics of IP (Intellectual Property) in the Republic of Korea*. Geneva: WIPO.

World Bank 1993. *The East Asian Miracle: Economic Growth and Public Policy*. New York: Oxford University Press.

  2005. *Economic Growth in the 1990s: Learning from a Decade of Reform*. Washington, DC: The World Bank.

  2010. *'Exploring the Middle-Income-Trap'*: *World Bank East Asia Pacific Economic Update: Robust Recovery, Rising Risks*, Vol. II. Washington, DC: The World Bank.

  2012. *China 2030: Building a Modern, Harmonious, and Creative High-Income Society*. Washington, DC: The World Bank.

Yao, Y. 2010. "The End of the Beijing Consensus? Can China's Model of Authoritarian Growth Survive?," *Foreign Affairs Online* 2.

Yusuf, S., and Nabeshima, K. 2009. "Can Malaysia Escape the Middle Income Trap? A Strategy for Penang," Policy Research Working Paper 4971, Washington, DC: The World Bank.

Zeng, Ming, and Peter Williamson 2007. *Dragons at Your Door: How Chinese Cost Innovation is Disrupting Global Competition*. Boston: Harvard Business School Press.

Index

Printed in the United States
By Bookmasters